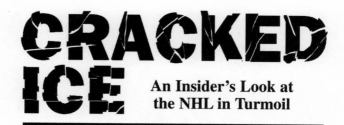

CRACKED ICE

An Insider's Look at
the NHL in Turmoil

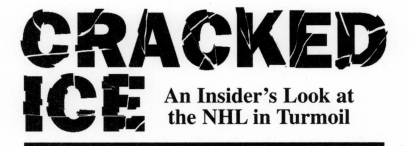

CRACKED ICE

An Insider's Look at the NHL in Turmoil

STAN FISCHLER

McGraw-Hill Ryerson

Toronto New York Auckland Bogotá Caracas
Lisbon London Madrid Mexico Milan New Delhi
San Juan Singapore Sydney Tokyo

Printed and bound in Canada

Care has been taken to trace ownership of the copyright material contained in this text. However, the publishers welcome any information that enables them to rectify any reference or credit in subsequent editions.

Published by
McGraw-Hill Ryerson Limited
300 Water Street
Whitby, Ontario
L1N 9B6

Canadian Cataloguing in Publication Data

Fischler, Stan, 1932-
    Cracked ice: an insider's look at the NHL in turmoil

ISBN 0-07-552626-3

1. National Hockey League. I. Title
GV847.8.N3F53 1995 796.962'62 C95-931877-1

Publisher: Joan Homewood
Cover and text design: Kimberley Davison
Editorial Services: Harry Endrulat
Photographs: Bruce Bennett Studios, reproduced with permission

This book was produced for McGraw-Hill Ryerson by Shaftesbury Books, a division of the Warwick Publishing Group, Toronto.

ABOUT THE AUTHOR

Stan Fischler is regarded as the dean of North American hockey writers. The prize-winning author has written more than 60 books on hockey. One of them, *The Hockey Encyclopedia*, which was co-authored by his wife, Shirley, is regarded as the bible of the sport. Fischler also writes a weekly column, *Inside Sports* which has been carried for over 20 years by *The Toronto Star* syndicate. Among other publications that have carried his byline are *The New York Times*, *Sports Illustrated*, *Newsweek* and *The Village Voice*.

The versatile Fischler is also a prominent hockey broadcaster, having done TV analysis for 20 years. Stan has taught journalism at Columbia University, Fordham University and Queens College. He recently completed an autobiography titled *Confessions of a Trolley Dodger from Brooklyn*.

A native of Brooklyn, Fischler lives in Manhattan with his wife and son, Simon. His other son, Ben, works in San Francisco.

For Simon, Ben and Shirley
– the starting team.

CONTENTS

ACKNOWLEDGMENTS   9

FOREWORD   10

1. A DONUT AND A DISAPPEARANCE:
   The Decline and Fall of John Ziegler   15

2. THE 1992 STRIKE AND REPLACEMENT
   OF JOHN ZIELGER   25

3. FROM ZIEGLER TO STEIN:
   Punching up the NHL's Image   39

4. THE NBA-ING OF THE NHL:
   Enter Gary Bettman   47

5. FACING DEATH AND HOCKEY:
   About Simon, Mike Keenan and a Heart   65

6. THE BETTMAN EVOLUTION   81

7. THE FALL OF BRUCE McNALL   91

8. PRELUDE TO CIVIL WAR:
   The Lockout Looms   111

9. THE GUNS OF OCTOBER:
War Begins in Earnest   117

10. THE DIRT FLIES AND THE IMPASSE HARDENS   121

11. GETTING HAIRY:
Digging in for the Long Haul   133

12. A DEAL IS MADE:
The 1995 Season Begins   147

13. GAME ON:
The Strange Season   153

14. FROM QUEBEC TO DENVER:
The Americanization and Possible Death of Hockey as We Know it   165

15. McMULLEN AND THE MICKEY MOUSE CLUB:
The Devils Strive for Respect   169

16. THE NHL IN THE LATE 1990s:
New Jersey versus Nashville   181

17. WILL THE DEVILS GET A NEW JERSEY?
The NHL Moves from the Ridiculous to the Bizarre   195

18. CHAMPAGNE VERSUS THE COURTROOM:
Climax of the Nashville-New Jersey NHL War   207

19. AND THE FINAL VERDICT IS…   219

20. D (AS IN DEVILS)-DAY
The Final "No" to Nashville   227

AFTERWORD:
The Life or Death of Hockey   235

ACKNOWLEDGMENTS

When I undertook the writing of *Cracked Ice* I anticipated that considerable research would be necessary although the book essentially is based on my own experiences through the administrations of three National Hockey League leaders.

Once the outline was in place, St. John's University student Rick DaCruz became my part-time librarian and major-domo in charge of filing relevant articles.

In the beginning our focus was on the lockout of 1994-95 and, frankly, we anticipated that it would be over and done with in a matter of one to three weeks. But it grew like the fabled Topsy and so did the hours which Rick invested in the project, not to mention the mountain of clippings which reached such proportions that they had to be transferred from my Manhattan office to larger quarters at Casa DaCruz in New Jersey.

To say that Rick had a Promethean task on his hands would be an understatement, but he remained unflagging in his pursuit of relevant material even after his graduation. Because DaCruz's time was limited, it was imperative to add other researchers. David Kolb, Dave Harsanyi, Keith Fernbach, Ann Marie Lynch and Anna Horton were especially helpful.

Ditto for Audra Ottimo of the New Jersey Devils' public relations department, Adam Schwartz of NHL publicity and Chris Botta, the crack editorial director of the New York Islanders.

Needless to say, *Cracked Ice* never would have been born if not for a publisher who believed in the project. From the get-go Don Broad of McGraw-Hill Ryerson inspired the book and when he left the firm, it was, thankfully, speeded ahead by his successors, Julia Woods and Joan Homewood. Their faith in the work rates a special "Thanks!" from this corner.

Rounding out the kudos, I reserve a special nod of gratitude to the potent and perspicuous Nick Pitt, who guided the manuscript through the minefields; not to mention the always affable and insightful Kimberley Davison, whose creativity gave us the book's cover.

FOREWORD

I saw my first hockey game before the Japanese bombed Pearl Harbor.

I earned my first paycheque in the hockey business before Toe Blake's Montreal Canadiens launched their first dynasty by winning five straight Stanley Cups.

And I haven't stopped writing about the ice game since.

In the forty years since I began writing professionally about the National Hockey League, I have experienced innumerable changes.

The advent of the goalie mask was one such change. It began when I watched Jacques Plante's mug get dismembered by an Andy Bathgate blast at Madison Square Garden, an event that traumatized me.

Despite the damage done to Plante, I subscribed to the Toe Blake Theory that goalies should remain maskless. As more netminders chose to save their faces, I felt that a wonderfully intimate aspect of pro hockey was disappearing.

Then came protective helmets, curved sticks and the slap shot, all of which bothered me. But nothing was more disturbing than NHL expansion from six to twelve teams in 1967-68.

That was a killer. Only one who had been raised on the six-team NHL could possibly imagine the sudden quality decline when the new expansion teams actually became high-grade versions of American Hockey League clubs. The 1968 Stanley Cup final between the Montreal Canadiens and the brand new St. Louis Blues set hockey back light-years as far as I was concerned, yet somehow, The Game survived.

In time, expansion teams flexed their muscles and by 1974 the Philadelphia Flyers had won their first of two straight Stanley Cups.

Then came the birth of the World Hockey Association, raids against the NHL, international matches with the Soviet Union and the inevitable NHL-WHA merger.

As startling as all of these changes may have been, each had a positive element that left me without rancour. How could I rail against goalie masks if they save a netminder's life? Who was I to tell Stan Mikita not to wear a helmet after Bill Masterton was killed because he wasn't wearing headgear? Where did I come off criticizing expansion or the WHA since it was the latter that enabled me to get my first broadcasting job?

It was all progress and I eventually came to understand that – for the most part – progress was leading to The Game's betterment, although I'll always maintain that the curved stick was an egregious mistake.

But a new element and emotion intruded when the National Hockey League Players' Association called its first strike in 1992. Hockey liberals, pro-unionists and the anti-Alan Eagleson Brigade might call the walk-out progress; particularly since it was directed against John Ziegler's misguided regime.

I do not stand among them. Liberal on some issues, conservative on others, I regarded the strike among the most nauseating events of my hockey journalistic career; and still do. Etched in my memory forever is a discussion I had with union leader Ken Baumgartner.

Make no mistake, I've always liked Baumgartner as a person and considered him a valued player for the New York Islanders for about a dozen games. But on this night when Baumgartner attempted to rationalize the runaway salaries that he and some of his colleagues were making, then I knew big-league hockey was in big trouble. Not long after that, my old pal Kevin Lowe launched a similar peroration about "underpaid" hockey players.

"Dammit," I said to myself, "this guy believes it as much as Abraham Lincoln believed The Gettysburg Address."

Later that evening, my hockey colleague – now with ESPN – Vic Morren and I walked out of the Plaza Hotel toward the Columbus Circle subway station in Manhattan. An early spring dusk was falling over New York City as we strolled through the perimeter of Central Park.

"Something awful is happening to the game of hockey," I said to Morren.

"I know what you mean," he replied.

"It's greed-to-the-radical-fifty," I went on, "and unless the NHL can can put the lid on it, hockey as we know it is never going to be the same."

It never was. Incredibly, the union scored a T.K.O. over Ziegler and the NHL ownership while salaries climbed and climbed and climbed. A fourth-line player such as Troy Crowder, who wasn't worth $100,000 on the best day he ever had, suddenly was demanding twice that amount and wound up being a coveted commodity by the Detroit Red Wings despite his innumerable shortcomings.

From time to time both NHL executives and agents would insist to me that runaway inflation simply could not continue without a big-league hockey version of the Wall Street Crash of 1929 that led to The Great Depression of the 1930s. Yet almost blithely the likes of Bruce McNall, Neil Smith and Michael Shanahan, to name a few, tossed money at stickhandlers as if it were growing on trees.

I watched these episodes with a mixture of awe and downright fear until the Great Lockout of 1994-95. Now wealthier than they ever had been, NHL players seemed oblivious to losses being suffered by many teams. Union boss Bob Goodenow betrayed a crass insensitivity to small-market teams such as Quebec, Winnipeg and Hartford. Player representatives such as Bruce Driver simply refused to believe owners like John McMullen when they attempted to open the books and show them that, yes, they were taking a fiscal beating.

The lockout stunned me to the very core, both professionally and emotionally, because I knew that it signalled one of the most dramatic changes our favourite game ever endured. What's more, I believed implicitly that the changes it wrought would do to the NHL's fabric what World War I inflicted on Europe's political mosaic when the armistice was signed in 1918.

When the lockout began in October 1994, I suggested to Don Broad, then with McGraw-Hill Ryerson, that a book chronicling major league hockey's turbulent period – from the 1992 strike through the lockout – would be a valuable addition to any history of the game.

"The lockout should be over in a week or two," I told Broad over lunch early in October 1994. "Even if it goes as long as a month, the changes in hockey should be profound."

Broad agreed and the concept for *Cracked Ice* was born. Like the generals who predicted that the Great War of 1914 would end in a matter of weeks, we were unable to believe that the Lockout would go on and on and on, past Christmas 1994 and through New Year's Day 1995.

As I began writing the manuscript, I realized that to make a coherent history of the turbulent period, I could best do it through my own eyes and that I should fix a starting period. I chose the John Ziegler presidency since I had covered it closely since its inception and also because it impacted directly on events of the 1990s through to the present.

I decided to follow the Ziegler years through the 1992 strike, his demise as president and the subsequent rump administration of Gil Stein leading to the Gary Bettman era. In that period, I had come to know and very much like Bruce McNall, who would impact on the NHL the way the San Francisco earthquake reverberated through California. Because of my experiences with these and other major hockey characters like Alan Eagleson, I decided to personalize the history and tell the NHL story through my eyes, biased though they may be.

Originally, I had planned to end the book with one chapter after the lockout ended. Everything seemed to be in order until the 1995 playoffs began and a seemingly foreign entity known as Nashville began intruding into the picture.

Nashville as an NHL site? It seemed impossible to anyone who had followed hockey as long as I had. Yet this was part and parcel of the new NHL era; one where luxury boxes became more important than ordinary seats; where venerable arenas such as Chicago Stadium were renamed after corporations; and where players were traded not because of a stickhandler's skill, but rather because of what the player was earning or wanted to earn.

Nashville's bid to steal the Devils from New Jersey was symbolic of hockey in the 1990s and I found myself right in the middle of this arresting story that was filled with characters that Central Casting couldn't have produced in Hollywood.

Thus, I decided that the last chapter would be about the Nashville - New Jersey tug of war. And it was; except that the story began to take on a life of its own with dramatic twists and turns that became mind-boggling to one who had thought he had seen just about everything in four decades on the NHL beat.

Instead of one chapter, Nashville - New Jersey became an entire section of the book simply because it deserved to be and because the suspense it generated was even more gripping than the lockout, which had plenty of drama in its own right. (Even as I write this in October 1995, the New Jersey - Nashville Saga still hasn't seen its last paragraph.)

All of which is a long-winded way of saying that I'm bringing you a Fischler-eye-view of hockey from the first seat on the roller coaster. It has had its ups and downs, for sure, but it has been one hell of a ride.

I hope you like it.

Stan Fischler, New York, October 1995

1

••

A DONUT AND A DISAPPEARANCE:
THE DECLINE AND FALL OF JOHN ZIEGLER

It is far too simplistic to assert that one incident contributed to the decline and fall of John Ziegler as NHL president. Of this I speak firsthand, having followed Ziegler in my journalistic capacity, from the beginning to the end of his presidency.

Ziegler's enforced departure was due to several elements and incidents, including the power-loss of his chief supporters, Alan Eagleson and Bill Wirtz, as well as his apparent capitulation to union boss Bob Goodenow following the 1992 players' revolt.

But one tremulous episode among the many set off the avalanche that eventually buried Ziegler under a mountain of bad publicity. Future hockey historians will refer to it as "The Donut Incident," although there were no crullers involved, as far as Ziegler was concerned.

The unforgettable mess developed, as many hockey messes do, from the fire of a heated Stanley Cup playoff game. New Jersey's Devils, who never before had been in a postseason tournament, had gained a berth on the final night of the season, edging the New York Rangers.

From a league viewpoint, this was not a happy event. Even during the Ziegler regime, the Rangers were regarded as the jewel of American-based NHL franchises; the club right smack in the middle of the world's media capital; the one which could produce considerable positive ink by doing well in the playoffs. For the "Broadway Blueshirts" to miss the playoffs completely was not exactly a disaster, but certainly akin to one.

For the Devils to edge them out was even more onerous because New Jersey's owner, John McMullen, from time to time had been one of Ziegler's critics.

The Devils not only reached the playoffs, they proceeded to upset the favoured Islanders and Capitals in rounds one and two, respectively, before meeting Boston in the semifinals. The Cinderella Devils were given little chance of toppling a Bruins' club led by the inimitable Raymond Bourque on defence. I expected New Jersey to go out in five games tops.

However, coach Jim Schoenfeld had turned his squad into believers and managed to leave Boston after the first two games with an even split. It now was Friday night at Byrne Meadowlands Arena, Game Three, with emotions beginning to run high. In terms of artistry, the third match would be rated a three on a scale of one to ten.

I was, as usual, covering the games for SportsChannel New York, the cable service that broadcasts both the Islanders and Devils matches. During the contests at Byrne Arena, I had a very strategic location – directly between the rival benches at ice level. I could see the whites of both coaches' eyes; particularly Schoenfeld whose eyes were popping out over what he considered inept officiating.

Although Schoenfeld's club was overwhelmed, 6-1, referee Don Koharski did not help matters. To the Devils' fans his work had a distinctly pro-Boston edge.

Schoenfeld later candidly allowed that he suspected his players would lose after the third shift of the first period, but he was still seething at the end. Instead of following his players into the dressing room – directly opposite to our television studio – Schoenfeld remained at the players' bench. At game's end, referees use the same ramp to reach their dressing room, so the Jersey coach figured the longer he waited the more likely he could deliver an eye-to-eye repudiation of Koharski's work.

Even before the game had ended and Schoenfeld began his vigil, waiting for Koharski to come off the ice, I had removed myself from between the benches because I had to get into the SportsChannel studio for post-game interviews. The following description of events comes from several eyewitness accounts and published records of what was said and done.

The consensus among some pro-Devils obervers is that Koharski could have defused the whole incident and forever have avoided the fracas which ensued. Instead of plunging headlong into the cauldron by skating over to Schoenfeld, Koharski could have kept his distance, remaining at centre ice for a longer period and motioning Schoenfeld into his locker room. There was no rush for Koharski. He didn't have to flee the arena; all he had to do was wait it out, even if a half-hour was required.

Moreover, the NHL's security chief, Frank Torpey, was standing next to Schoenfeld and was in an ideal position to usher the enraged coach into the vomitory exit and out of harm's way.

Koharski eventually skated directly toward the players' bench, where the encounter with Schoenfeld was as inevitable as the Titanic hitting the iceberg. Linesmen Ray Scapinello and Gord Broseker accompanied the referee. Schoenfeld's coaching aide, Doug McKay, was with him as the Devils' big, red-headed leader confronted Koharski with flowing invectives.

Koharski brusquely continued forward, but Schoenfeld managed to get himself in front of the referee again. "You f— walked right into me," Schoenfeld reportedly yelled. "I'm standing there and you stepped on my f— foot."

At this point McKay intervened, trying to place his left arm between the coach and the referee. One report noted that Scapinello ran toward Schoenfeld, but bumped McKay who then bumped Koharski. The alleged inadvertent blow pushed the referee off the rubberized runway and against the wall.

At least two witnesses present, who had no connection with the league, insist that at no time did Schoenfeld lay a hand on Koharski. But the referee, according to one report, shouted at the coach as if Schoenfeld was the culprit: "You're gone now! You're gone. You won't coach another f— game." By this time the full-fledged melee was taking place right outside our interview room.

Now aware that Koharski was implying that the coach had manhandled him, Schoenfeld shot back, "You f— fell and you know it. You know you fell. I didn't touch you. You're full of s—. You're crazy. You're crazy."

Koharski continued snapping, "You're gone," with a postscript that he hoped the incident was on tape. (At least one TV news cameraman recorded the episode.) As the referee turned right toward the officials' room, Schoenfeld provided the imperfect squelch: "Good, 'cause you fell, you fat pig. Have another donut!" (It would become one of the most quoted lines in NHL annals.)

Witnesses reported that Koharski continued bellowing before making another turn out of sight and into the officials' room. By this time, the corridors leading to both dressing rooms were in an uproar, crowded with print journalists, camera crews and some NHL officials.

Apparently realizing that Koharski would file a complaint and make sure the coach got the worst of it, Schoenfeld declared, "He slipped, but he said I pushed him. Anyone who was there knows my hands were by my side. I had a point to make, but he obviously didn't want to hear it."

Koharski did officially complain to the league. Although NHL vice-president Brian O'Neill normally handled disciplinary problems, many thought that this one appeared severe enough to merit president John Ziegler's personal intervention. Not so. Ziegler was not around. Instead, as was his droning style, O'Neill gathered evidence, but pointedly refused to evaluate the tape the Devils offered to send to him. An expected in-person hearing involving Schoenfeld, Koharski and O'Neill never was held.

By noon on Sunday (Mother's Day), when Game Four of the series was scheduled to be played, O'Neill had rendered his arbitrary decision. Schoenfeld was suspended for vilifying Koharski. The NHL vice-president phoned Devils' general manager Lou Lamoriello with the news. Upon hearing the decision, Lamoriello demanded a hearing, but O'Neill – Ziegler's alter-ego who, inexplicably, still had not left Montreal – refused.

O'Neill then was advised by Lamoriello that the Devils would seek to nullify the suspension through court action. But first, Lamoriello vainly attempted to locate Ziegler. Then he contacted the NHL's top lawyer, Gil Stein, informing him that the Devils would seek a temporary restraining order to nullify Schoenfeld's suspension.

John Conte, a lawyer and Devils season-ticket holder, filed a show-cause order on behalf of Schoenfeld, a portion of which read:

"The referee, without warning to Plaintiff, Coach JAMES SCHOENFELD, pushed past him, and through use of threats and intimidation, caused a certain concern and anxiety among those in the area, and stumbled through no fault or cause of Plaintiff Coach JAMES SCHOENFELD.

"To avoid charges of misconduct due to his threats and harassment, Referee DONALD KOHARSKI deliberately filed a grievance with the National Hockey League, well-knowing the sanctions that could be imposed on Plaintiff Coach JAMES SCHOENFELD."

Events moved swiftly and dramatically: 1. At 6 p.m. O'Neill announced from Montreal that Schoenfeld had been suspended for Game Four; 2. At 6:30 p.m. NHL officiating supervisor John McCauley was tipped off that the regular game officials would strike if Schoenfeld appeared behind the bench; 3. At 6:40 p.m., under NHL pressure, McCauley approached the New Jersey off-ice officials about the possibility of three of them handling the fourth playoff game in the event that the regular referee, Dave Newell, and linesmen, Gord Broseker and Ray Scapinello, pulled a walk-out.

I had been at the rink since early afternoon preparing for our evening SportsChannel telecast of the game. By 6 p.m. the pressroom was a frenzy of conjecture, as both print and electronic journalists grasped the significance of the impending crisis and awaited bulletins as they arrived.

Although the teams took their regular warmup at 7:10 p.m., there was a sense in the hallways outside the dressing rooms that the game was not likely to start on time. Furthermore, there was a chance that it might not be played at all despite a capacity crowd of 19,040.

Meanwhile, two egregious omissions were damaging the NHL's reputation. First and foremost, its highest officer, president Ziegler, still was nowhere to be found, although L'Affaire Schoenfeld-Koharski had escalated well into its second day. Then there was the question of O'Neill's probe. New Jersey Superior Court Judge James F. Madden took due note of the latter in his review, stating, "...the NHL's investigation consisted of them calling one person (Koharski), then another (Schoenfeld). In the middle of an important series like this, particularly when they have something like a videotape. What can be more conclusive than a photographic production? Plus the fact that after (O'Neill) made up his mind, the Devils asked for a hearing and everyone runs into the woods and gets lost."

Judge Madden issued a verbal temporary restraining order at 7:20 p.m. which meant that Schoenfeld could coach the Devils in Game Four. Madden delivered his verdict by phone to McCauley who was at the rink. He had ordered the NHL to "desist and refrain from suspending Schoenfeld pending a formal hearing and notice of specific charges against him."

At the time I was riding a belt line between my studio opposite the Devils' locker room and the pressroom about 200 feet down the corridor. Once the players had completed their pregame skate it had become apparent that the game would be delayed. And still no Ziegler, although theories abounded, including one that he was tending to a family emergency.

At game-time the Devils called a press conference during which the club's vice-president for public relations, Larry Brooks, read a statement from Lamoriello: "The New Jersey Devils cannot tolerate the injustice that has been done to Jim Schoenfeld and our organization. We are owed the right of a hearing and appeal. Two weeks ago, when (our player) Brendan Shanahan became involved with a member of the Washington Capitals, the league conducted a hearing in my office within 36 hours of the altercation. Yet in this case, with the future of the franchise at stake as well as the reputation of our coach, Jim Schoenfeld, Brian O'Neill did not convene an official hearing."

No less potent was Lamoriello's postscript that "a hearing was required because the officials filed reports to the league which were clearly false. We cannot accept this."

The suggestion was that the linesmen and Koharski had trumped up the story that Schoenfeld had actually knocked over the referee. Witnesses insist that no contact was made by the coach and referee. The Devils refused to be intimidated – and they were absolutely correct in taking that stand.

The on-ice officials were dead wrong in their refusal to work the game. By contract they were obliged to take the ice; it was their duty to the league, to the players and to the fans. It was anarchy, compounded by the absence of president Ziegler.

At 7:45 p.m. the players took the ice as a prelude to the national anthem, but the referee and linesmen were missing. McCauley then informed coaches Schoenfeld and Terry O'Reilly that the NHL-assigned officials had refused to take the ice. After a confused few moments on the ice, the players gradually returned to their dressing rooms.

The Byrne Meadowlands Arena was filled to capacity with fans awaiting the game's start, although no official notice was provided about the delay. Once the regular officials stated that they would not go on, McCauley rounded up three off-ice officials – Paul McInnis, Jim Sullivan and Vin Godleski, each of whom had considerable officiating experience on the collegiate and amateur level. McInnis donned the black-and-white striped referee's uniform while Sullivan and Godleski wore yellow scrimmage sweaters. Those sweaters would inspire the term "Yellow Sunday."

NHL board chairman Bill Wirtz was contacted. He told the officials that they had a contractual obligation to officiate the game. When they again refused, he ordered Denis Morel – the standby referee – to substitute, but Morel also declined.

Jim Beatty, a Toronto lawyer representing the officials' association and the individual who was counselling Newell et. al., proposed a compromise which would place Schoenfeld in the press box with headphones, orchestrating his club from above. Bruins' general manager Harry Sinden rejected the idea. Notorious for his criticism of officials, Sinden snapped, "We don't need you guys." Thus, Sinden was lining up behind the league – and, in effect, Lamoriello.

I was in and out of the studio; at once trying to obtain the latest information and also working with my colleagues Gary Thorne and Peter McNab in the overhead booth. At one point Devils' owner John McMullen popped his head out of the Devils' trainer's room.

"Will we have a game?" I asked him.

"I'd better not talk to you now," he demurred, "but I think we'll work something out."

They did. McInnis, 52, Godleski, 51 and Sullivan, 50, eventually took the ice and handled the meanspirited game. Considering the pressure, the importance of the game and the fact that they were working before a full house, the three imports were both heroic and splendid as the Devils won the game.

All in all it was one of the most intense events I ever had the pleasure of covering. An afterglow of excitement permeated the arena long after the final buzzer had sounded. In the bowels of the arena near the pressroom, an area had been set aside for post-game interviews. Godleski, Sullivan and McInnis were there mingling with friends and media. I walked over to the trio and shook their hands. "You did a really fine job tonight, guys," I said.

They smiled. "No comment," said Sullivan, a retired New York City cop.

Little did they know it at the time, but their decision to officiate would mark the beginning of a long-running feud between the league officials and the New Jersey off-ice people, not to mention the referees and the Devils.

Godleski would later tell me that linesman Pat Dapuzzo, who had been nurtured through the New Jersey hockey ranks by the likes of Godleski, would pointedly ignore his former mentors in protest against their action.

Once the fallout of the game had ended, attention shifted to the NHL high command and its next move. More particularly, the question on every hockey person's lips was, "What happened to John Ziegler?" The president's extended absence had turned into a huge embarrassment to the league.

On Monday O'Neill still was at the helm in distant Montreal and minus the president. He announced that the NHL would conduct a formal hearing on the Schoenfeld matter on Tuesday in Boston. This pleased the Devils who firmly believed that the officials' charges were fabricated and that witnesses and videotape would back up Schoenfeld.

Meanwhile, inexplicably, the officials called off their walk-out and acknowledged that they would work the remainder of the series. Nevertheless, they had broken a contract while placing the playoffs in jeopardy. All three should have been suspended and fined. Instead, no disciplinary action was taken – a spineless move by the NHL and one that signalled to the officials that walk-outs would not result in punishment. It would be a decision that in years to come would have far-reaching effects on the power and independence of referees and linesmen.

By this time Ziegler's absence had become the source of conjecture through-out the league, providing a field day for columnists and television commentators. When the president finally surfaced again publicly on Tuesday, May 10th, he ducked questions concerning his whereabouts during the New Jersey crisis.

"Where I was is my personal business," he insisted. "I answer to the board and nobody else." The media were astonished by this arrogant and obdurate comment.

Ziegler's rationale was that he had chosen to take a break between league business and the following round, the Stanley Cup finals. Perhaps it was a rea-sonable excuse, but under the circumstances the perception that he was ducking his duty became a major issue which his many enemies in the media seized with delight. Not surprisingly, the president – notorious for watching most NHL games at home rather than at the rinks – was asked when he had last been at a game in person. Again Ziegler declined to comment.

At the conclusion of the nearly three-hour hearing, Ziegler required another hour to deliver his ruling. Schoenfeld was suspended one game and fined $1,000. The Devils received a $10,000 fine and the series resumed.

"It's the kind of thing you wished never happened," said Ziegler. "But the league will survive." (One wag was heard to snipe, "It's a marvellous game, to be sure, to have survived this guy for 11 years!")

The league would survive, but John Ziegler's presidency would not. Yellow Sunday alone would not topple his administration because Ziegler still was propped up by the Wirtz-Eagleson duo, along with several other governors with less power but fully supportive of their chief executive. Other blunders would have to take place to undermine his regime – and they did.

One which was self-inflicted concerned the president's Achilles heel – pub-lic relations. Somewhat diffident in public, Ziegler perceived that he had been unfairly victimized by the media. He tended to downplay the role of his public relations department leaving it in the care of Steve Ryan, an affable fellow whose primary expertise was in marketing and merchandising. While Ryan was titular head of the p.r. bureau, he rarely had others to help him.

The p.r. role was ably handled by John Halligan, despite unseen "controls" by Ziegler, until 1986 when the veteran pro moved over to Madison Square Garden where he ran the Rangers' publicity office. Ryan lured author-hockey nut Jack Falla into the p.r. job, but it turned into an overnight disaster. A writer by trade, Falla couldn't adapt to the Madison Avenue mode and exited the job almost as quickly as he entered.

Next in line was Gerry Helper, a sincere, competent type whose surname befitted his work habits. Helper lasted at the NHL's New York office until 1991 when he opted for a job as publicist for the new Tampa Bay Lightning franchise. In the interim Ziegler made a decision that not only could be considered obtuse but thoroughly counter to the direction the NHL should have gone.

Incredible as it may seem, Ziegler decided to dismantle the public relations department in his New York (main) office. The publicity function would hereby be handled long distance from the league's outpost in Rexdale, Ontario, which heretofore had been limited to such functions as officiating, scheduling and other lesser duties. At best, it was a monumentally unwise move; Ziegler's answer to his media critics.

This was completely counter to the policies of competing major sports such as the National Basketball Association – the NHL's prime challenger – Major League Baseball and the National Football League. Each correctly reasoned that it was imperative to have a robust, aggressive and very evident p.r. department in the world's media capital.

When I directly challenged Ziegler on his decision to eliminate the New York p.r. office, his rationale was typical of the thinking that had bedevilled the NHL under his administration. "We're streamlining our organization," he said.

"What does that mean?" I asked.

"We're in the age of electronics," he replied. "We can get all the information we want from Toronto in a matter of seconds."

Not having a league public relations presence in New York City was akin to Bill Clinton not having a press aide and media department at the White House. Ziegler ignored the criticism. He signed a pair of expensive Toronto media specialists who had specialized in politics. Bill Wilkerson and Fraser Kelly operated a Toronto p.r. outfit and they became Ziegler's consultants.

So quiet was the hiring that for months nobody among the press was aware that Ziegler had employed the pair. But gradually they slipped into the picture and I met them – one-on-two – one morning at the league's New York headquarters.

Two things were immediately clear: 1. They knew virtually nothing about hockey; 2. They had a mandate from Ziegler to revamp the public relations sector. Their response was to further solidify the Canadian operation which would be conveniently close to their own Toronto office. Wilkerson in particular had become a much more public figure within the NHL hierarchy, although he never was officially on staff. Gary Meagher, who had been handling NHL publicity out of Toronto, remained the official league spokesman and a competent one at that.

Every so often Wilkerson would prove himself effective as a go-between when Ziegler and his media antagonists would clash. Once, I wrote a column for *The Hockey News* suggesting that Ziegler had not been forceful enough in repudiating carpetbagging owners.

A few days after the column appeared, I received a harsh, handwritten letter from the president, more sharply critical than I thought the column deserved. Apparently, Ziegler had mentioned the letter to Wilkerson since the p.r. man called me suggesting that we meet for breakfast.

I left that meeting impressed with Wilkerson and wondering whether the president ever would get the hang of public relations.

Some observers believed that he was loosening up; that Wilkerson was having a soothing effect on Ziegler; that the president could still recoup the prestige lost by his disappearance in the 1988 debacle, as well as other leadership transgressions that had occurred over the years.

Ziegler might have cleared the hurdles except for a chain reaction of circumstances, beginning with the decline of Wirtz's power, the eventual ouster of Alan Eagleson as union boss and a series of harsh journalistic works by such diverse writers as a sports editor for a small New England daily to a Vancouver husband-and-wife team with little previous knowledge of hockey.

The combination of David Cruise and Alison Griffiths' book, *Net Worth*, and Russ Conway's seemingly endless expose of NHL misdeeds in the *Lawrence Eagle-Tribune* (Massachusetts) helped to irrevocably turn the tide against John Ziegler. It finally reached the point where the combined efforts of Wilkerson and Kelly were ineffective.

But the ultimate coup de grâce was supplied by the players themselves, who called the first league-wide strike in NHL history. The strike and Ziegler's tepid personal response to it proved to be the chute that slid him right out of the presidency.

This was sad because, when all was said and done, Ziegler seemed like a pleasant, decent man away from the ice.

2

•••

THE 1992 STRIKE AND
REPLACEMENT OF JOHN ZIEGLER

To the average hockey fan, the idea of a players' strike seemed incomprehensible. During the decade spanning 1982-92, salaries continued to rise despite the fact that the National Hockey League was bereft of a network television contract in the United States. By contrast, Major League Baseball, the National Football League and the National Basketball Association all were beneficiaries of major "rights" fees from U.S. networks.

Playing in the NHL during most of the Ziegler regime was a decent deal for a skilled performer. Wayne Gretzky, now playing in Los Angeles, was making more money than ever and the once tiny list of stickhandling millionaires was growing by the year despite some half-hearted attempts by ownership to curb the inflationary spiral.

Despite his innumerable blunders in the areas of leadership, marketing and public relations, Ziegler entered the 1990s in reasonable control of his organization and gubernatorial constituency. He continued to supervise and to rule by carefully selected committee, isolated his foes and maintained a strong personal and professional alliance with union boss Alan Eagleson. The president's house, at least superficially, appeared to be resting on reasonably strong piles that had been driven in years earlier. But, as Ziegler soon would learn, major fissures began appearing in the foundations.

The cracks were caused in such diverse precincts as Edmonton, Alberta and Lawrence, Massachusetts. I learned of the "Edmonton Connection" years earlier. Back in the early 1970s when Eagleson was reaching the peak of his powers, I challenged his stewardship of the union and, in return, felt "The Eagle's" wrath. Through his union's offices, Eagleson attempted to ban me from all the team dressing rooms on the grounds that I was spreading seditious anti-union propaganda.

Rather than accept his ban, I challenged it. At the time, I was New York Bureau Chief for the *Toronto Star* and decided to use the newspaper clout in my Eagleson war. The Ontario Press Council believed that I had a good enough case to order a hearing at which Eagleson was present. They ruled that Eagleson had wrongfully attempted to impose an anti-Fischler ban. He publicly apologized – almost unheard of for Eagleson at the time – then put his arm around me and indicated that we'd now be friends.

I was amazed at The Eagle's absence of rancor and his instant willingness to patch up our feud. Frankly, his hail-fellow-well-met attitude thoroughly won me over. I soon came to regard Eagleson as much a friendly source as I had previously treated him as a foe. Now, in our new relationship he proved a reasonably good provider of information and certainly a ready and easy quote. No matter the topic, The Eagle was ready to chirp with a reply, a newsman's delight.

But as his power grew, so too did concern about his multi-roles. On the one hand he was czar of the union; on the other he was a player agent, leader of Canada Cup tournaments and, of course, a pal of NHL power brokers, especially John Ziegler and Bill Wirtz.

Whenever challenged about his many hats, Eagleson would matter-of-factly dismiss the suggestion of impropriety with a wave of the hand and a chuckle. "I make no secret about what I do," he would say. His contention was that he could adequately serve his player constituency, the Players' Association, as well as the other organizations without damaging his or their credibility.

For considerable time Eagleson was able to maintain his multiple roles. Canada's journalistic establishment didn't challenge him for apparent reasons. It lauded The Eagle's accomplishments and also enjoyed his company, too much to seriously challenge hockey's newest icon.

In the United States, where Eagleson was considerably less known, *Sports Illustrated*'s managing editor Mark Mulvoy went after The Eagle. After what seemed like years of research, the magazine's "exposé" – apparently bedevilled by legal constraints – was lukewarm rather than hot, and caused hardly a tremor in the Eagleson empire. The word went out in the journalistic fraternity, if *Sports Illustrated* couldn't bring Eagleson to his knees, nobody could.

Which explains why I paid little attention to a large brown envelope I received in the mail one day, postmarked Edmonton. The name on the return address was Rich Winter, someone I had vaguely remembered as an agent, but not one of the stature of Eagleson, Art Kaminsky and others who dominated the business at the time.

I couldn't imagine what Winter wanted of me until I opened the envelope and began poring through the material. Page after page dealt with Winter's personal indictment of Eagleson and his practices. It detailed alleged abuses, conflicts of interest and assorted other examples of Eagleson's supposed misdeeds as the union leader.

For sheer bulk alone the package was impressive, but in my case Winter's timing was wrong. It arrived during a week when I was snowed under with writing and television assignments, allowing me virtually no time to study the documents. Nevertheless, my curiosity was piqued, so I phoned Eagleson to obtain his comment on the contents and on Winter.

I got the impression that Eagleson did not consider Winter a threat. "I wouldn't waste my time with him if I was you," he said.

After hanging up, I took another look at the mass of documentation and then put the envelope in a steel drawer, closed it and conveniently forgot about it and Winter.

Eagleson wasn't so lucky. Whatever his faults – and his critics will waste no time elaborating on them – Winter was smart and not lazy, nor easily deterred. While other agents such as Kaminsky were willing to assail The Eagle from time to time, Winter had launched an impressive crusade and would not be daunted.

Undiscouraged by journalists like me, who tended to dismiss or ignore him, Winter redoubled his efforts. By the mid-1980s he had an ally in a California-based agent named Ron Salcer, who was fast becoming a name in the business. Winter and Salcer soon enlisted ex-NFL Players' Association leader Ed Garvey to support their dump-Eagleson movement. By the late 1980s it began gaining momentum; Eagleson appeared unaware that a hurricane was about to blow over his carefully-crafted tower of hockey cards.

Garvey – an expert – began zeroing in on The Eagle's modus operandi. In 1989 he wrote a report on Eagleson's spending practices. "There are no limits on his travel expenses," Garvey noted, "and he has refused to allow us to examine his expense records. We are not really looking for a dinner here or there, we were trying to find out if you, his employers, are able to review his records. The answer is no."

As the crescendo of criticism finally caught the media's attention, Eagleson had to take note of his tormentors. Those of us who had frequently dealt with The Eagle began realizing that, right or wrong, his scalp was in danger as the decade of the 1990s began. As for the media, there was just too much smoke in The Eagle's complicated dealings for there not to be a fire.

Eagleson's treatment of his critics essentially remained the same; they were jealous know-nothings who, more often than not, ignored his contributions to The Game or were outsiders trying to make a name for themselves inside a burgeoning sport.

"I'm sick and tired of worrying about Ed Garvey," said Eagleson. "I am concerned about the players in the National Hockey League, not some of these outsiders who have not contributed anything to the game."

Knowing Eagleson much better than I did Garvey, of whom I knew very little, I accepted Eagleson's critique – again. Yes, The Eagle was flawed, but he had done much to raise the union's standards. He had helped his constituents to steadily-rising salaries, whether his critics wanted to accept it or not. I and most of my journalistic colleagues were willing to plod the same route because at least in print, Eagleson remained the Teflon man.

There was, however, one fatal exception. Russ Conway, the determined reporter who had become sports editor of the *Lawrence Eagle-Tribune*, had been a longtime friend of Hall of Famer Bobby Orr and other former Boston Bruins, some of whom had felt ethically and financially betrayed by Eagleson.

By national standards, the *Eagle-Tribune* is a newspaper unknown beyond New England. The same could be said for Conway as a reporter; that is, until 1990 when he launched his investigation of Eagleson's performance in office.

However, The Eagle already was heading out the NHLPA's door. The Winter-Salcer-Garvey axis had gained so much support that Eagleson finally was forced to launch a search for a successor with a target date for his ultimate resignation from the union in 1992. Meanwhile, the groundswell of interest in Eagleson's performance grew, thanks to the late night probing at the *Lawrence Eagle-Tribune*.

Despite the newspaper's and Conway's relative obscurity, the two worked to bring down hockey's most powerful figure. Conway already had a track record as an investigative reporter and – no less important – had the support of his editor, Daniel J. Warner, who provided infinite time and sufficient resources for Conway to probe the union boss. This was very unusual for a small, New England newspaper.

"Sometimes duty causes us to go beyond local boundaries," said Warner. "Conway saw such a duty when he detected over the years of covering his beat, that something was seriously wrong inside the National Hockey League. So he went inside to take a look."

Over a period of a year Conway interviewed more than 200 people including retired and active professional players, NHL officials and others in the hockey world. Many of the interviews were taped and in-depth. According to the reporter, more than 1,600 phone calls were made or received and more than 150 documents, totalling thousands of pages, were reviewed.

In time Eagleson and Ziegler got wind of the investigation. During one telephone conversation with me, The Eagle dismissed Conway in the same manner that he had Rich Winter years earlier. Eagleson understood that Conway was pals with Eagleson's ex-client-turned-adversary Bobby Orr and insisted to me that the entire assault on his honour was Orr-inspired and therefore more a matter of jealousy than substance.

Conway forged ahead. When he attempted to obtain interviews with Eagleson and Ziegler, he was rebuffed. "They answered with letters from lawyers," said Conway. "Ziegler also ordered NHL employees not to talk with me about the investigation."

No matter. Conway persisted and the more he dug, the more delectable information he discovered. In September 1991 he published the first of many instalments in a series titled "Cracking The Ice – Intrigue and Conflict In The World Of Big-Time Hockey." Not surprisingly some of Conway's prime targets were Eagleson and Ziegler.

"Behind the upheaval in the NHL," Conway wrote in the third paragraph of his first instalment, "are found charges by players that they have been betrayed not only by the league but also by their own union's executive director, R. Alan Eagleson."

Conway's probe accelerated as Eagleson's protesting momentum decelerated. In the summer of 1990 a Detroit lawyer-agent, Bob Goodenow, had edged out another agent, Steve Bartlett, as NHLPA executive director. It was to emerge as one of the most telling turning points in the history of the NHL. From that moment on, Goodenow began laying the groundwork for new Collective Bargaining Agreement talks that resulted in the strike of April 1, 1992, and a metamorphosis of hockey politics.

Notorious for his hard-nosed style as a player-agent, Goodenow was the beneficiary of a number of events, not the least of which was the Conway series, as well as a book authored by a Canadian husband-and-wife team with no known hockey connections.

I first heard the names Alison Griffiths and David Cruise in 1990 via a phone call from the former who identified herself as a writer from Victoria, British Columbia. "I'm researching a book on hockey," she said, "and was wondering whether you could help?"

An introduction such as that had come across my wire dozens of times and I readily agreed to provide any useful information she needed. It didn't take long for me to deduce that Griffiths and Cruise were embarking on a powerful bit of journalism, particularly when she began grilling me about Eagleson.

I told her about my experience with Eagleson – the anti-Fischler move within the NHLPA – and its settlement. She asked me for additional contacts and I provided them on the assumption that Griffiths would have done the same had the positions been reversed.

That marked the first of many conversations with Griffiths. Occasionally I had telephone chats with her husband who seemed less involved in the project. If I came away with one impression above others, it was that neither was what we in the industry regarded as a "hockey person." I mentioned at least once to Griffiths that this could be a terrific asset to her rather than a liability. Judging by the results, it apparently was more plus than minus.

Cruise and Griffiths had previously won awards for such non-hockey works as *Fleecing The Lamb* and *Lords Of The Line* and were now applying their diligence with equal verve to the NHL. Griffiths had mentioned in passing one day that their original purpose was to focus on Eagleson, the character. It was only after significant probing that they widened the scope of their work to an all-encompassing assault on the hockey establishment.

The book was slated for publication in the fall of 1991, and as often is the case with such editions, the authors attempted to obtain as much publicity as possible. One way to do so was to send advance copies to those who might be willing to help the project along.

Since I then was writing a weekly column in *The Hockey News*, I was a prime source of space for Griffiths and Cruise and since the couple were going to be spending time in New York City, they suggested that we finally meet for an interview.

With the approval of *The Hockey News*' editor Steve Dryden, I told Griffiths and Cruise that I'd read the book before our meeting and then arranged my questions before the interview. We agreed to meet at the Paramount Hotel in Times Square, a hostelry which in another era had been the hotel for visiting NHL teams.

Net Worth, their brand-new book, arrived in the mail a few days before they arrived in Manhattan. I immediately plunged into it with enormous interest. From the start, I sensed that it would be a very special read and by the time I had read a dozen pages, my attention was riveted to the text.

Net Worth eventually became a bestseller and played right into Bob Goodenow's hands. Here was a book that he could distribute to every one of the union members as a "bible" listing the debits and transgressions of the Eagleson-Ziegler-Wirtz triumvirate and the plusses that would come from the enlightened new NHLPA boss. To no one's surprise, it also solidified the Players' Association's resolve as it entered into negotiations for the 1991 Collective Bargaining Agreement.

Having covered hockey professionally since 1954, I was into my 37th year on the NHL beat when talk of a possible strike began wafting across pressrooms throughout the league. When I heard such talk, I laughed – and argued – with people and players.

Strike! Players were now averaging more than $300,000 a year and the fiscal skyrocket still was climbing toward the stratosphere. These were athletes who played an average of three times a week and were getting paid vacations for the months of June, July and August. They were usually catered to hand and foot; they often operated businesses on the side; they were quartered at the best hotels; they dined at the best restaurants; and they were often asked to actually perform for less than 25 minutes per game. For a deal like that, receiving an average salary of $300,000 in 1991 seemed like a pretty good deal to me.

I didn't think a strike was much in the minds of many players, the media or the fans, although one of them, a friend of mine from the New York Islanders, was very vehement about it. Ray Ferraro had heard me do an interview on New York's sports-radio station WFAN about a potential strike. "It won't happen," I said, "because hockey players simply are not that stupid to turn down the cushy life they have."

Ferraro phoned and suggested that I had missed the point; that the union was misrepresented by its previous leader and now it was playing catch-up and maybe a strike was a necessity. We talked for more than a half-hour and agreed to disagree. Never did I believe that the players – most still from Canada – would walk out on themselves, the fans and the ownership.

But I hadn't taken into account the cleverness and ferocity of Bob Goodenow's leadership since he took over from Eagleson; nor had the owners. However, Ziegler must have understood that, in labour terms, they were in bed with a crocodile.

My encounters with Goodenow were very pleasant. We shared a table at a *Hockey News* award luncheon and spent considerable time discussing the strike of the Hamilton (Ontario) Tigers' players in 1925 that led to dissolution of the team and its move to New York (Americans). Goodenow proved very helpful in supplying me with lists of agents for *The Fischler Report*, my weekly hockey newsletter, and seemed a most cordial fellow.

Obviously, Goodenow was putting his best face forward. "He's not the same affable guy when you get down to real business," an agent stated a few weeks later. "Bob called the other day and bawled the hell out of me about a contract I had negotiated. He said I wasn't tough enough."

In time I would hear similar complaints from other agents; the prevailing theme was that Goodenow would jump all over them if he felt they weren't fighting hard enough for their clients.

The union boss would become the "hardballer" he wanted his colleagues to be. The proof was in the negotiations. In September 1991, Goodenow broke off Collective Bargaining Agreement talks with the owners. Ziegler warned that if the union got its way, the average NHL salary by 1994 would be $680,000. This time he was close to being prescient. Ziegler, trying to be stern, further cautioned that the teams couldn't absorb it.

By now player skepticism about the NHL operation in general and Eagleson in particular had mushroomed to such an extent that rank-and-file stickhandlers simply couldn't care less about Ziegler's projections. They obviously thought the prexy, to quote the Bard of Avon, "doth protesteth too much."

It hardly mattered to NHLPA members that they were richer than ever and expansion guaranteed them more job opportunities than big-league hockey players had ever enjoyed. Whenever a critic of runaway inflation – like myself – would complain to a Ray Ferraro, he would answer that nobody was twisting the owners' arms to pay the salaries.

He was right, to an extent. Owners such as Bruce McNall in Los Angeles and Mike Shanahan in St. Louis (the Blues' chairman, but not owner) had been overspending on the likes of Wayne Gretzky and Scott Stevens. "Some owners have opened the floodgates," said Flyers' owner Ed Snider. "We have gone the way of our brothers in baseball and basketball in terms of overspending, but we don't have the TV money to bail us out." (This admission, incidentally, from the owner who would, in 1993, pay $15 million cash, plus players, just for the rights to Eric Lindros.)

The stalemate between owners and players moved into the season's homestretch with no breakthrough. Goodenow was forcing a showdown and the issue was a better deal for his players. He was prepared to make the owners blink. In the mind of some critics the players were going too far. One of these critics was Pat Doyle of the *Winnipeg Sun*.

"The players want and want and want," said Doyle. "They fret and frown over free agency. Their wish is to come and go as they please and, under present NHL legislation, it's their belief that harsh compensation limits movement.

"Not true. Mark Messier wanted out of Edmonton; he's in New York. Dale Hawerchuk wanted out of Winnipeg; he's in Buffalo. Adam Oates wanted out of St. Louis; he's in Boston. Doug Gilmour wanted out of Calgary; he's in Toronto.

"So, who needs free agency? If you desire a change of scenery, all you have to do is demand, whine, pout or sulk; or, all of the above. Eventually, you'll get your wish."

What Goodenow and the union really wanted was a fight. They had developed the notion that, no matter how much money they were making, they would be perceived as wimps. "If we back down now," said one player, echoing the prevailing macho thought, "we're stupid. It will be perceived as a sign of weakness."

Notice, there was no mention about how much better the average player's standard of living had become, although there remained a precious few NHLPA members with the courage to put Eagleson and his contributions in a more realistic perspective. One of them was veteran forward Bobby Smith who had been an NHLPA executive for nine years.

"It has become very popular to dump on The Eagle," said Smith. "People are making a mistake commonly made, judging things that happen in 1983 and 1986 by 1992 standards. No one was paying $50 million for franchises then. A lot of teams weren't making money.

"That's not the reality now. Times have changed. Salaries are higher than anyone thought they would be. Alan has been unfairly slighted."

Unfortunately, Smith's voice was muffled by the union leadership and, particularly, by Goodenow. Those of us who believed that the already well-off players would avoid disrupting the orderly flow of the season were sadly mistaken.

Incredibly, the strike happened. It was early April 1992. I had a first-hand view of it, primarily because most of the major meetings between owners and players were held in Manhattan, close to my home. The elegant Plaza Hotel at the southern tip of Central Park became press headquarters and it was there that much of the bad guessing among the media took place.

This is not meant so much as a criticism of my colleagues as it is an attempt to portray to the average fan how distant the rank-and-file newsman standing on the outside actually is from the inside reality.

I recall one meeting that took place in the morning. The owners broke for lunch and, as they paraded down the corridor, we attempted to get some clues as to the direction in which the talks were headed. For a moment someone caught Flyers' president Ed Snider smiling and, immediately, this was interpreted as a sign that progress was being made. (It wasn't.) Yet this type of misinterpretation was more the rule rather than the exception.

On Saturday, April 4, 1992, Day Four of the strike, the *Toronto Star*'s Bob McKenzie threateningly suggested that the Monday board of governors' meeting "will ultimately determine" if the strike "is going to be long and destructive."

He went on to quote Minnesota (soon to be in Dallas) North Stars' owner Norman Green: "If we don't reach an agreement on Monday, it won't be done."

Of course, there was no agreement on Monday or Tuesday or Wednesday or Thursday – but it would be done, nonetheless. In the meantime, Goodenow bared his fangs and Ziegler exposed his sensitivity. When the dust of battle had cleared, the union leader's grasp of the jugular and the president's inept and soft defences would ultimately doom Ziegler and cast Goodenow in the role of the menacing power broker.

Eagleson, for all his bluster and his alliances with ownership, was a true hockey aficionado. Those who dealt regularly with The Eagle sensed that he truly loved the game. Whatever his personal goals, Eagleson wanted the NHL to succeed for hockey's sake nearly as much as his own.

Goodenow was another question and required much more study. But his critics were now being heard from. "Goodenow has transformed the 30-second sound byte to a sleep exercise," said *Toronto Sun* columnist Steve Simmons in what may have been the understatement of the decade.

On this night at the Plaza, as the union boss rejected Ziegler's plaintive offer, I suffered an ache in the pit of my stomach that delivered a message: the NHL as I knew and loved it never would be the same, at least not as long as Goodenow ran the show.

My former intern, Vic Morren, now a hockey producer for ESPN, was with me at the time and shared virtually the same emotion. Not long afterward, we walked out of the hotel and, by accident, happened to meet Kevin Lowe, the then Edmonton Oilers' defenceman with whom I had written a book, *Champions*. I was somewhat astonished as Lowe indicated that the strike might be a long one and even more surprised as he mentioned how difficult the owners' position was for the union to accept.

As Morren and I headed toward the subway station, we turned to each other. "Here's another guy who's making a ton of money and he's still not satisfied," I said.

Another memorable vignette took place on the first Sunday of the strike. That morning word circulated among the media that Mark Messier was calling a special press conference to articulate the union's position. It was an unusually cold spring afternoon when Messier, Andy Moog, Mike Gartner and other union executives gathered at a posh Park Avenue hotel. The idea was to persuade the media of the union cause and, supposedly, answer questions.

Sounding very much like a high school sophomore reading from the "New Testament," Messier tried to articulate the players' position. He sounded more unctuous than sincere and the question-and-answer period which followed did nothing to convince me that the unionists were a suffering lot.

I spent most of the week in and out of the Plaza as my anxiety quotient became more intense. With each day it seemed more likely that the sides wouldn't come to a compromise. By mid-week Ziegler produced a third "final proposal" which was promptly rejected by the union. The president called it a "sad, sad day in NHL history," even suggesting that this could be the end of the NHL.

"I don't know who is more stupid," said Bruins' general manager Harry Sinden, "the owners for proposing the deal or the players for rejecting it."

I appreciated Sinden's hard line, but I also believed Ziegler was sincere vis-à-vis the NHL's overall welfare, although I'm sure that many would say I was duped by the president's style. I was only a few feet from Ziegler as he actually shed a few tears – "Could this be the end of the NHL, forever?" – during his Plaza Hotel press conference.

But, the betrayal of the tears did as much harm to the president's image as anything since his "Koharskigate." Rather than empathize with the president's feelings, the media seized upon the sight of a weeping leader and re-created Ziegler as a weak-kneed wimp. The president's statements were a bit too whiny for most of the fourth estate.

Describing his offer on April 7, 1992, Ziegler virtually pleaded, "If it will make the players happy, if it will be the thing that gets them back to what they do best, playing the game, I will call it a surrender. I will call it an unconditional surrender. All they have to do is go back and play hockey."

Ziegler's words cemented Goodenow's resolve. The NHLPA head dug in his heels and soon two words that would be bruited about as much as any in the next three years were first uttered in the NHL, "salary cap."

Aware that the rival NBA had become an immensely profitable (for both owners and players) business, NHL owners began studying pro basketball's strategy, from marketing to budgeting. One aspect of NBA planning that caught their attention was the salary cap which was crafted under the David Stern regime as a means of regulating salaries while enabling players to enjoy fair profits. That it worked to everyone's advantage was evident by the NBA's overall popularity both at the gate and on television as well as by the salary figures themselves. Many professional basketball players still were averaging over $1 million annually under the new NBA salary cap.

Ziegler warned Goodenow that the NHL would pursue implementation of an NBA-style salary cap. "If they wish to save this business," said Ziegler, "they'd better be interested (in the concept of a salary cap). If they think a partnership is, we pay and they get and take no risk, they've got the wrong idea."

Owners sought a 15 percent cap on salary arbitration raises and an arrangement whereby league-wide salary increases would be limited to 15 percent. Judging by the manner in which the pay scale was climbing, exploding even, this all made sense.

Chicago's Wirtz, who was familiar with the NBA cap because of his association with the Bulls, pushed for its implementation. "That's what all sports need

– a salary cap," he said. "The only thing that's fair is sharing revenue on a 50-50 basis."

Even assuming that Bill Wirtz and John McMullen were talking sense – and I thought they were – it was too late. Goodenow smelled blood. The strike was now more than a week old and playoff monies, which the owners so dearly coveted, would be lost if a settlement wasn't reached almost immediately.

On Tuesday, April 7, 1992, the owners produced an offer and set a deadline of 3 p.m., Thursday, April 9th, for the players to accept it or face termination of the season. The players rejected it, but the owners left it on the table to find ways of breaking the impasse,

"I thought the season was over then and there," said Blackhawks' owner Bill Wirtz. "I'm usually an 'up' kind of guy, but I was down then."

Many of us had come to the conclusion that the season would, in fact, be lost. Goodenow appeared intransigent and impenetrable. The word among some members of the fourth estate was that Ziegler needed a settlement in order to save his job.

On Wednesday, April 8th, New Jersey Devils' president-general manager Lou Lamoriello convened a luncheon-gathering of metropolitan area hockey writers. Lamoriello delivered his – and the NHL's – position before throwing the floor open to questions. It was evident from the hostile tones and questioning of the newsmen that they were emphatically on the players' side. Lamoriello remained composed throughout the grilling but at one point, Frank Brown of the *Daily News* got up and began filibustering about the union's right to strike among other things. It was an interesting interlude but certainly not on the agenda. Perhaps I should have kept my mouth shut, but under the circumstances it was impossible. When Brown finished, I submitted that the time had come to impede the runaway salaries; that the owners should be doing that right now, whether the players liked it or not. I offered variations on the theme as passionately as possible because I fervently believed the players were demanding too much. When I had finished my peroration, I realized what I knew from the very beginning; I was in the distinct minority. No problem. I had gotten that off my chest and returned home to continue coverage of the strike. From time to time Ziegler and Goodenow would huddle in semi-secret locations including one quick visit to Toronto by the president and several owners.

Pessimism permeated the Plaza's press headquarters until 6 p.m. on Thursday night, April 9th, three hours after the NHL's deadline had passed. Goodenow, a practitioner of 11th-hour negotiations, had reconvened with Ziegler.

Some of the old-line conservatives quite correctly were willing to go head-to-head with Goodenow and sacrifice the playoff riches, but the board of governors had divided into factions between liberals such as Norm Green and Howard Baldwin of the Pittsburgh Penguins and right wingers like Wirtz, McMullen and Jerry Jacobs of Boston.

"I'm not going to give up the store for one playoff year when the whole future is at stake," said Wirtz.

Had ownership accepted Wirtz's plan of battle and met Goodenow's challenge, the governors might have outlasted the union and beaten the new union boss before he won the respect of his troops. It was not unlike Germany's (illegal) occupation of the Rhineland. The German high command gambled that neither the stronger French nor English armies would call his bluff. Had either or both moved against the weaker, smaller German occupiers, Hitler would have been defeated, embarrassed and possibly even prevented from ever occupying Austria and Czechoslovakia.

For an assortment of historical reasons, the Allies flinched and the result was World War II. Likewise, on Friday, April 10, 1992, word filtered throughout the Plaza Hotel pressroom that ownership was about to flinch. The salary cap, which might have imposed some economic sanity with a decelerated payroll skyrocket, was in no part of the agreement. This was the most egregious omission, the one which would become a long-term time bomb that would explode in October 1994.

But ownership had no "book" on Goodenow's modus operandi and underestimated his willingness to play brinksmanship politics. "Bob says 98 percent of a negotiation gets done the last two days," said Wirtz. "I don't understand that, but everyone's got his own style."

Owners made concessions up and down the line. The clubs agreed to recognize that the players own exclusive rights to their individual personality, including their likeness. This would prove to be a major cash cow for the stickhandlers.

The trauma the Canadian owners were suffering, and the pressure from Kings' owner Bruce McNall, agents and marquee players such as Wayne Gretzky and Mark Messier accelerated the rapprochement which crystallized on Friday evening, April 10, at the Plaza. Those of us who had been in and out of the hotel all week sensed that the drama was reaching its climax around 9 p.m. when camera crews began setting up in a pressroom off the main lobby.

Many of us expected the chief protagonists to arrive before 10 p.m., hopeful that they would accommodate those who were on a deadline. But this was not to be. Now the clock was approaching midnight and some TV crews had packed up and left. Suddenly, the room came alive with the buzz that always accompanies the prelude to a peace pact, whether labour or war.

Ziegler and Goodenow finally entered from stage right, adjusted the microphones and the president declared, "We reached a meeting of the minds and an agreement in principle."

He looked wan, as anyone might after a ten-day marathon. It was difficult to discern whether either of the combatants had a physical edge on the other. I could see no significant differences, even in the smiles, as they indulged photographers with the usual post-conference handshakes.

By sheer coincidence, my SportsChannel cameraman had packed up his equipment and loaded his car's trunk just as Goodenow and an aide were leaving the hotel. It was raining and there were no cabs in the immediate vicinity. Goodenow needed some help.

"You want a ride?" I asked.

"Do you have room for two more?" he replied.

Pat Watters, the cameraman, drives a big Oldsmobile. There was more than enough room. Goodenow and his pal climbed into the back and we headed west to his hotel. He seemed pumped without saying very much. The talk drifted to innocuous subjects. Goodenow was not giving away any state secrets, but inwardly he must have been savouring an emphatic victory.

My hope, among many, many others, was that something good would come of the conflict. Bruce McNall, who soon would replace Wirtz as chairman of the board of governors, was typically optimistic. "Long-term," McNall opined, "the strike will be very positive. You'll have a movement to where the sport needs to be, to a partnership between players and owners."

It sounded good at the time, but McNall was dreaming. He either underestimated Goodenow's motives or chose to ignore them altogether in a Candide-like imitation. Naturally, Goodenow mimicked the "partnership" theme and the naive – or hopeful – believed him.

But Ziegler's bosses were less naive. They sensed that they had a bum deal, that the president had capitulated and that new leadership was necessary. The wheels of change had begun moving against Ziegler whose litany of problems dating back to 1988, and prior, were weighing against him.

This time the president's allies couldn't help him. Wirtz had been board chairman too long and the young Turks wanted him replaced while Eagleson's wings had been clipped by the advent of Goodenow. There was talk of a brave, new NHL world on the horizon but it would be one without John Ziegler at the helm.

3

....

FROM ZIEGLER TO STEIN:
PUNCHING UP THE NHL'S IMAGE

You know the gag about the chap who kept hitting himself in the head with a big wooden mallet? When someone asked why he persisted in such apparent madness, the fellow replied, "Because it feels so good when I stop."

When John Ziegler resigned - after a monumental push - as NHL president in June of 1992, the mallet stopped hitting big-league hockey in the head. Not that "Ziggy Stardust's" fade to the wings automatically jump-started the sport to the top of the charts, or even to a U.S. network TV contract, but it at least signalled an end to the league's 16-year migraine. "During Ziegler's reign," TV sports executive Gil Miller mentioned to me one day, "hockey became the fastest growing game in the world; except in the National Hockey League!"

Evidence was available. Consider these doozies:

* Despite having 16 out of 24 teams based in the United States, Ziegler closed the NHL's New York City public relations office in 1991. The league was without a publicity outlet in the U.S. which often left the media moguls strapped for data. "I called the New York office for some information about Eric Lindros," said Madison Avenue p.r. executive Chuck Alexander, "and the woman who answered didn't even know who he was. Eventually they referred me to Toronto."
* When the league's crown jewel, Pittsburgh's Mario Lemieux, was chopped down in the spring of 1992 by New York Rangers' slugger Adam Graves, Ziegler was not immediately heard from. "Ziggy Stardust," as he is known to *New York Daily News* columnist Bob Raissman, uttered not even one adjective of protest while such august journals as the Washington *Post* and the *New York Times* skewered him.

* Marketing (this is just a euphemism for sales) was never a part of Ziegler's lexicon, or his persona. Even in the most obvious moments when the NHL could have reaped immense dividends.

   Wayne Gretzky once was invited to be on "The Tonight Show" but found himself stranded in Chicago by a blizzard. The Great One could have reached L.A., but only by private jet. "Wayne offered to pay half out of his own pocket," said then Edmonton Oilers' defence-man Kevin Lowe, who was with Gretzky at the time, "but the league wouldn't foot the other half. Wayne never made it, and the NHL blew the Carson show." Sometimes it was simply flabbergasting.

* "Think small" was Ziggy's philosophy for dealing with everything from promoting marquee players to promoting himself. "I once recommended to John that he have his title upgraded from 'president' to 'commissioner,' but he shot me down," my pal Harry Ornest, former owner of the Blues, mentioned. "Now that he's gone, the league is doing what Ziegler would never do: have a commissioner ... AND make him available to the media."

   That was only one of the many changes as big-league hockey buried its Ziegler past. "What's needed is a total stripping down of the machine and a rebuilding," said TV analyst John Davidson. "Already we can see that the new administration is open to new ideas."

Total them up and you'll find as many cures for the NHL's ills as Eric Lindros has dollar bills. The transition would be painfully slow, but new leaders such as Bruce McNall couldn't wait to turn over a new puck. "We want to get out of the Dark Ages," said McNall, who succeeded Blackhawks' owner Bill Wirtz as chairman of the board of governors, "and already we're beginning to see the light."

One reporter said "Cousin Brucie's" problems were priorities, such as, if you have 100 very important things to do yesterday, which ones come first tomorrow? "Getting us back on U.S. network television is right up there with my primary objectives," said McNall. "We've got the best attraction, but we've got to get it across the country."

However some Madison Avenue mavens believed Tie Domi had a better chance of winning the Lady Byng Trophy for sportsmanship than the NHL had of signing with NBC, CBS, or ABC. They insisted that the league's negative charisma quotient was directly attributed to players punching one another in the mouth. Fighting, they said, must go. Washington Capitals' general manager David Poile agreed. "We've got a great product," he said, "but we've given ourselves an image problem. We're walking a fine line between a great day and a bad one."

Like wizards crouched over a smoking cauldron, the NHL image-changers were searching for the elixir that would transform the toad into a prince and make the game less akin to "Wrestlemania on Ice" and more of a Utopian spectacle that combined clean hitting, lyrical skating and slick stickhandling. They strove for the day when Baryshnikovs of hockey such as Pat LaFontaine could strut their stuff without taking a stick in the mouth. Imagine – may Bob Probert forgive us – an end to fighting as an NHL staple. Some power brokers said it would happen.

"This is a time for change," said then-Minnesota North Stars' owner Norm Green. "People used to feel that fighting was an integral part of the game, but the people of the 1990s are different from the people of the 1970s. It's tough to explain to a mother whose youngster is about to play hockey what the rationale is for fighting."

Ever since Tyrannosaurus Rex first stickhandled a boulder past a Brontosaurus, the rationales that connected hockey and fighting have been tradition and money. As former Toronto Maple Leafs' owner Conn Smythe proclaimed long ago, "If you can't beat 'em in the alley, you can't beat 'em on the ice." Besides, Smythe noted, fans pay money to see hockey players fight. Over the years, propagandists have endorsed the punch in the mouth as a "safety valve" for otherwise frustrated stickhandlers, and since attendance climbed to around 90 percent of capacity by the start of the 1990s, Ziegler reasoned that fighting was not hurting the gate. Some owners believed that was right.

"We've sold every seat for years, and we're not in favour of radical changes in the rules," said Detroit Red Wings' executive vice-president Jim Lites. "Aggressiveness is part of our game."

True, but suddenly hockey purists were making a keen distinction between clean aggressive play and gratuitous woodchopping. Exhibit A was Adam Graves' Paul Bunyan act on Lemieux in the 1992 playoffs. His bludgeoning of hockey's most majestic star was so outrageous that it invoked continent-wide criticism of goonery. Lemieux unabashedly charged that the Blueshirts had "a contract" out on him and that the game was "too dangerous" in its current state. Penguins' owner Howard Baldwin immediately proposed that the league disinfect itself of such muggings and filter out the filth while allowing the virtuosos to gain centre stage once and for all.

There was only one problem: the officiating. Hockey referees are a unique breed, a hybrid of zebras crossed with ostriches. They have eyes and they wear stripes, but they bury their heads while thugs endlessly perpetrate "restraining fouls" and muck up what should be a magnificent spectacle. On a given night the refs will allow at least 50 percent of the obvious fouls to go unpunished. But not without reason, some claim.

"Too much goes on for one man to handle," said Scotty Bowman, who coached the Pittsburgh Penguins to the 1992 Stanley Cup. "We have to have three referees. There's interference, there's putting hands on the stick. With the one-referee system, the official only tries to pick out the most flagrant fouls." Davidson agreed, adding: "Eliminating the fouls that hold back the game's speed should be one of the league's highest priorities."

One of the many problematic aspects of hockey officiating, according to my friend Harry Ornest, himself a former hockey referee, was that the president (meaning Ziegler) of the NHL himself had known less than nothing about the officiating. "Ziegler not only knew nothing about the officiating," said Ornest, "but he made no effort to learn. He was irresponsible in this, when it should have been a major function of his job. But John fancied himself an elitist – above these petty concerns. He was almost childish in this respect."

"Nobody was allowed to speak on anything without some kind of censure," said *VancouverProvince* columnist Tony Gallagher. "You talk about the libel chill – in this fiefdom, speech was never free. It was the Hear-No-Evil League."

Censorship cut right across the NHL board. It even infected the script prepared for Hollywood's Alan Thicke in June of 1992 at the NHL awards gala, which was carried over Canadian Broadcasting Corporation's TV network.

Thicke was forced to edit out references to the NHL players' strike. "The people who criticize me for toothless humour should have been sitting in the damn board room and seen how many teeth were there before the chickens got their hands on them," said Thicke.

Partly because of the gag rule, the players themselves seldom had anything to say. Or, if they did speak, too many of them sounded more like Mortimer Snerd than the articulate athletes they were. Compared to their basketball brethren, stickhandlers are colossal bores, regurgitating bromides ("We've got to play 60 minutes") as if reciting the Gettysburg Address.

More frustrating yet for interviewers such as myself, the league had become sprinkled with a new breed of nontalker: the European import. In the 1992 entry draft a record 11 Eastern Europeans were chosen in the first round. The Tampa Bay Lightning's No. 1 pick, Czech defenceman Roman Hamrlik, had mastered enough English to report that his favourite food was "ham and eggs." After that the interviewer was in trouble. Ditto for writers who were hopeful of schmoozing with the Ottawa Senator's top pick, Alexei Yashin, a Russian who was great with "da" and "nyet," but otherwise could pass for Gary Cooper. However, the language barrier was something the league, and the media covering the sport, had to accept, as it mined the mother lode of former Iron Curtain players.

This immigration may not have been a joy for journalists, but it did wonders for the league's talent quotient. "One reason why we finished first overall," said Rangers' president Neil Smith in 1994, "is because of the way [Russian] Sergei Nemchinov performed as a rookie. And you can say a good reason why the Penguins won the Stanley Cup was because of the help they got from [Czech] Jaromir Jagr. The Europeans are here to stay."

They had to be, if only to fill the rosters of an ever-expanding league. For a $50 million entrance fee Ottawa and Tampa Bay obtained minimal talent – Lightning president Phil Esposito described it as "all the crap thrown our way" – but maximum hope. Despite their impoverished lineups, leaders of both franchises were as optimistic as a newly-elected president on Inauguration Day. "We've sold out every one of our (10,500) seats," said Senators' general manager Mel Bridgman, "and some of them are going for one hundred dollars a pop."

After a year of fiscal embarrassment, the Lightning appeared to be shaping up, and if the Tampa experiment succeeded even more NHL seeds would be planted in the Sun Belt. "I can see another team in Florida," said Minnesota's Green (whose team was about to decamp the north and become the Dallas Stars), eyeing the Miami market, "and one in Texas. That would give us a nice spread in the warmer states and open the league's network possibilities."

Perhaps, but all of that was small potatoes compared with the NHL's prime challenges, otherwise known as the Three L's: labour, Lindros, and leadership.

Reverberations from the spring of 1992's 10-day players' strike were just being felt at the box office around November of that same year. Losing teams such as the Sabres raised their ticket prices 16 percent to 27 percent above 1991's numbers. Like other clubs that were hiking prices, the Sabres pointed to sky-rocketing salaries as the prime reason. In Buffalo's case the payroll had gone up 69 percent in the past three years.

Prime-market clubs such as the Rangers and Kings had been able to feed the fat-cat players, but smaller-market teams such as Winnipeg and Hartford were unable to compete financially with the big-city boys. Under the circumstances, even the rich players were beginning to worry about the NHL's survival.

"We have to come up with a plan that makes it more attractive for players to play for smaller-market teams," said Mark Messier, "so that it doesn't matter what size of the city or the market is. If there was a system like [the NBA salary cap] you'd see a lot of players would want to play in the smaller Canadian cities because those are the kinds of cities where they grew up."

Tell that to Lindros. The Ontario-born behemoth made beauteous Quebec City seem like the Black Hole of Calcutta with his unprecedented refusal to play for the Nordiques. The NHL then began to hold its breath, hoping that the "Next One" would be as good as the "Great One" when the Philadelphia Flyers paid Quebec $15 million in American funds (about $20 million Canadian) plus $3 million worth of traded players, as well as $22 million over six years to Lindros.

How good would Lindros be? At six feet four inches tall and 225 pounds, he loomed as an oversized Messier, which would be plenty good indeed. The lad was a steamroller in the slot, and could also score. All signs suggested that he would fill seats in the manner of Gretzky. There was one big if, though: "Eric the Large" had yet to play an NHL game. "He may be the greatest thing since sliced bread," said Edmonton Oilers' GM Glenn Sather, "but he had better be the whole loaf."

While the hockey world awaited "Lindrosmania," the NHL also was casting about for a new leader. Ziegler was dropped through the trapdoor so quickly that even his most rabid executioners were left empty-handed, without an instant replacement. Almost overnight there was a feeding frenzy. The list of potential successors included everyone but Dan Quayle (and even he would have obtained support had he known that hockey was played on ice).

In the interim the league knighted chief counsel Gil Stein as acting president. Stein quickly did one of the most arresting flip-flops since Dr. Jekyll and Mr.

Hyde. Known as a quiet, dour legal eagle nesting in the NHL's Manhattan aerie, Stein suddenly flew busily into dozens of interviews like a sporting David Letterman. Every day he seemed to be in another city, making quips and spreading the NHL gospel (more like selling himself) while promising reform. Said one NHL GM: "Gil visited more NHL cities in one month than Ziegler did in 15 years."

When one listened to Stein, it was possible to believe that a brave new world of hockey was just around the corner. He promised all manner of changes, from better media relations to enhancing the image of hidden stars. Obviously the man had a grip on things. "The NHL is 75 years old," said Stein, "and hockey is still one of the best-kept secrets in the United States."

Ziggy was directly to blame for that. As Ornest told me, in what has to be one of the best summations of the Ziegler presidency, "John proved that he never failed to miss an opportunity to miss an opportunity."

What fascinated me most about the summer of 1992 was Stein's hellbent bid for the new commissionership. I had known Stein ever since his days as legal counsel for the Philadelphia Flyers in the early 1970s. Any student of NHL politics understood that Flyers' owner Ed Snider was Stein's patron and when Stein moved to the league's New York office as its legal eagle, Stein became one of the most important aides to Ziegler.

To those of us who dealt with Stein on a one-on-one basis – not very easy, I might add – he oozed an avuncular affability. He was given to quick quips, but just as suddenly would turn serious. Under the Ziegler regime, Stein had remained in the background – even further back than Ziggy – rarely granting interviews.

But the moment Ziegler departed, Stein was anointed "interim" president. Stein realized instantly that he had a shot at the top job. How he would obtain the commissionership was another story, since there never had been an NHL commissioner before, nor such an open field for the position.

I phoned Stein one day and suggested a meeting so I could discern his thinking. He told me that he was taking a couple of trips, but would be glad to sit down when he returned. In the interim I followed his tour, which many believed was merely a blatant attempt to promote himself for the top job.

"He probably will win the NHL's top job on a permanent basis," said William Houston in the *Globe and Mail*. "But Stein's age (64) is a problem."

On a visit to Toronto, Stein said that fighting was presenting the NHL with an image problem and added that he thought it could be removed from the game completely. He added that a U.S. TV contract was critical to the league's success and said he would be talking to the heads of ABC, NBC and CBS.

Aware of Ziegler's media phobia, Stein went on to promise a "more open" and less abrasive relationship with the press. During an 18,000-mile transcontinental "goodwill" junket, Stein reiterated constantly that he was seeking "input" from the newspeople and fans.

"But during his meeting with us," added Houston, "he did not ask one question. Is this a fact-finding mission or a goodwill tour?"

Finally, I got the call; Stein was ready for our interview. Our meeting in his spiffy, well-appointed mid-Manhattan office was pleasant enough although it seemed as if Stein was a bit edgy. I immediately brought up the question of his age being a detriment to his bid and he laughed it off. Like Houston, I got the distinct impression that Stein was less interested in improving league conditions than he was his own bid for the commissionership. I left his office less impressed than I had hoped I would be, but convinced that he would make a powerful run.

Conceivably, he could have led the pack to the finish line but Stein's heavy-handed campaigning began turning off key influential owners. Moreover, in his new position of power, McNall could influence the decision-making procedure. McNall once said to me, early on in the search, that "since the NBA is so successful, maybe I should try to get (Commissioner) David Stern to come over to our league."

Stern had no intentions of leaving his basketball realm nor did his first deputy Russ Granik. If McNall still was interested in an NBA guy of note, there was one left, the third banana, Gary Bettman. Sure enough, McNall went after Bettman while the NHL went through the costly motions of hiring a headhunting firm to screen candidates.

As summer turned to fall 1992, Stein remained front-and-centre in all discussions of succession, because he now occupied the throne – the term "interim" president was simply changed to president. He made no bones about his interest in staying at the top. Other prominent hockey people also were mentioned, including Washington Capitals' president Richard Patrick and general managers Bill Torrey and Glen Sather.

Stein's preoccupation with the commissionership had one lasting negative effect on the league's economic structure – ownership's desire for implementing a salary cap.

Following the 1992 strike settlement, both sides agreed to form a joint study committee to produce a restructuring of the business and avoid runaway inflation. Written into the Collective Bargaining Agreement was a vital clause that should have been addressed head-on by Stein and his NHLPA counterpart, Bob Goodenow.

"Based on NHL economic studies and projections, the league and its member clubs believe that a continuation of the current system would have a serious negative impact on the business of hockey and hence the parties.

"Accordingly, the NHL clubs have expressed an intent to develop and submit to the NHLPA as promptly as possible a proposal for restructuring with a salary cap and a revenue-sharing concept...

"The NHLPA commits that, as soon as reasonably practicable after the joint study committee report issues, it will begin bargaining in good faith with the clubs in an effort to reach agreement regarding restructuring by September 15, 1993."

Unfortunately, the joint study committee never was formed. As the Canadian Press observed, "Stein was too preoccupied with running for the office of NHL commissioner to worry about the joint study committee."

This would be a tragic omission. When the 1994 lockout took place, the union refused meaningful discussions on restructuring and the salary cap – as their signed agreement demanded – using the alibi that the joint study committee never had been formed.

As for Stein, his energetic bid for the chief executive's role was thwarted in the most unlikely place by the most unlikely opponent.

4

THE NBA-ING OF THE NHL:
ENTER GARY BETTMAN

Once Gil Stein had a full season (1992-93) to preside over the NHL as its president, he appeared to have the inside track for the soon-to-be-created commissioner's position. After all, an incumbent almost always is favoured in a political contest and Stein had been around the league for 15 years, enough time to develop friends in high places – also enough time to collect critics, even enemies, which Stein seemed to do with equal ease.

"Stein's work ethics were almost as inactive as Ziegler's had been," commented former owner Harry Ornest, with his usual dry wit. "In fact, I would have described their jobs as 'half-vacations, with big perks!'"

Bob McKenzie noted in the *Toronto Star*, "His (Stein's) appointment as president was thought to be interim by most everyone except himself." It was a most accurate appraisal of Stein's ego at work.

If nothing else, Stein was creative as he attempted to solidify his presidency. He recognized the importance of public relations and pledged to reopen the NHL's New York p.r. office. Unlike Ziegler, he showed up in as many arenas as possible and he recognized the need to clean up the game. With McNall's backing an edict was issued that called for the limitation of restraining fouls such as holding, interference and hooking that braked the more artistic performers.

These logical and often-discussed (under Ziegler) moves were enthusiastically received by many critics. Many, who had known Stein as the league counsel, were astonished by his personality change. It was almost as if Darth Vader had become Dale Carnegie, or visa versa.

But what critics insisted was Stein's dark side also managed to make itself apparent with several shocking moves. Shortly after taking office, he dumped long time vice-president Brian O'Neill. The move caused considerable despair in

Montreal. As Clarence Campbell's trusted deputy and heir apparent, O'Neill had relatively little authority.

Except for rare cases, O'Neill had handled all disciplinary matters, acting as Ziegler's stand-in during the infamous Koharski-Schoenfeld affair in 1988. O'Neill had his supporters and his share of detractors, myself among them. But, supported by Ziegler, he enjoyed protection from certain veteran hockey leaders. His abrupt firing by Stein shocked some in the NHL community but not everyone. It was a surprise, surely, although not nearly as much as Stein's new disciplinary moves.

At a time when the public was clamouring for increased punishment for misbehaving players, Stein incredibly went in the other direction. He launched a policy whereby suspended players would only be benched on non-game days. In effect, it was no punishment at all, it was merely silly.

One decision he rendered, which I thought made a lot of sense, was to redo the rules so that players could discard their helmets and play bareheaded. This would have added personality to a depersonalized game and create more identity between fans and players. It made a lot of sense – as long as rules against excessive stick work and boarding would ensure that helmetless players could enjoy a reasonable measure of safety without the headgear.

Unfortunately, Stein did not sufficiently promote the non-helmet campaign, nor fortify it with the legislation that would have made it practical rather than the subject of ridicule among the media and a large bloc of players. That, however, was the *cause celebre* that developed over Stein's nomination to the Hockey Hall of Fame; a move which inspired an independent probe and subsequently, a highly critical ruling against the president.

The Hall of Fame episode, however, took place long after Stein's presidential campaign concluded. A few months after the 1992-93 season had begun, the McNall-led board of governors had reduced the competition for commissioner to two individuals. Amazingly, only one of them had a hockey background and that was Stein, but his chances had been flawed by his questionable tactics over the past half-year.

Even more astonishing was the other aspirant for the top job. In a league notorious for its cocoon-like inbreeding, it was rare enough that an American such as Ziegler – and then Stein – would have the presidency, but at least their roots were in hockey turf. It was generally felt that ultimately Ziegler's successor would be a personality connected with The Game, be it Richard Patrick, whose grandfather Lester Patrick was in the Hall of Fame, or Bill Torrey, whose Islanders had won four straight Stanley Cups. Another possibilty was Ken Dryden, the goalie-author who had developed some absurdly Messianic quality after obtaining a law degree and then writing a book – *The Game* – which attained a biblical quality in some areas, although *Sports Illustrated*'s Mark Mulvoy once confessed to me that he found it a bore.

Neither Dryden nor Patrick made the final cuts. It came down to Stein, who in the end never had a genuine chance, and Gary Bettman, who had been a complete unknown outside the hockey industry, but was well known in NBA circles as one of David Stern's lieutenants.

As third in command for the enormously successful National Basketball Association, Bettman was credited with stimulating the league's growth in several realms, including marketing and public relations. He was regarded publicly as the "Father of the salary cap" and the man who negotiated a new contract with NBA officials – although some insiders privately whispered that Bettman had simply done the paperwork on these deals and that it had been Stern and the second in command who had actually done all of the spadework.

I called Bettman the day his name appeared in the *New York Times* as Stein's prime competition. He was at his NBA office when I phoned and was as affable as David Letterman, sounding more like a fellow you'd share a beer with at a local pub than a high-priced member of the sports establishment.

"I hear you've got the NHL job," I said, "and I'm doing a (SportsChannel TV pre-game) show tonight. Can I run with it?"

Bettman then revealed what would be his style with the media. If he trusted you – and he had no idea which way to go with me since we had never talked before – he'd give you off-the-record information or, as the case may be, even provide some on-the-record material.

"It's not official yet," he said, "so I don't want to say anything. But the minute I can talk, I'll sit down with you for an interview."

That sounded fair enough to me, so I decided to cool it until Bettman was ready to talk. In the meantime, I decided to feel him out. In all the years I had known Clarence Campbell, John Ziegler or Gil Stein, I never felt comfortable enough to tell them a joke.

But Bettman seemed different. He had what New Yorkers would call a homey, "candy store" quality to him. He instantly signalled that schmoozing (Yiddish for idle gabbing) was one of his favourite pastimes. I gambled on a relatively bad joke that I had just heard and he managed a chuckle while allowing that on a scale of one to ten, this bit of humour ranked about three.

No matter, Bettman was disarming and relaxed enough to indulge in some humour while also bantering about the sports business. A few weeks later he was officially appointed commissioner – Stein would remain "president" until June 1993 whereupon he would become special advisor to the commissioner. True to his word, Bettman called me to set up the interview.

We convened on a leather couch in his NBA office which soon would be vacated. It was sprinkled with an assortment of promotional items from autographed basketballs to mugs with team logos. He was, as he always would be (except for one occasion), so vibrant one would have imagined that he had stepped out of the morning shower only minutes earlier.

Before beginning the on-the-record interview, he launched into a number of topics, picking my brain about future decisions. One of his most critical would be the appointment of an aide-de-camp who was well versed in hockey.

"If I were you," I said, "I'd keep Brian Burke in mind. He's at Hartford (as the GM at the time), but I think he'd make the move."

Bettman knew nothing about Burke so I amplified, pointing out that he had a law degree, had played the game, had been a player-agent for a while and was hard-nosed, yet excellent with the media. I had no idea whether he was seriously considering my thoughts, although I suspected that he had. (Burke got the job months later.) Bettman shot back that he had been very impressed with Glen Sather, president and GM of the Edmonton Oilers.

"You'll never get him to move to New York," I said. "He likes Western Canada too much and has already rejected a lot of offers to move east."

Nevertheless, Bettman pointed out that he admired Sather enough to try to convince him to come or, that failing, try to get someone like him. I shot back that Burke was as close as he would get to a Sather; maybe even better since Sather had no background in law.

He asked me about the officiating. I told him that the refereeing department required a top-to-bottom overhaul and he had better make it a top priority. I also mentioned that I had just written a book of lists which included "John Ziegler's Eight Biggest Mistakes As NHL President." He wanted to hear them so I obliged.

1. He disappeared during the 1988 Devils-Bruins' playoff crisis and to this day nobody knows where he was at the time.
2. His media relations were somewhere below minus-the-radical 50.
3. He appeared to spend more time in Europe than he did in North America.
4. He was seen so rarely at NHL games, that he could have been put on the Endangered Species list, there had been so few sightings!
5. He closed the league's New York public relations department leaving the NHL as the only one of four major sports without a publicity presence in the world's media capital.
6. He fought – rather than listened to – his friends who became his critics.
7. He couldn't be found in the spring of 1992 when Mario Lemieux was chopped down by Adam Graves and a presidential decision was demanded by the public.
8. He ridiculed his employers – the 24 NHL governors – by saying the league needed a union-management partnership. "We need someone to protect the owners from themselves!"

He was amused and even more interested when I told him I was writing a column for *The Hockey News* in which I would list a few dozen pieces of advice. But it was time for the interview. He was quick to answer and rarely went off the record. The dialogue follows:

STAN FISCHLER: What are your top priorities as commissioner?

GARY BETTMAN: Over the next year, I've got to stabilize the franchises that need help, and I've got to stabilize the relationship with the Players' Association. Quite frankly, the two are interdependent upon each other.

SF: What do you see as your key to success? What makes Gary tick?

GB: Hard work. There's no substitute for applying yourself 199 percent in everything you do. When you have to deal with an issue or a problem or a project, you've got to know more about it than anyone else does. Then you've got to apply yourself to it, and then you've got to make it happen, dotting every "i" and crossing every "t." There is no substitute for execution in detail.

SF: What are your shortcomings?

GB: I may be too hard on myself. I have trouble accepting less than things going 100 percent right. When they don't, I tend to look at myself first in terms of what I could have done to make a difference, to make it perfect. Fortunately, here we haven't had too many missed steps at the NBA, but I believe I may drive myself too hard. But that's what happens when you are a type A personality.

SF: The NHL owners gave you a mandate. What are the top items on this mandate? What are they paying you to accomplish?

GB: I think what they want is a focus, an agenda, a vision for the future. We are going to try to take this sport to levels that it has never seen before. We need a good labour agreement. We need good marketing. We need good promotion. We need good television. We need to focus internationally. We need to do the things that a major professional sports league in the 1990s must do.

There are going to be some issues – collective bargaining and television. There are going to be some new opportunities, new technologies. I think we can improve our marketing, our promotion, especially the promotion of our players. It's going to be my job to set an agenda that deals with all these issues and takes advantage of all the opportunities.

The sum and substance of all this will be to have a healthy sport that has a fan base much broader than it is right now.

SF: What's wrong with the game as you see it?

GB: I think fundamentally, it's pretty sound. People focus on the issue of fighting. I get asked that in every interview, so you don't have to ask me now. I don't know whether or not that's a problem. But I'm going to form a judgment on it relatively quickly. Some people say it's not a big problem, but it could be better. Some people say it's a terrible problem.

I've had a couple of chats with a couple of former players and some hockey people. I'm going to touch on all bases and try to come to a view that makes the most sense. But basically, I think the game is a wonderful game. There are great athletes doing amazing things on the ice at an incredible speed. Basically, I think we are dealing with a terrific sport.

SF: Is it as salable as basketball?

GB: I don't like drawing that comparison for a lot of reasons. I think it's much more salable than it has been sold, so whether or not it's compared to something else is not the issue. This is its own sport; it's hockey. I think it can be sold much better and much bigger than it has been.

SF: How are you going to deal with Bob Goodenow? What is the solution to this knotty problem? There is a hypothesis that there will be a solution without a strike because the players have never had it so good. How do you see it?

GB: I don't know whether or not they've had it so good. I don't know enough about the specifics of this industry. I know the general trends and everything, but I'm going to have to get educated on that.

The way we're going to do it is that Bob Goodenow and I are going to work very hard at it together. I'm going to understand everything he understands and that he thinks, and I hope that I'm going to get him to understand everything that I know and I think. From there – since we both have a big stake in the same thing and that is the success of the NHL – we're going to reason with each other and try to come up with a framework.

I've always had a very good relationship with the National Basketball Players' Association. We haven't always agreed on everything, but we have a relationship. We can talk, we can communicate. I understand where they're coming from on issues. I think they understand where I'm coming from, you need to have that kind of relationship – a strong, businesslike, trusting relationship – to create the type of partnership that is going to be necessary to build that sport.

Goal number one is going to be to start dialogue with Bob Goodenow. We've got a time frame. I would have preferred to have the luxury of a little more time, but I think I have enough of a head start on the issues. I think I have enough understanding of labour relationships in professional sports.

I've been collecting the data. I have mounds of books over here that I have to read, and I'll do that and get myself up to speed very quickly. And Bob will help bring me up to speed.

SF: Is revenue sharing a realistic possibility?

GB: I don't view revenue sharing as the be-all and end-all. In other words it may not be necessary.

I'll give you an example why. You've got four teams in the league, and the gross for the league is $4 million. One team is grossing $2 million, another team is grossing $1 million, and the other two are grossing $500,000. If they're all spending $4 million or more in expenses, not just players but expenses, and there's no profit, sharing the revenue isn't going to help.

What you need to do, especially when you are dealing with an under-appreciated sport, is grow the revenue pie and create new sources of revenue that can be shared among the teams. That will deal better with the problem than dividing up what may be inadequate revenue anyway.

I think the pie that we're dealing with is too small. I want to make a bigger pie. To get hung up on revenue sharing in an industry that may be in its financial infancy may be putting it backwards.

What we need to do is come up with a framework. If we create a structure that should enable all the teams to operate successfully, but then some don't, we have to look at a whole host of things. We have to look at management. We have to look at marketing. We have to look at the markets. Then we have to see how to respond to it from there.

SF: How do you plan to give encouragement to fans and ownership in sites such as Hartford, New Jersey, Long Island and Minnesota, so they can redevelop vibrancy?

GB: You've got to look at each market specifically. Hartford's had a particular series of unique problems based on prior ownership. You've got to work through that and get stable ownership in place, and it's being worked on. Richard Gordon has done a terrific job up there, and it takes time to bring it back.

The Long Island market has in the past supported the Islanders in a big way. Then they had some problems, but there's now a new management team in place. I'm hopeful, and I believe that they are on the right track. They used to have 14,000 season ticket holders there. Let's also focus on the fact that Long Island is in the middle of a big-time recession which may have an impact, and those things are cyclical. I'm not familiar with Jersey, although I know the Nets have had some problems in the NBA.

You've got to look market by market. You've got to do the right things. Then if you've tried everything and you've had good management, you've made the right investments in time, energy and money, you've tried everything possible and you've got new ownership, then you've got to look at the market.

I get hung up on this. People say big market, small market. I never, even in the NBA context, I never refer to it as big market, small market. I reject the notion. There are plenty of teams in small markets that do great when they are the only game in town. And then there are some teams in big markets that don't do very well because there's either too many professional sports teams or even more in there own league.

Markets that were strong and vibrant 10 years ago aren't necessarily the same markets. Salt Lake City is a great example of a booming market that people at one point thought was too small to sustain an NBA franchise.

These problems are not subject to blanket generalizations in terms of curing them. You have to look at what happened. Have there been problems in ownership? Have there been problems in the market? What is the building like? What are the economic conditions? You've got all those things and you work on them one at a time.

One of the things I'm going to do is work with the owners of franchises that are having problems, look at their problems, look at potential solutions, then stabilize them. I want a stable league office, a well-run office, and I want to push that down to the team level as well.

SF: Where do you see the next expansion?

GB: I'm more focused now on the two new teams in Anaheim and Miami. I have no doubt that they are going to be successful, but we're going to get them assimilated and we've got to get them competitive.

I want to stabilize the existing teams. We've got three other recent teams. I saw Ottawa play and they need some work, but they play hard. As long as we're on the right track and everything is stabilized, I want that taken care of first before we look at expansion. Expansion in this sport is going to happen down the road if we do everything right because there is going to be more fan interest and we are going to need to expand to satisfy that fan interest.

There are a whole host of cities, especially in the Texas sunbelt region. I read an article yesterday about the ECHL, which is drawing 5,000 a game in Memphis. They're drawing 3,500 a game in Binghampton. We are talking about real interest across the board in hockey. We're going to help develop that interest and then respond to that interest.

SF: What did you learn from David Stern?

GB: An awful lot. You don't have enough tapes here for me to tell you. Other than having exposed me to all the aspects of running a professional sports league, he's a wonderful people person, he's incredibly smart, he's incredibly hard working, he's got a great set of values, he's got a great business acumen and savvy, and I hope that he's passed all those things along to me. Some people think he has, in some measure, and that may be the reason why the NHL reached out to me. I owe him a lot.

SF: Why did you want the NHL job?

GB: The short answer is that I happen to like the sport. I love the sport. I have since I was in college. I think that it's an incredible challenge and an incredible opportunity. I think the Ice Age is coming.

SF: Will ownership give you enough power to do what you have to do?

GB: They're going to let me do what I have to do because I'm going to set an agenda that's going to put this league on a course that's consistent with the visions the owners, I believe as a group, have as well.

Coming in I heard a lot about factionalism, disputes and everything else. I then witnessed two days where they unanimously granted two terrific franchises and they unanimously elected me. I spent two days in Florida meeting with all the owners and talking to them. They were interviewing me, but I was interviewing them as well because I didn't need a job; I had a good one. I was extremely favourably impressed by the ownership group. On an individual level, they were all terrifically nice, and I enjoyed the rapport we developed. I developed a lot of respect for them. I think they're smart businessmen. In the past I think that they have been unfairly maligned because I think it's up to the commissioner to set an agenda and lead. It doesn't mean I think the commissioner sits on a throne and throws lightning bolts and orders subjects around. That's not my view. You set an agenda, you communicate the agenda, you work hand-in-hand with your constituent groups: the owners, the media, the fans. You try to bring everyone together in an agenda that will grow the sport. I think that they are ready for it.

Bruce McNall may have helped to part the seas a little bit. He is viewed as a progressive owner. He has a great deal of respect among the other owners. There's a new era coming. It doesn't matter what the constitution says. I'm going to have the powers on paper consistent with the other professional sports leagues, but that's on the side. I'm going to lead with an agenda. The business aspects of the sport have to be well run so that people can enjoy the sport, and that's my agenda.

SF: How important is establishing a network television contract?

GB: It's very important. It's interesting. It's a chicken and an egg because you've got to build a fan base to get the network contract, which I'm committed to doing. But with the network contract, I'm going to build a fan base. It's going to snowball once I get it going.

This is such a difficult sports' marketplace. It's so fragmented that it's different then it was 10 years ago. Baseball in its regular-season games does a 3 (rating), 3.5, maybe a 4 if it's a really good game. The expectations now isn't as great as it was.

NHL hockey will be able to provide reasonably priced, good network programming for the sports division. As long as I can demonstrate that there is a decent following – it doesn't have to be spectacular numbers – that will give us something to grow on.

We have a relationship that runs out in four years. That's going to give me an opportunity to get the sport on a plane that's going to make the networks and the advertisers and the sponsors come on board. Hopefully, we can generate some more fan interest. We will work very hard with ESPN to make sure that their package is as successful as possible. Maybe along the way we can try some things, more than the handful of games that ABC is prepared to do, since they are related to ESPN. We'll deal with sponsors to do some promotions. We will market the marquee players better and I think increase the fan base. I think that being back on ESPN will help with the exposure, and I'm looking to the point when we're ready for prime time on the network.

SF: What's your view on pay-per-view?

GB: For a sport that needs more exposure pay-per-view isn't the short-term answer. We need the widest possible exposure that we can get. Pay-per-view might work in the short-run for the hard-core fan that can't get, on the usual outlets, the exposure that he wants.

I'll give you an example. You grew up in Boston. All your life you are a die-hard Bruins' fan, and you move to Texas. What do you do? Pay-per-view in that context might make some sense. I believe there's a market of people.

Let's assume that you lived in St. Louis and you just moved from Winnipeg and you miss the Jets. You get the St. Louis games locally, but you want to buy an additional game that you can't otherwise see. The last thing you need to do is put the Stanley Cup finals on pay-per-view. I want more people to see the Stanley Cup finals, not less.

SF: Do you see Europe as a spawning ground for more NHL games?

GB: I was responsible for the NBA games played in Europe. Northern Europe is particularly ripe for the NHL interests because a lot of players come from there. But you have to start first with licencing, sponsorship and television. Then, you move on to the occasional exhibition or regular season games. Then, if the interest is strong enough, you think about whether it's feasible to have franchises on the continent. Right now, it's too far down the road.

SF: What's your short-term goal vis-à-vis North America and Europe?

GB: To stabilize the sport in North America. Doing TV (for Europe) is easy. I can get a few people. I can get us exposure, use the satellites and all that. We'll do some of that because the opportunities are there and there's interest. Doing expansion in a big (European) way has to take second fiddle to making sure that we are in good shape here in North America.

I'd like to snap my fingers and implement everything that's in my head, but it's not going to happen in 24 hours. I've got to take care of the basics.

SF: What's your gut feeling on an NHL Dream Team playing in the Olympics?

GB: It would certainly get the sport a lot of exposure, but I have real concerns about the practical and logistical problems in doing it. In the NBA it took years to get it right. I don't want to do it just to do it, because if it's not done perfectly and we can't achieve the benefits that we want, then it's not worth doing. With a four year lag time to 1998, it may very well be another story.

SF: Who are you bringing over to the NHL from the NBA?

GB: Nobody except my secretary (Debbie Walsh). I was under contract to the NBA, and I have been released from my contract on the understanding that I won't take anyone else with me. I'm leaving a big enough hole in this organization that I don't have to create any others.

SF: How are you planning to change aspects of the NHL offices?

GB: I'm going to put the organization under the microscope, look at the strengths and weaknesses and make the appropriate changes, if any, necessary to make the NHL run as well as any professional sports league in the world. I have a philosophy: If the league – NHL Enterprises – is being well run, and everything is smooth and stable, people aren't going to know we're there; they're just going to focus on the game. When you focus on the game, it's an empty-netter. It used to be a slamdunk; now it's an empty-netter.

In the early 1980s, the NBA was perceived to have a ton of problems. It solved the problems, eliminated the distractions and the people started to focus on the game. I want people focused on hockey because it's a great game.

SF: You dealt with the NBA referees' union, which seemed a little surprising.

GB: It's funny. Shortly after I was named commissioner, I was at Byrne Arena watching the Rangers and the Devils. After a second-period interview, I walked over to the officials' locker room, introduced myself, and I said to them, "This is great; I just finished a year of negotiating with the referees in the NBA and I thought I was done for three years. Now I have to do it again!" I was the chief negotiator with the NBA and at the time nobody would have accused me of being a basketball person. But obviously I know the sport well enough that I can sit across the table with the referees. I know what the issues are. I've become an expert because I have to. I'll learn every aspect of the operation including the officials. Officials are important and they always feel underappreciated. They're always the visiting team; it's a tough job.

SF: What are you going to do about the NHL's three offices (New York, Montreal and Toronto)?

GB: No question we are going to open a PR office here in New York. I'm going to have to understand the need to have three offices. And they're going to have to operate under my management style.

SF: Who will handle discipline under your administration?

GB: The hockey operations people. I'm responsible for everything that goes on. But I don't think I should be involved in every disciplinary action that's meted out. But on major incidents, I'll get involved, while the run-of-the-mill stuff will be handled by hockey operations.

SF: What about Gil Stein?

GB: I like him. He's bright. He's a link with history – what transpired, what's going on. If something comes up, I can go to him and say, "Has this happened before? What did we do? And why?" He can be helpful.

SF: Any thoughts about luring more women to the game?

GB: I do know that somewhere between 40 and 50 percent of the people attending games are women. It's important to get kids as they are growing up. It's very important get the next generation of fans. We just need more of everybody. I want full arenas.

SF: What about the salary cap?

GB: Ask Bob Goodenow. I don't mean that facetiously. There's going to be a system that makes sense, a system that's fair to the owners and the players, a system that's jointly arrived upon by the league and the players' union.

Maybe it's an NBA-style salary cap. Maybe it's a new type of salary cap, and maybe it's a system that hasn't been invented yet. I know about this stuff. I know how to create these systems. I know how to invent these things and the owners are counting on me to come up with a system that makes sense to the NHL, and that's a system that I have to come up with, with Bob Goodenow.

SF: Which owners did you know best before you got the NHL job?

GB: Abe Pollin of the Capitals because he owns the Bullets; and Stanley Jaffe, the president and CEO of Paramount (Rangers); and the Gund brothers from Cleveland Cavaliers' days (the current owners of the San Jose Sharks). Since then, I've met them all.

SF: One thing different from the NBA is that you are going to be dealing with the Canadian psyche as well as the Americans.

GB: I understand the Canadian love affair with the game. I want to take that love affair and give it to more people. Basketball was always perceived as a U.S. game. It now may be the second – or first – most popular sport in the world. I'm going to be very sensitive to the Canadians and tread very lightly as to the sensitivity that may or may not be there. I want to be viewed as somebody who cares for the game, takes care of the game, and will do good things for the game.

And that ended the interview. At the start, Bettman was saying – and doing – all the right things. Unlike Ziegler, he established a peripatetic relationship with the media. One might have suspected that the commissioner's theme was "Bring on the cameras! Bring on the pencils!"

I got a firsthand view of Bettman at work shortly after he moved to the hockey realm. All executives have styles. Ziegler was reserved, painfully humorous on rare occasions and extremely loose when with his friends. Bettman displayed a New York neighbourly approach. Whenever one addressed him as "commissioner," he instantly injected a "Call me Gary" into the conversation.

He was sensitive enough to the fact that hockey people regarded him as "a basketball man," that Canadians viewed him as an American interloper into their game and that whomever the bigots were in the NHL crowd, they would take due note of the fact that he is Jewish; in fact, the first leader of big-league hockey of Hebrew roots.

To his credit, Bettman neither played up nor played down his background. Those who knew him from his pre-NBA and NBA days, however, had reservations about his ability to smoothly orchestrate the executive role. One mutual friend, Marty Blackman, a Madison Avenue consultant who works with athletes and ad agencies on television commercials, expressed some concern to me.

"What I'd be worried about is whether Gary becomes too confrontational in the manner of some New York trial lawyers," said Blackman. "That could turn off people and I consider it a factor that he should address."

When I mentioned this to Bettman, he pooh-poohed the suggestion as one would to a Nervous Nellie. He suggested that Blackman was exaggerating to make a point and, really, this was not a part of his style. The message: not to worry. The question in my mind was: how well does the commissioner take to criticism? The answer would be well and not-too-well in the months to come.

One thing was obvious; I had developed a closer rapport with Bettman in a month than I had with Ziegler in 15 years. That was not so much a knock at the more reserved, deposed president, but more a statement about Bettman the person.

What I liked most about him was his ease of communication and what seemed to be sensible ideas about reorganizing the league. I decided to give him some of my 22 points of free advice in my *Hockey News* column:

1. When in doubt, do exactly the opposite of what John Ziegler would have done.
2. Prepare yourself this instant for a colossal explosion over the the NHL pension scandal. And distance yourself about 3,000 miles from all involved.
3. Do the opposite of your myopic and lazy predecessor. Move the league's public relations centre out of an outpost in Rexdale, Ontario, and back where it belongs at NHL Central on Fifth Avenue in New York, the world's media capital.
4. Wear a Teflon suit when dealing with Canadian writers. They will automatically scorn you because (a) you're a New Yorker; (b) you're smaller than Tie Domi [Bob Costas or Pinky Lee]; (c) you didn't sign a $500 billion contract with CBS yesterday.
5. Never for a minute forget your constituency; 18 American teams and only eight north of the border. That's more than a two-thirds majority for Uncle Sam.
6. Never underestimate the resentment of some Canadian hockey people for their American counterparts.
7. If you don't think your public relations corps doesn't need trebling, check out the New York papers where hockey is fourth banana, despite Mark Messier, Brain Leetch et. al.
8. Make a distinction between phony, premeditative, goon fighting and legitimate, spontaneous bouts. Don't abolish legal fisticuffs, but pun-ish the illegitimate goons. Whatever you do, when you finally make a decision on fighting, articulate it loud and clear. And when the critics begin sniping, don't wimp out. Go on the offensive.
9. The referees will try to cow you now that their contract is running out. Don't be fazed. Their inconsistency and ineptitude has degraded the game to the point that a gag rule can't even subdue the critics. If they pull a strike; let 'em walk.
10. The Dream Team idea for the Olympics is for the birds. With creative thinking, the NHL can get as much positive ink on the continent as it

would a costly three-week interruption of the schedule. Don't fall for the easy-publicity propaganda.

11. Keep Gil Stein on board. He generated more energy in six months than John Zeigler did in a decade. [So, even Stan Fischler makes mistakes in judgement.]

12. Hockey players can be colourful, distinct personalities, but most come out looking like battleship gray androids because of the league's public relations program. Open them up to the world or the NHL will remain light years behind your favourite basketball league.

13. I know you disagree and have used a bunch of buzzwords to say so, but read my lips: revenue sharing is a must [partial, at least]. And when those rich New York Rangers bozos object, along with those in Detroit, Toronto, Chicago and Montreal, remind them that they're in the minority – by a lot. Tell 'em to join the club or get out.

14. Never stop talking to the fans; even those with a median income under $20,000 a year.

15. It's nice that Disney and Blockbuster are in our midst, but don't let those hockey-come-latelies wag your tail.

16. Listen carefully to Marcel Aubut's idea for shootouts to settle ties in the regular season. Then, approve it for the best reason of all; because the plan will add excitement to the game.

17. Stop expansion at 28 teams.

18. Give expansion teams a break. The protected list should be trimmed to 13 players. While you're at it, institute a National Basketball Association-type lottery.

19. Upgrade linesmen to referee status. Have three referees, the same as in professional basketball.

20. Promote the heck out of street and roller hockey as America's city game alternative to basketball.

21. Don't for a second forget that hockey people are not like basketball people and something that works for hoops doesn't necessarily work for pucks.

22. Don't hang out at Madison Square Garden any more than you do at the Spectrum, Nassau Coliseum, Chicago Stadium, Byrne Arena or Great Western Forum.

If I do say so myself, I was right on 21 out of the 22 points. The one strike was number 11; my suggestion that he keep Gil Stein aboard. Some NHL insiders believed that Stein could be an effective background man to aid Bettman's transition to the new office. Stein was gifted with the annual Lester Patrick Trophy ("for service to hockey in the United States"), a largely ceremonial-political award. From past experience, I learned that the Patrick winners usually are politically correct personalities who, in effect, are paid off with the prize although it should be noted that there have been several deserving winners such as Brian and Joey Mullen.

Stein accepted the Lester Patrick Trophy before public disclosure of his attempt to rig his own induction into the Hockey Hall of Fame. "As his term as president was coming to a close," said Bob McKenzie in the *Toronto Star*, "Stein found it necessary to hatch the bold but flawed scheme of orchestrating his own induction into the Hall of Fame, using his last-gasp powers of president to influence the outcome of the election."

While this would be Bettman's first taste of NHL cyanide and while it wasn't fatal to his administration, it was a portent of negative things to come, including a charge that the Ottawa Senators had tanked their end of the schedule to ensure better draft selection.

My information was that the more Bettman analyzed the Ziegler administration, the more he became convinced that the old hockey way was the wrong way. One by one, the "Zieglerites" were cashiered. Joel Nixon, the universally likeable vice-president of broadcasting, was put out to pasture, replaced by Glenn Adamo. Steve Ryan hung on a bit longer but eventually gave way to Rick Dudley as head of NHL Enterprises.

After my second face-to-face meeting with Bettman, I had become magnetized enough by his modus operandi – not to mention personality – to consider the unthinkable and actually work for the NHL.

There were a few big-time problems: 1. I was under contract with SportsChannel New York as an Islanders' and Devils' broadcaster; 2. I was writing a regular *Hockey News* column; 3. I had a long list of writing assignments ranging from books to magazine articles; 4. I loved television too much to forsake it.

First, I had to establish whether Bettman was interested in me. During our third chat, he indicated that he was, but the position remained uncertain. "We need somebody who can write and who can edit," he said. "Eventually, we'll put out a weekly newsletter like the NBA does. We'll need somebody for that."

"I have obligations to SportsChannel and others," I pointed out. "I won't leave TV."

"Maybe you can do work for us as a part-time consultant," he shot back.

Now it was clear that he meant business and I had some serious thinking to do. Did I really want to become part of The Establishment? Did I want to enter the corporate world after having spent my lifetime of employment on the other side of the typewriter? Dare I leave the glorified world of television where my mug was seen on the tube three times a week in season? Dare I forget what happened to others? I was acutely aware of Jack Falla's unfortunate experience after leaving the writing world for NHL p.r.

These were difficult decisions, accentuated by the fact that Bettman would soon want answers and I was immersed in a delicious regular-season NHL race involving the Devils and Islanders. Both clubs were bound for the playoffs; the

Islanders led by a rejuvenated Al Arbour while the Devils were being driven by Herb Brooks.

Before I could even come close to making up my mind, Bettman hired Steve Solomon away from the American Broadcasting Corporation to be his second in command. Solomon's savvy in the TV realm would be essential as the NHL attempted to regain a foothold with one of the major American networks. Although he wasn't a "pure" hockey person, Solomon did have family involvement in the sport. His grandfather had been a major investor in the New York Americans' NHL club when it was a rival with the Rangers at the old Madison Square Garden in the 1930s. From our brief meetings, I came away impressed.

Shortly thereafter, the 1993 All-Star game was held in Montreal. I was covering it for an American radio syndicate and also planned to meet Bruce McNall for an interview. The trip would whet my appetite for the NHL job even more.

We arrived on a Thursday night to prepare for the NHL Oldtimers' game and the skills competition on Friday evening at The Forum. It was during an eight-hour period, from mid-morning through early evening, that I got to see Bettman in action. First he was cornered by Canadian Broadcasting Corporation cameras, then it was the print media and, finally, local radio.

He had time for everybody and when I asked him for 20 minutes for a magazine piece, the commissioner led me behind closed doors so we wouldn't be interrupted. His manner was extra-friendly and I got the distinct impression that he soon expected to bring me aboard – presuming that we could work out the details.

Shortly after I returned to New York, Bettman phoned and invited me to a meeting with himself at the NHL offices. He made it clear that an NHL job was available to me. Then, he asked, "What do you know about Arthur Pincus?"

Wow! Pincus had been a Sunday sports editor with the *New York Times* and had since moved to the *Washington Post*. I couldn't figure his hockey background, but Bettman said he was being considered for vice-president of public relations. "I know him from his *Times* days," I said in a deliberate, non-committal way. "That's an interesting choice."

Frankly, I didn't know what to make of it. I could tell that Bettman figured he was aiming high and there was that "prestige" aspect of the *Times* and *Washington Post* that must have entered the commissioner's thinking. (But so many times corporate heads guess wrong when they think newsmen can simply shed their journalistic clothes and climb into a flack's suit.)

"I'm also going to have a vice-president of corporate communications," Bettman added. "We have someone from Reebok in mind for that."

He mentioned the name Bernadette Mansur, which meant absolutely nothing to me, and then cut to the meat. What Bettman planned was a p.r. hat-trick announcement; Pincus, Mansur and me.

"But you still haven't told me what I'm going to do," I said.

Bettman talked about me being the league archivist, editor, head of an unborn book sector; a sort of vice-president of publishing, for want of a better title. "You write the job description," he concluded with one of the best offers a newsman could expect. "We'll talk next week."

Now the pressure was on me – and mounting. There was no way I could take the NHL job unless I was able to continue my television work and, SportsChannel did not want me to leave. Finally, I told Bettman to go ahead with his announcement about Pincus and Mansur without me. I was locked in by TV – and loved it.

On the one hand, the NHL offer was tantalizingly tempting; particularly the idea of working with a galvanic character such as Bettman. But on the other, I enjoyed the television work more than ever.

Meanwhile, I followed the Islanders down the homestretch of the 1992-93 season and observed Bettman handle the first crisis of his administration while I tried to cope with the ultimate crisis of our immediate family.

5

∙∙

FACING DEATH AND HOCKEY:
ABOUT SIMON, MIKE KEENAN AND A HEART

The 1993 New York Islanders-Pittsburgh Penguins playoff series was one of the most exciting I've ever covered. Although heavily-favoured, the Stanley Cup champions, led by Mario Lemieux, were being played as equals by Al Arbour's squad.

The series reached its climax Saturday evening, May 8, at Nassau Coliseum. New York won the opener, 3-2, at Pittsburgh, then lost 3-0 on the road, then lost again, 3-1, in Uniondale. This was the fourth game of the series at Nassau.

A Penguins' win would virtually seal the series. But, if the Islanders could tie the playoff at two games apiece, who knows, they might even pull off a colossal upset.

At the time, my younger son, 15-year-old Simon – his brother Ben was six years his senior – was attending Northwood, a boarding (prep) school in Lake Placid, New York. A freshman, Simon chose Northwood principally because of its hockey program and the desire to experience life away from home on his own. Independence was the operable word.

Simon was a goaltender but with only limited experience, largely because he had committed himself for four winters to alpine (downhill) ski racing – and even made it to the New York State championships his last year as a Junior IV racer.

However, around the ski season, he enrolled in a hockey program at Sky Rink, a few blocks from Madison Square Garden, participated in Bob Nystrom's Summer Hockey School for a week and was backup goalie in a Yonkers, New York house league. This craze for goaltending had come about first because he started out a poor skater (although by now he wasn't bad – he had taken power-skating lessons with Laura Stamm) and because goalies got into rinks for free in local pick-up leagues (figuring that the poor parents had already paid a fortune for goalie equipment!).

Then, when Simon was about nine or 10, I was invited to do mock play-by-play at a hockey fantasy camp at the famous old Borscht Belt (Jewish Catskill) resort, The Concord. Simon got to suit up and "play" with the stars, and there were some genuine stars: Dale Hawerchuk, Mario Lemieux, Luc Robitaille, Dan Quinn, Larry Robinson and Marc Bergeuin. In fact, the first goal scored on him was by Robitaille and the second, by Mario!

That incredible experience, coupled with the fact that he sat at ice level in the Meadowlands parallel to his idol Chico Resch's goal for two periods, during the infamous "Mickey Mouse" game (Wayne Gretzky had called the young Devils a "Mickey Mouse club" shortly before his Edmonton Oilers were to play there), clinched it for Simon: he wanted to be an NHL goaltender.

Having such positive experiences as a goaltender and hungry for more, Simon had done a powerful job of lobbying to go to Northwood and I, reluctantly, agreed that he could get more ice time at Northwood.

Unfortunately, he was sixth out of six goalies, obtained limited ice time and gradually grew to dislike Northwood and the extraordinarily frigid 1992-1993 winter in Lake Placid (it snowed the June day my wife picked him up after finals, for instance!). Still, when he did get to play, it was thrilling because the Northwood varsity team played in the 1980 Olympic rink in downtown Lake Placid.

At least once a month Simon and a friend or two would train down to Manhattan on a Friday night and remain with us until Sunday morning when they completed the Amtrak round trip back to Northwood. On the weekend in question, I arranged for Simon & Co. to accompany my wife, Shirley, to the fourth playoff game at Uniondale.

A thoroughly absorbed Islanders' fan (he was five when the Isles won their fourth Cup, in 1983), Simon was tickled to see a playoff game and enamoured of the manner in which his heroes conducted themselves. Spearheaded by penalty-killer Tom Fitzgerald's two short-handed goals, the Isles rallied for a stirring 6-5 victory that permanently impacted on most who viewed the match.

I always enjoyed having Simon at games, but this one was so special and ended so euphorically, I was filled with transports of joy when I got behind the wheel of our Honda and began driving Shirley, Simon and his friends back to Manhattan. But as I drove, the ecstasy diminished with every mile. From the car's rear, the interior was punctuated by spasmatic coughing that carried right through to my very core.

It was Simon hacking away so intensely that I began asking myself whether I should permit him to return to school the next morning. When we arrived back at our apartment, I mentioned my concern to Shirley and we decided we'd wait until the next morning before deciding. The problem, of course, was that Simon had to be up early and at Pennsylvania Station by 10 a.m. to catch the train.

Shortly after he awakened, I suggested that it might be wiser for him to remain in the city and see a doctor on Monday. With typical teenage bravado, he insisted that he'd be okay, that he'd see a nurse (or doctor) in Lake Placid and not to worry. Since I wanted not to worry and since my wife figured it was all right for him to head north again, I raised no objections.

Later in the week Simon phoned and seemed completely recovered. I remember admonishing myself for being overprotective. Somehow I managed to forget that he had suffered through "walking pneumonia" during the winter and assorted other ailments which we considered ordinary for a growing boy.

Meanwhile, his Islanders went on to defeat Pittsburgh before being eliminated by the Canadiens. School ended in late spring and he returned home to prepare for a summer job as a junior counsellor at a day camp near our country home in the Catskill Mountains. He appeared to be perfectly normal. One Saturday morning we went to the beach at Riis Park and played a hard game of paddle handball in a broiling sun. I remarked to myself how well Simon held up under adverse conditions. But I also recall that when I encouraged him to take a swim with me later, he said he was tired and just wanted to stretch out. No sweat, teenagers like to nap on Saturdays.

But there were other signs that something was wrong with Simon, physically. First, about a week after returning from Lake Placid, he complained of an earache. Our regular doctor checked him out, found mild signs of an ear infection and recommended an ear, nose and throat clinic. The prescription didn't work, so she tried another. There were other symptons but each taken on its own hinted at only a passing ailment. We thought it might be allergies and took him to see our allergist. He noticed a rapid heartbeat at the time, but attributed it to the fact that Simon was taking antihistamines, decongestants and an antibiotic – all of which could mean an elevated heart rate.

One Friday afternoon in late June, Simon – who had been a competitive mountain-bike racer, too – and I took a leisurely cycle in Riverside Park, adjoining the Hudson River. Our destination was my cousin Gerry's apartment about 2 1/2 miles away. The sun was bright, the air warm but not overbearing and the ambience – if you will excuse the expression – swell.

Normally, Simon would speed ahead of me and then circle until his father caught up, then take another spring and wait. This time, he kept pace with me and, to my astonishment, halted and got off his bike after we had pedalled up a rather modest hill. "I need a rest, dad," he implored.

That seemed strange to me, but after a brief respite we resumed our ride and, yet again, after another climb, he requested a rest for a few more minutes. Little did I realize that Simon was just a weekend away from suffering heart failure.

On Monday, June 28, the Devils held a press conference to announce a new coach. Simon had had a difficult weekend. His ear continued to bother him and a lethargy overcame him as well as nausea. Shirley was so frustrated over the doctors' failure to isolate any cause for his problems, she didn't know who to contact next. On Sunday night she obtained a prescription for his nausea and on Monday she scheduled an appointment at Manhattan's Eye and Ear Hospital for another examination.

At approximately the same time as Devils' president-general manager Lou Lamoriello announced that Jacques Lemaire had been named head coach (to replace Herb Brooks), Simon collapsed in the doctor's office of heart failure. Unfortunately, nobody knew precisely why he had taken ill, but he was rushed (with Shirley) to St. Vincent's Hospital by an Emergency Medical Service ambulance.

When I phoned home to get messages from my office manager, I was told that Simon was in a hospital – mistakenly named Beth Israel – and "probably had an attack of ulcers."

After regaining my composure, I dashed to my car, along with colleague Steve Viuker who had accompanied me to the press conference. Ulcers? Simon never had a hint of ulcers but, perhaps, the symptoms were there after all. By the time I returned home, word had gotten through that they were at St. Vincent's. I headed for the subway and spent 20 agonizing minutes riding to the hospital.

Upon arriving in the emergency room, I found Shirley and Simon surrounded by doctors and emergency medical service people. All I could think about was the original message, "a bleeding ulcer" and wondered what was going on with the procedure.

I was quickly introduced to the EMS people, one of whom was rather corpulent and perspiring profusely. I was able to give Simon a hug and kiss and some measure of reassurance although I hadn't a clue as to his true condition.

Neither, as I would soon learn, did the Pediatric Emergency Room people at St. Vincent's. The original guess of "bleeding ulcers" apparently had been discarded almost immediately. They had taken him into the emergency room and immediately decided he was in anaphylactic shock, despite Shirley's attempts to tell them he had been taking the new medications for more than 24 hours and there was no way the kid was in anaphylaxis. Unfortunately, a part of the treatment was pumping him full of liquids, and within moments of my arrival Simon was choking and coughing up pink froth.

At this point the medical crew realized that they were probably killing Simon rather than saving him and they tried to catheterize him (a thin tube inserted up the penis, with no anesthesia), so that they could get the liquid back out of him as rapidly as possible.

It was then that I discovered how brave my son really was under the most excrutiating conditions. Not that he laughed off the pain. Far from it. But he coped with the trauma of it all with a blend of stoicism and fortitude that surely surpassed anything I could match under similar conditions.

Twice they tried the catheterization, which they soon decided was two times too many. I think it began to dawn on everybody in the room that Simon – with no previous history of heart problems; a healthy athlete – was somehow, unaccountably, in heart failure.

Suddenly, I remembered that both Simon and his older brother Ben, had been diagnosed with heart murmurs. But, after careful checking, our pediatrician had determined that both had "systolic" or harmless heart murmurs which they might well grow out of (Shirley had had a systolic murmur when she was a child). In both cases it was said to have no relation to future ailments as they grew to adulthood.

After considerable examination it was determined that Simon would be removed to an Intensive Care Unit where he would be further examined and diagnosed. At this point neither Shirley nor I had any indication that his young life was teetering on the balance, nor did we know what to expect in the next 24 hours.

In the relative security of the Intensive Care Unit, Simon was checked regularly and seemed to feel a bit more comfortable. My main task was ferrying cans of Seltzer to him from the soda dispenser down the hall to his bedside.

A Dr. Lee, who supervised the Pediatric ICU, indicated that Simon's condition could improve overnight. That would have been comforting had the doctor known precisely the nature of Simon's ailment at the time; which he didn't. He did, however, ask us questions about whether anyone else had mentioned lately that Simon had an enlarged heart. No one had. He told us that the head of Pediatric Cardiology, Dr. Liu, would be performing an echocardiogram on Simon soon. In the meantime, Simon was being given several medications we had never heard of intravenously.

Shirley remained overnight at Simon's bedside. I eventually took the subway home, walked Cleo, the Airedale, flopped in bed and wondered what was going on.

As promised Dr. Liu performed the echocardiogram and then disappeared for most of the day. Unaware of the details, I returned to St. Vincent's in the afternoon and happened to arrive as Shirley left the ICU for respite.

Instinctively, I sensed bad news when we embraced although I never imagined the gravity of Simon's condition. After hugging him, Shirley and I were called aside by Dr. Liu. She clearly did not want to converse in front of Simon and led us to an empty children's playroom. "Your son is very ill," she said. "His heart is in poor condition, almost useless."

It was if a grenade had exploded in my stomach. "Heart. Useless." The words resonated uncontrollably, mystifyingly. We're talking about a 15-year-old who had competed in a world cross-country mountain-biking event, who had played a 21-point game of hard paddleball in a noonday sun only weeks ago.

Four words kept repeating: how could it be?

But it was, and Dr. Liu made it clear that decisions were necessary. St. Vincent's was ill-equipped to deal with acute myocarditis or cardiomyopathy, which were said to be the most likely causes of Simon's heart failure. She insisted that the one place to go was Columbia-Presbyterian Babies' Hospital, then admitted that she had already taken the results of Simon's "echo" and x-rays up to a colleague there. Everyone (whoever that was, and we would find that out very soon) who had looked at the tests agreed that Simon should be moved to Columbia-Presbyterian Babies' Hospital as soon as possible.

Dr. Liu arranged for a bed that night (Tuesday, June 29) and we sent for a private ambulance to take Simon to what would be his "home" for the next two terrifying months.

A pair of pleasant, heavily-accented Russian paramedics finally arrived at about 8 p.m. that very hot summer evening and loaded Simon (with Shirley) into the rear patient's compartment. I would again take the subway home.

As I helped them aboard, I experienced a doleful feeling that Simon might not survive the night, that I might never see him again. Yet I tried not to betray my thoughts and put on an encouraging face. "You'll be okay, guy!" I said as the ambulance door closed and then turned toward the subway.

Simon had become aware of his deteriorating condition earlier in the day and, somehow, coped with it without any emotional breakdown, although I'm not sure how he managed to do so. He maintained that amazingly strong disposition throughout the ordeal which began in earnest when he checked into Columbia-Presbyterian and was taken to the Pediatric Intensive Care Unit of its Babies' Hospital building.

At this point you may be wondering what all this has to do with hockey. In fact, throughout the ordeal – from getting the communique at the Lemaire press conference to the start of the new season – hockey people were directly involved in the grieving, waiting and healing process this hideous event was about to become.

Shirley and I had been invited to speak at a USA Hockey symposium in Boston during a weekend early in July. At first we had hoped that Simon's illness would be minor enough for us to head for Massachusetts. But once we began getting results at Columbia-Presbyterian, we realized that we were going nowhere.

Then, there were my dealings with Bettman and the NHL. Now all bets were off. I had phoned Bettman shortly after Simon's hospitalization. "Don't even think about us," he said, sounding very much like the parent he is. "Do what you have to do with Simon."

We learned that sometime in the past – perhaps a month, perhaps several months – that Simon had suffered a virus, and the virus had reached his heart. The destructive process then began and culminated with the collapse on June 28th. By the time he reached Columbia-Presbyterain, Simon's heart was fuctioning at only 13 percent.

Life became an endless nightmare at this point. When Shirley walked into the Pediatric Intensive Care Unit (after sleeping on a chair in a lounge outside the PICU) on the morning after Simon's admission, she found him unable to speak and partially paralyzed on his right side (and this was only moments after he had spoken to his nurse). Simon had had a small stroke, or Trans-Inschemic Accident, and although he began to recover his speech and movement almost immediately, the episode was terrifying. It turned out that Simon's poor labouring heart was "throwing out" blood clots. They later found one in a lung which was compounding the situation by setting up a situation of incipient pneumonia. Now he was on a medication that was keeping his heart pumping and a medication that thinned his blood so that he wouldn't form any more clots; we couldn't keep track of all the medications being pumped through his thin, rapidly-weakening body.

The bad news just kept coming. As I look back on it now, I see Shirley and me sitting there, stunned and numb, while the doctors kept rolling out a new litany of horrors. They were wonderful, calm, confident, positive; we were terrified, confused, basically in shock and denial.

After the doctors performed a heart catheterization on Simon, which allowed them to peek into the heart itself, as well as take tissue samples, they had some answers and treatments to try, some hope (albeit slim, as we could sense by now).

Simon's life was in grave danger. But the doctors told us that they had definitely found inflammation in the heart tissue, signs that a virus had once been present. Cautiously they said they might be able to treat the virus with medicine and restore his heart to a semblance of normalcy. If that didn't work, only a heart transplant would save the lad.

I can't tell you the profundity of the shock of hearing those words: heart transplant. It was impossible to take in that they were talking about our son – our skier, skater, biker, soccer-playing son. It was at almost this precise moment in time that the basketball star Reggie Lewis dropped dead on the playing court, of what they later confessed was cardiomyopathy. With what Simon was undergoing at the time, it seemed impossible to label him "lucky." But, if he hadn't collapsed in a doctor's office, he probably would have died.

For a week Shirley and I hoped and prayed. For one brief period on a late Friday morning, as they began to withdraw Simon from the medication which kept his heart pumping, we all hoped Simon had beaten the virus, beaten the imflammation. But no, almost to the moment they told us the medication would all be out of his blood stream, Simon's heart rate skyrocketed and simultaneously his blood pressure began to disappear. Simon's heart was irreversibly, irretrievably, irreparably destroyed. Our son was going to have to have a heart transplant. The unthinkable, the impossible had become our kid's only possible reality.

At first, I had decided to keep Simon's condition from all but family and close friends, but word leaked to *Daily News* columnist Bob Raissman who wrote an oblique item about the hospitalization. I figured if Raissman had the item, I'd better contact my pal, Phil Mushnick at the *Post*, which I did. The hockey community got wind of it when we had to cancel the trip to Boston. Soon, the outpouring of emotion became a bit overwhelming.

A huge card, signed by the members of the U.S. Olympic team arrived along with good wishes from coach John Cunniff and USA Hockey bigwigs.

At this point, I decided to become more proactive. I figured an appearance by a hockey personality or two might be a tonic for a lad who was weakening by the day. I phoned several friends including Todd Diamond, a former intern who had become an aide to agent Mark Gandler, a good pal.

"How would he like a visit from Alexei Kasatonov?" Diamond asked. Kasatonov had completed his second year on the Devils' defence and was one of my favourite people although he was bashful about being interviewed. Diamond arranged for the Russian to come to the hospital on Friday, July 9th, 1993, which turned out to be one of the true bittersweet days of our lives.

That was the morning we were informed that nothing would reverse what had happened to Simon's heart, and that measures would have to be taken to keep the destroyed heart working until (hopefully) a transplantable one arrived.

It had been an emotionally draining morning for Simon, who slipped into a nap shortly after lunch. He had been occupying a bed in the far right corner of the Intensive Care Unit. Because of its location, it seemed almost cozy, if such a feeling is possible in the frenzied confines of an ICU.

When Simon napped, I usually busied myself with work that I brought with me and on this day, I was jotting notes for a hockey book when I felt a tap on the shoulder. It was Diamond and rubbing shoulders with him was Alexei Kasatonov, his steely eyes softened by his deep, warm grin.

"How are you?" he asked, his English still deeply accented. I was overwhelmed. To this point I had never really expected anyone from hockey to visit, especially a foreigner like Kasatonov who really didn't know me that well. But there was something strong about our bond and I imagine it was evident from the well-coupled eye contact whenever we would meet.

Dammit! Simon was fast asleep and considering his condition, there was no way I would awaken him. One of the nurses pointed out that there was another young patient, a few beds down, who was a Devils' fan, and wondered if Alexei would mind stopping at his bed?

"Certainly, I will," he said and proceeded down the corridor until he reached the teenager who was overwhelmed by the sight of the Russian. Diamond mentioned that this was one of Alexei's first trips to Upper Manhattan, a heavily-Hispanic neighbourhood and he had left his wife down front in the car.

"Don't worry," Kasatonov insisted, "I will stay."

Simon slept for another half-hour during which Alexei and I schmoozed about the hockey season. Finally, a nurse came around for a checkup and awakened him. A couple of seconds passed before he realized that a New Jersey Devil was at his bedside. He grinned and extended his hand which disappeared inside the Russian's ham-like grip.

Kasatonov struggled with his English but said volumes with his eyes. He reached into a large, plastic shopping bag with the name GERRY COSBY SPORTING GOODS on the side and said, "I have something for you."

He rustled the plastic and pulled out a large but strange-looking hockey jersey. After doing a doubletake, Simon realized that it was part of the Russian National Team uniform.

"From the Olympics," said Kasatonov. "For you." Simon had already received his share of flowers and cards, but the Russian Olympic Hockey jersey was something to which he could relate to better than just about anything he had received. He grasped it tightly and profusely thanked Alexei. They talked hockey for a few minutes and then Kasatonov and Diamond begged off; it was time to leave.

It's so difficult to measure how much a morale boost a visit such as that means to a patient like Simon. Kasatonov gave no inspirational speech and communicated very little except his concern for my son, but that was more than enough. The gift of the Olympic jersey – so treasured a momento – was much more than anyone of us had expected.

If a visit from someone who lacked English communication skills could be a boost, I imagined that an English-speaking NHL personality would be even better. I phoned the Islanders, Simon's favourite team, and learned that all of the players were out of town. Ditto for the Devils, his second favourite club; they, too, were away. That left me with the Rangers, far from being on my son's hit parade.

When I called the Rangers public relations man, Barry Watkins, he was very understanding. "Mike Richter might be in town," he said, "and maybe even Mike Keenan."

Keenan. I thought for a moment and without hesitation said, "Sure, if you could get either or both, let me know."

I hung up and then I began hesitating. My relationship with Keenan had taken several strange turns ever since our first encounter nearly two decades ago. I had been broadcasting hockey for several years and was writing a *Hockey News* column, among other things, when I received a phone call out of the blue.

"This is Mike Keenan," said the voice at the other end. He must have sensed that I didn't have a clue as to who Mike Keenan was all about because he quickly added, "I'm coaching the Rochester Americans."

Of course, of course, I said to myself. I should have known that but why would Keenan call me? To my knowledge I had never insulted him.

"I want to coach in the NHL," he elaborated, "and I figured you might help me."

Flattered, I was. Nobody had ever phoned me for an NHL job and here was Mike Keenan wanting a boost from Stan.

"The first thing we have to do," I said, "is figure who might be looking and then make a couple of calls."

At the time there were very few likely openings. As promised, I contacted a couple of people but to no avail. I finally told Keenan I couldn't help him, he thanked me politely and that was the end of our first encounter. A few years later he got his wish and wound up as head coach of the Philadelphia Flyers. We would meet from time to time in NHL hallways both before and after games and casually gab.

But our next meaningful encounter took place in Toronto at the *Hockey News'* annual awards luncheon of which Keenan was an honouree. I was seated next to Keenan and his wife, Rita, each of whom was an absolutely delightful table mate.

Keenan was the antithesis of the ogre who had been portrayed by players as "Adolf" (as in Hitler) while Rita was a pretty, articulate and sensitive Jewish woman who told me that some of her family were Holocaust victims. On the other side was their daughter Gayla, about the same age as our Simon; very sweet, very well-behaved and very out-of-place amid the hockey crowd.

My affection for Keenan grew when I learned that he was a biking enthusiast. We exchanged cycle tales and even vaguely talked of pedalling somewhere together sometime in the distant future. Interestingly, the conversation hardly ever dwelled on hockey which was fine for all of us.

In my eyes, the most noteworthy aspect of the chat was Keenan's remarkable calm, warmth and insights. He was so totally unlike his image that I wondered whether he needed a new press agent or if he simply pulled a Jekyll-Hyde depending on the season. I also wondered about Rita. She was so totally unlike any "hockey wife" I had ever met. Not that others weren't attractive, intelligent and witty, but Rita seemed to be two cuts above everybody else.

Keenan and I never bicycled together – although we did talk about it from time to time thereafter – nor did we spend much time in lengthy conversation during the season or after. Eventually, he moved from Philadelphia to Chicago where he coached the Blackhawks amid the same aura of imminent player-coach warfare that enveloped the Flyers' dressing room.

By this time Keenan had been around the NHL so long that his reputation preceded him wherever he went, and it was not uncommon for the media to allude to him in terms that were more suitable for a Charles Addams' cartoon than big-league hockey. Nor was it unusual to hear Blackhawks' players complain about Keenan's mania for discipline and the atmosphere of hypertension that characterized his stewardship.

This was not news to me. My close friend, Munson Campbell, had been pals with Blackhawks' owner Bill Wirtz for many years and was operating one of Wirtz's many liquor dealerships. Campbell, therefore, became my best contact vis-a-vis the Blackhawks, since he was in direct communication with Wirtz on a weekly basis.

"Billy is fed up with Keenan," Campbell told me one day. "He can't take him anymore. As soon as he can, Wirtz will fire him."

It didn't happen right away because, as usual, Keenan kept his club competitive and attractive to watch. But the military academy ambience prevailed and one summer, as I prepared my annual NHL preview for *Inside Sports* magazine, I wrote a squib about the Blackhawks. One of my choice morsels suggested that if the dislike-for-Mike atmosphere had any effect it would cause a tidal wave in Lake Michigan.

The article hit the stands about a week after training camp began which is when my office phone rang.

"Jim DeMaria (Blackhawks p.r. man), Stan." His voice was unusually austere. "Mister Keenan would like to talk to you."

Uh, oh. It didn't sound good, but I wasn't quite sure what Keenan had on his mind. Before I could think of the *Inside Sports* item, he was on the blower.

His voice was tingling with tension. "That article you wrote in *Inside Sports*."

"Yes."

"Was that line you wrote about me supposed to be humour?"

"It was an attempt to be funny."

"Well, I didn't think it was very funny."

We went back and forth for awhile. At one point I believed he simply was trying to intimidate me and yet at another, I suspected that he was sensitive enough to actually feel hurt by the barb. Who knows, maybe it was both.

I was jolted by the call, but also pleased that I hadn't bent to his onslaught. After we hung up, I reread the *Inside Sports* item and remained convinced that Keenan had vastly overreacted to the squib, but then again, Keenan has spent his NHL career overreacting; or overacting, as the case may be.

Wirtz – via Bob Pulford – eventually fired Keenan and I next met him at the All-Star game in Montreal when Gary Bettman was taking command of the NHL. Keenan appeared relaxed as we chatted at rinkside, acting as if our clash had never happened. He even offered me his phone number and suggested that I call if I needed any information. Maybe I shouldn't have been surprised at his total friendliness, but I was.

Thus, when Keenan was appointed Rangers' coach, I looked forward to a resumption of our relationship – friendship would have been an exaggeration. Now, here I was: Simon was in crisis, Keenan was in town and I was looking to him for help.

Actually, I'm not certain what kind of help I had expected. The hockey community had learned about Simon's plight and each day we would receive tokens of encouragement, from cards to letters to autographed pictures from Tie Domi, one of my friendly enemies. There was a phone call and autographed stick from Gretzky, another stick from Lemieux. Trevor Linden sent his playoff jersey; in fact, we had received so much hockey equipment and gear, that we could have opened up a shop! But so far, only Kasatonov had actually lugged himself all the way up here to Morningside Heights.

Keenan's persona offered more strength-giving potential than most of the others and, despite our past differences, I thought it would be beneficial if he visited.

It was another Friday, this time it was July 16th, when we got the news that Simon had actually gone on the Columbia-Presbyterian transplant list. This was the actual outward admission that our son couldn't live unless they took out his heart and replaced it with the heart of another. It was still too much to comprehend.

Now it was a matter of waiting – and hoping – for the call that told us a healthy heart was on the way.

Once again, Simon took it with fortitude and with nary a tear in his eye. My wife, Shirley, and I were shaken and attempted to fortify ourselves with the knowledge needed for the next step. The doctors gave us an elaborate handbook that explained all the pitfalls and procedures enroute to the transplant and beyond. To say the least, we were overcome by the challenge.

What we needed now was some kind of a family tonic, and it came on a Saturday morning in the form of the two Mikes, Keenan and Richter. The goalie was the first to arrive; quietly gliding in, looking more like a college sophomore than an NHL goalie. He went right over to Simon and handed him a bag filled with Rangers' goodies that included a T-shirt, pins and other tidbits. Richter kidded the kid about not being a Ranger fan and got a broad – yet semi-sheepish – grin in return.

Richter plopped himself in a big leather chair at bedside and began chatting with Simon when, within a minute, another figure appeared in the doorway. I got up to greet the coach who walked briskly toward the bed, gazing straight at me. Instead of a handshake, he wrapped his arms around me and squeezed the squeeze of a parent who had a special feel for a sick kid. I've been squeezed a few hundred times in my life but none equalled the Keenan hug for a simple message delivery: hang tough, my good friend!

For an hour the two Mikes, myself, Simon and, later, Shirley, traded stories, exchanged views and distracted ourselves from the trouble around us. Keenan's demeanour alternated from witty to intensely intellectual as he would carefully explain an aerobic program he thought Simon might try after – we hoped – he obtained his new heart.

Uncannily we all seemed to realize simultaneously when it was time for the two Mikes to leave, and except for Simon, of course, all stood up as one. As they headed for the elevator, Keenan spun around and grabbed me a second time. I was inwardly hoping that he would. Shirley and I were terribly anxious about the uncertain days ahead and needed outside reassurance. Mike's hug tightened the emotional vise. If he said anything, I couldn't hear, but I was feeling plenty.

The elevator arrived and they both disappeared through the doors. We returned to the room. "It's enough to make you a Ranger fan," I said to Simon.

He thought for a moment. "Well," he said, "I don't know about that." Spoken like a true Islander fan with a fresh reverence for the two Mikes.

I had been so touched by the two visits, I wondered how I could possibly give the two Mikes fair journalistic treatment. Dare I criticize Keenan who had given me such immense emotional support? Would I ever put the knock on Richter no matter how badly he played goal?

The answers were difficult and, for the moment at least, did not have to be answered. But they would prove perplexing down the line when I returned to the arena, resumed my professional life and once again began writing and discussing their performances. Believe me, it was not easy.

Shortly after Keenan and Richter had departed, the three of us understood what Simon faced in the next weeks; waiting, hoping and praying. There was no way of knowing when – or if – the heart would arrive. There was no way of knowing how long Simon's severely wounded heart could last despite the medications. We wanted to think that he could last for months (as it often took months to receive a heart), but we sensed that it could be less – much less.

In the meantime, the hockey community continued an outpouring that was almost overwhelming: a stirring letter from Pat Quinn and another from Devils' owner John McMullen. New Jersey president Lou Lamoriello remembered that Simon had lionized former Devils goalie Craig Billington – since traded to Ottawa – so he dispatched a Devils' Billington jersey with a funny note about Simon being true to his hero.

As the days passed, we had hoped that the "magic" drug Dibutamine would sustain Simon's heart until the new one arrived, but soon it became clear that he was weakening. Where once he could climb out of bed and walk to the toilet, now he could barely take a step or two, at the most. And still no replacement heart.

Distractions and encouragement were necessary. A steady stream of Simon's friends and some relatives helped immensely. One day, completely unannounced, goalie Sean Burke and forward Jim McKenzie of the Whalers drove all the way from Hartford and showed up in the kid's room. Simon knew and remembered Burke from his 1988 heroics as a Devils' rookie. McKenzie was a complete newcomer, but a very gregarious fellow who immediately won over the lad. Burke talked goaltending and McKenzie talked about everything else. It was a key visit.

Even more so was the visit of Islanders' forwards Mick Vukota and Derek King. As a Long Island fan, Simon had been hoping that one or two of his favourites would show up, but none had been around in the early part of July. Then, old friend Vukota called, said he was coming and asked if he could bring along his Sega hockey video game. By all means, I said.

Vukota and King said they were coming up on a Friday afternoon but they didn't say when. Simon, in the meantime, was at the whim of doctors and nurses; constantly being wheeled around for tests and X-rays. On this day, he had made several trips and fell asleep exhausted. He awakened at about 4 p.m. and about three minutes later the two Islanders knocked on the door. (Simon was at the moment out of PICU and in a private room on a cardiac care floor in the Babies' Hospital.)

Like Richter, Vukota carried a shopping bag from which he lifted out a set of black wires connected to a video-game console. It was the same system Simon had at home, which somehow, none of us had thought to bring.

Just as we had hoped, the visit of the Islanders was extra special. King, who always had seemed to be a withdrawn personality, was terribly witty in a low-key way while Vukota was Vukota; effusive, occasionally brash and at his best when discussing the art of winning at electronic hockey.

"Kinger beats me up all the time," chuckled Vukota, referring to the video game and not the ice version where King had been renowned as a soft player.

King was highly amused and went along with the gag; the pair japing back and forth as if they were sitting in the Nassau Coliseum dressing room. This time the hockey talk had more meaning to Simon because it involved the Islanders. We bulled about the 1993 playoffs, the missed chance against Montreal, the craziness of Darius Kasparaitis and the flubby Rangers. We talked until dinnertime and then the two players had to leave to head downtown. Simon thanked Vukota for the video game and they were out the door.

There was no way for Vukota to know this at the time, but the simple gesture of delivering the Sega had a profound effect on Simon in the days ahead. His condition had deteriorated to a point where he was virtually confined to bed. Somehow, the game became a distraction at critical moments when his attention had to be diverted from the anxiety of waiting for the precious gift of the heart.

It wasn't the only Islander visit, either. Just a few days later Isles' director of publications, Chris Botta, showed up with goalie Mark Fitzpatrick in tow. Fitzpatrick had just been traded to Quebec for Ron Hextall. He was then claimed by Florida from Quebec in the Expansion Draft, but was still in the area. Fitzpatrick, too, had been stricken by a mystery ailment a few years earlier – and had sufficiently recovered to resume his NHL career. This was another boost for Simon, and for me as well.

On Thursday, August 5th, a doctor on the cardiology team, Dr. Marianne Kichuk, informed me that the Dibutamine was losing its effectiveness, that Simon would have to be returned to Intensive Care and placed on another more potent medicine. Without articulating it, Dr. Kichkuk intimated that Simon was dying.

I phoned Shirley, who still was at home, and spilled the news, unedited. This was no time to mince words; at least that was what I thought at the time. When I returned to Simon's room, he mentioned that he already had spoken with the doctor.

"Dad," he said, almost matter-of-factly, "things aren't so good, are they?"

I tried to create a verbal cushion. Yes, you would have to return to Intensive Care, but you'll be all right. The Dibutamine will be replaced by another drug that will sustain you – I knew not how – until the heart arrived. He appeared somewhat reassured and then thoroughly distracted when his friend Doug arrived. That was just the break I needed.

Two hours later, while I tried to relax in the waiting room, Dr. Kichuk walked in and said the precious words: "It looks like a heart is on the way."

It was. When Shirley walked in shortly thereafter, she had obviously been shoring herself up to spend a desolate night with Simon before he went down to PICU for what could be the last time, when she was confronted with a weird scene of what I could only call scared jubilation: a heart was on its way and Simon was being readied for surgery. It would be almost 1 a.m. on Friday, August the 6th, before he disappeared into the icy operating room.

By 7 a.m. he was in the PICU, tubes and machines all over. But, by God, he was already conscious and trying to speak around the respirator and over the medications they had given him to actually paralyze him. Simon's subsequent recovery bordered on the incredible, until he underwent his first attempt to reject the new heart only a week after the transplant. Other complications would occur, but by August 25th, Simon Fischler walked into his own home.

His life never would be the same. He might not ever play goal again but there was the hope that, despite the many obstacles he would face along the way, he could enjoy a reasonably normal life.

In the meantime, I had hoped to return to a reasonably normal hockey life, although the sense I had was that the ice game never would be the same for me, or for that matter, the NHL.

6

....

THE BETTMAN EVOLUTION

When Gary Bettman took command of the National Hockey League, I warned him face-to-face that no matter what he did, there would be a residue of Canadian chauvinists who would criticize him no matter how pure his intentions, no matter how sage his decisions, nor how business-like they were.

And since there never has been a faultless NHL leader, it was inevitable that Bettman would err; which he did. But even before the commissioner committed his first faux pas, he was under the gun north of the 49th parallel.

After all, Canadians realized that their beloved game no longer was the same and never would be in the foreseeable future. It had become Americanized beyond recognition and the franchise score when Bettman succeeded Stein was 18-8 for Uncle Sam. The rout was on.

On the administration front, where the movers and shakers live, the tilt was even more precipitous. Americans were now running Canada's national sport from top to bottom. For example, the "Big Three" among hockey's power brokers – board chairman Bruce McNall, Bettman and NHL Players' Association boss Bob Goodenow – were all U.S.-born.

At 650 Fifth Avenue, the NHL's fortress, Bettman, with precious few exceptions, filled almost every available league command post with non-Canadians. Brian Burke, the new senior vice-president, was born in Providence, Rhode Island, and grew up in Minnesota. Almost all the vice-presidents, from Steve Solomon to Glenn Adamo to Arthur Pincus to Bernadette Mansur, were New Yorkers or close to Gotham in spirit.

This was a far cry from an earlier era when Toronto's Conn Smythe and Montreal's Frank Selke Sr. ran the league. The president, Clarence Campbell, and his aide, Brian O'Neill, both were Canadians.

Bettman's Americanization of the NHL did not go unnoticed in Canada where two major complaints were heard: 1. The league is orchestrated by U.S. attorneys; 2. They are insensitive to the needs of Canadian markets and would just as soon unload Winnipeg, Edmonton and Quebec in favour of larger American cities.

"I can sympathize with Canadians whose noses are out of joint," *Toronto Star* columnist Bob McKenzie told me. "How would Americans feel if the baseball commissioner was Japanese?"

Unlike some of his colleagues, McKenzie allowed that quality of performance as well as the new administration's sensitivity toward small Canadian markets remain key bases for judgment. Burke cautioned the Nervous Nellies north of the border not to worry.

"We feel the Canadian component is critical," said Burke. "The bulk of players and media interests are north of the 49th parallel. It's important that we promote professional hockey in Canada."

Burke, like others at 650 Fifth Avenue, had become acutely sensitive to criticism. "I resent this American attorneys notion," he told me. "I would be just as offended if someone said, 'Oh, this guy shouldn't be hired because he's black or this guy shouldn't be hired because he's Jewish or Chinese.' It's 1993. Wake up and smell the coffee. The best people should get the jobs."

Not all the critics were in Canada. Vicki Contavespi, a reporter for the prestigious *Forbes* (financial) magazine, had been a hockey fan for a number of years and looked forward to writing an upbeat feature about the new administration. *Forbes* had only recently published a positive story on the NBA and featured a sidebar on how Bettman's NHL was poised to be the next NBA.

In researching her article, Contavespi phoned Goodenow and inquired about the union's new "Be A Player" campaign. The NHLPA's director explained that older players do not receive pension money and that all monies from "Be A Player" would go to them. "I began to delve into that and my *Forbes* piece was the end result," Contavespi told me.

The headline over Contavespi's story in the January 31, 1994 issue of *Forbes* was hardly the kind that would be savoured by the NHL's relatively new public relations honchos. "BAD BLOOD ON THE ICE" was followed by a subheadline, "Can Gary Bettman do for ice hockey what David Stern did for basketball? So far, the outlook is hardly promising."

Hmmmm.

At a time when the press-conscious Bettman was obtaining generally positive publicity, the *Forbes* piece was like a literary land mine for the denizens of 650 Fifth Avenue. After lavishly praising Bettman's former boss, David Stern, Contavespi then asserted that, "Bettman, by contrast, is alienating hockey's players."

Among other items, she mentioned that players felt they were missing out on revenues for hockey-jersey sales and that retired players were still battling over $40 million in pension money they felt they were owed. Her story concluded with the fact that union members had been skating without a contract since the beginning of the season.

She wondered why Bettman hadn't focused his attention on that issue, an assertion that grated Bettman. "Well, excuse me," he replied to her. "I also have 400 other things that are front-burner items and I have a league to run on a daily basis."

But the woman from *Forbes* had the last word. Contavespi acidly concluded her commentary with two sentences: "A commissioner out of his depth? So it seems." It was awfully – and perhaps unnecessarily – tough stuff.

Since all of the 26 NHL club owners are businessmen, virtually every one of them reads *Forbes*. Many reacted angrily to the feature and some clearly suggested that the Goodenow had planted it with Contavespi, a charge that she later vigorously denied. Not surprisingly, Bettman, Inc. was unhappy with her piece.

"The league was very helpful to me until the *Forbes* story came out," said Contavespi. "I actually received a call at my home from (NHL VP corporate communications) Bernadette Mansur before my story came out. She accused me of setting out to do a hatchet job on Bettman, which I thought was unprofessional.

"Arthur Pincus (NHL VP public relations) tried his best to have any mention of a lawsuit filed by retired players against the league be removed from my story. *Forbes* refused that request because the information was factually correct."

Contavespi, a soft-spoken, unobtrusive reporter who has since become a private investigator, was dismayed over the NHL reaction to the story. "I did not set out to do a hatchet job on Bettman," she insisted in our conversations. "I had nothing against him and had never even met him. But I've come to the conclusion that Bettman has an attitude; of that there is no doubt. He is very arrogant; and coming from the NBA he would be arrogant. The NBA had the world by the basketballs and Bettman came to the NHL thinking he could run it like Stern ran the NBA." Perhaps, but others suggested that Contavespi was unduly harsh too early in Bettman's reign.

Bettman's critics argued that his NBA background precluded him from having a genuine "feel" for hockey. The sacking of Stu Hackel from the TV department was cited by some as a classic example. Hackel was well-respected throughout the league for his knowledge and contacts. He had been with the NHL for many years.

"Bettman didn't understand the culture of hockey," Contavespi argued. "He had no idea how the 'boys' thought. In my article, I called Bettman 'pugnacious' and that wasn't a compliment. I think he has a short man's complex."

Then again, Bettman didn't expect everyone to like him. He understood there would be criticism even from critics who liked his performance. Me included. I was terribly unhappy with his handling of the Dale Hunter-Pierre Turgeon affair during the spring of 1993. Late in the final game, Hunter, whose Washington Capitals were about to lose the series, sneaked up on the New York Islanders' centre and cross-checked Turgeon from behind into the side boards.

It was as dastardly an act as any I've seen in a half-century of watching hockey. The result was even worse. Enjoying the best year of his career, Turgeon suffered a shoulder injury that sidelined him for the next series – except for a token appearance in Game Seven at Pittsburgh – and rendered him ineffective against the Canadiens in the Cup semifinals. Some Turgeon watchers insist he never was the same player after his recovery.

My belief, shared by many journalists, was that Bettman's first major disciplinary case should have set an example for years to come. A year-long suspension would have been justified. Instead, Hunter was suspended for the first 21 games of the following season.

"The Islanders' fans wanted summary execution of Hunter," said Bettman, "and the Capitals have continued to say that I was much, much, much too severe. That tells me we hit it on the mark."

Nevertheless, Bettman was clobbered by some New York media heavyweights including *Newsday*'s Mike Lupica but shrugged off the criticism and proceeded to his next crisis which was the embarassing Gil Stein affair. As a liason from the Ziegler regime, Stein might have been a useful aide-de-camp for Bettman based on his long years with the league and his contacts, but when the media got wind of the Hall of Fame shenanigans, Stein got it from all barrels and Bettman had to move swiftly to defuse the incident before it damaged the league.

He made a brilliant move, engaging an independent probe that eventually found Stein culpable. When questions about Ottawa's lack of effort in late season games were raised, the commissioner again went to his investigative consultants and emerged smelling like a rose.

After months of criticism for his failure to hire a right-hand "hockey man," he selected Brian Burke, the one I had recommended to him in the first place just after he had taken office. I wouldn't for a minute suggest that I was responsible for Burke's appointment, but I found it fascinating to see how many NHL personalities Bettman considered – Glen Sather among them – before making his final decision.

There were those who thought that Burke got the job by default; that many general managers rejected the position because they were dubious about working for Bettman. Some simply didn't want to work in New York City, but Burke, as I had said at the start, fit all the criteria. He's smart, a lawyer, played hockey, has dual citizenship, was an agent and general manager. Moreover, Burke is media friendly, answering any and every question put to him by the press.

He's also notoriously combative and during his Vancouver stint as Canucks' boss Pat Quinn's senior assistant, Burke singled out *Vancouver Province* columnist Tony Gallagher for criticism in what amounted to a war between the two that still hasn't ended. Its evolution offers an arresting view of team-media relations when a newsman is perceived as overly hostile.

During one exchange in August 1991, the Canucks' Glen Ringdal, vice-president and director of marketing and communications, wrote a stinging letter to

Gallagher's editor-in-chief, Brian Butters. Ringdal asserted that neither Burke nor Quinn "has any desire or intention to speak to or grant interviews to Tony no matter which media outlet he represents."

Burke-Quinn also ordered that Gallagher "not be accorded the access to club personnel generally given to other reporters."

The reason, according to Ringdal, was that the Canucks' personnel "have been personally offended on numerous occasions by Tony's scurrilous editorial attacks on our company and its people."

Butters responded with a letter on August 6, 1991, rejecting the ban out of hand. "The fact you don't care for Gallagher's reporting on Canuck affairs is beside the point here," wrote Butters. "Gallagher's job as a contract columnist for the *Province* is to call the shots the way he sees them."

Butters concluded by saying, "The Canucks are attempting to interfere with the ability of a specific individual to make a living."

Gallagher continued making a living as the *Vancouver Province* hockey columnist where he remains to this day. The feelings between Gallagher and Burke appear to have changed little. The Canucks' attempt at stifling Gallagher was an abject failure.

While Gallagher might not have seconded Burke's addition to the Bettman cabinet, others did at the very least because he was a "hockey man" in an NHL milieu that was increasingly being dominated by non-hockey people. Meanwhile, the Americanization of the NHL was becoming more and more galling to Canadian chauvinist journalists, the most obvious of whom was the *Toronto Sun*'s well-connected, outspoken columnist Al Strachan.

"Once the head (NHL) office was in Montreal," wrote Strachan, "but it's now in New York and staffed by Americans, mostly lawyers. Even the responsibility of overseeing the game itself was given to an American, Brian Burke, a Boston lawyer.

"Burke, who was born in the United States, got his law degree in the United States and always worked in the United States except for a few years as assistant general manager of the Vancouver Canucks. He acquired Canadian citizenship during his tenure on the west coast and therefore tries to convince people that he's a Canadian. In the new NHL, not one of 25 million real Canadians qualifies to be the chief executive in charge of hockey.

"This fact has not escaped the players, the majority of whom are Canadians."

Bettman and Burke dismissed the criticism out of hand; as well they should. Players, many of whom were either American or foreign-born, couldn't care less whether a Ubangi was running the NHL as long as the average salary kept climbing – as it was – and the league remained a stickhandlers' market – which it was, and still is.

But Strachan was right on when he noted that the influx of Bettman technocrats had altered the close feel for the game experienced by NHL workers during the coccoon-like Campbell, Ziegler and Stein regimes. The NBA-ing of the NHL put the accent on bigness and a more corporate feel than ever before.

"When Canadians ran the game," added Strachan, "even the owners had a hockey sense and the game's roots were in frozen-prairie ponds and cold arenas.

"The roots of today's game are in the board rooms. Decisions are made not because they may have a good or bad impact on hockey, but because of the manner in which they will be received by large corporations – and all those corporations are American.

"This is the new order and, unfortunately, it's here to stay."

Whether "the new order" would be capable of achieving its goals – primarily to lift the NHL toward the NBA's success level – would depend on its handling of two labour crises, the first of which was a strike by referees and linesmen in the early part of the 1993-94 season.

The zebras' walk-out was followed by anguished cries that the use of substitute officials would result in chaos beyond belief and, within days of scab officiating, Bettman's gamble would fail and, conceivably, his regime would crumble.

Opinions differ as to the effectiveness of the replacements. I covered several games which were handled by the non-union types and, in some cases, they were handled better than games orchestrated by the Don Koharskis, Bill McCrearys and Andy vanHellemond of the world. Granted that Paul Stewart's inevitable showboating was missing as was Terry Gregson's intensity, but by and large, the newcomers held up throughout the walk-out; if they hadn't, Bettman would have been toast.

The commissioner was fortunate. Had there not been enough substitutes, or had they been intimidated by the strikers, games would have been cancelled and Bettman would have faced intense criticism.

However, the commissioner and Burke planned well, lined up their replacements well enough in advance and had them in place when the walk-out was called. While the zebras had plenty of support, they also faced public opposition from those who believed that their on-ice performance hardly merited any raise in salaries.

During the early days of the strike, I had been in close touch with both sides of the dispute. Agent Don Meehan, who represented the zebras, was an old friend through his representation of Pat LaFontaine, while the NHL types, led by Bettman, chatted with me on a regular basis.

I clearly sided with ownership in this dispute, but was not averse to giving the other side its voice. One day I received a phone call from Kerry Fraser, who had been a pal of mine for years – we once considered writing a book together – and had become a spokesman for the striking officials. Fraser had been exceptionally supportive during my son's crisis and held a special niche in our hearts. Fraser knew that we had given time to the NHL on one of our telecasts from Byrne Meadowlands Arena in New Jersey and asked whether one of the striking officials could get equal time. My SportsChannel producer Jackie Lyons unhesitatingly agreed and I phoned Meehan to obtain a referee. The most natural would have been vanHellemond, who had been outspoken from the start of the strike and who was best known among the zebras.

I considered this an interesting test of personality. As long as I had known vanHellemond he had refused interviews with me, presumably on the grounds that he objected to my criticism of him and his colleagues. Now he was on the blower and I mentioned that I'd like him to be the zebra to articulate his union's position.

At first he seemed willing, yet there was some hesitation. He was in Toronto and the interview would be held in East Rutherford, New Jersey. Yes, he wanted to appear, but no, there were a few obstacles. I was fervently hoping he would come, mostly because it would demonstrate that in a contentious issue such as this, I bore no grudge and left my microphone open to the other side.

VanHellemond never phoned back. Instead, I received a call from Fraser explaining that he would be the guest, not Andy. His explanation sounded reasonable enough – travel, other commitments – but it left me with a sour aftertaste. I had the feeling that vanHellemond just couldn't get himself to go one-on-one with me and that was that.

Since the interview with NHL people had been conducted in our SportsChannel studio adjoining the Devils' dressing room, we expected to do the Fraser interview there as well. But when word of the striking referee's impending appearance reached the NHL high command, we were told that Fraser would not be admitted into Byrne Arena. Period.

Neither the NHL nor the Devils were pleased that we were giving equal time to the officials and they certainly would not allow him into the building – at least not as long as he was striking – without a ticket. And when Fraser obtained a ducat, he was not cleared to come down to the dressing-room area without a pass which he was emphatically denied.

Faced with these obstacles, SportsChannel had the option of either scrapping the interview or finding a location where it could be conducted. Lyons decided that the "best" spot would be in the Byrne Arena parking lot just outside the vomitory ramp where the TV trucks are located.

As we set up for the interview, winds were blowing fiercely off the nearby Hudson River and over the Meadowlands. The cold air was filtering through my overcoat as Fraser appeared from behind a row of parked cars. Typically upbeat, he apologized for us having to do the one-on-one in a parking lot and we insisted that it was no problem even though we were freezing our tootsies off.

After Fraser had made his points, I asked him if he saw the irony in this situation. Time after time, I had asked referees to be interviewed and time after time they had refused. But now that they had something to gain from going before the cameras, Fraser was suddenly available. There was nothing he could say about that and we parted shaking hands.

Needless to say, the Fraser interview did not sit well with the NHL general staff nor with the Devils' high command. Lou Lamoriello and Dr. John

McMullen, president and owner respectively, with whom I had become quite close, wanted no part of the zebras getting air time on a Devils' telecast, but what was done was done and in 10 days the strike was settled.

Anyone who suggests there was a winner or loser in this dispute is off-base. Officials obtained meaningful raises and other benefits – opponents would have preferred that they obtained not a penny more – while Bettman's gamble on using the scabs worked. Had the replacements cracked in the first days, as many had predicted, it would have been bye-bye Bettman. But the replacements performed nobly under adverse conditions.

"We got all the games played and we didn't miss a beat," Bettman glowed when we met in a corridor at Byrne Arena. "We had competent replacement officials who came under the most intense and unfair scrutiny. If this scrutiny was placed on any of our existing officials, I don't know that they could have fared better."

But the settlement did not settle the rancour in the zebra pasture. Many of the officials, speaking anonymously, blurted out their bitterness toward the commissioner who was viewed as an arrogant outsider. This view was magnified by several Canadian journalists who depicted him as an insensitive dictator.

I pointedly brought up the ill-feeling issue to Bettman after the strike. Typically, he tried to put a positive spin on it while remaining somewhat realistic.

"In terms of the residue of bad feelings," he said, "I don't think it's widespread among all the officials. It was business and people can't confuse that. I was charged to run this place in a credible way. When someone comes in and says, 'I want a hundred percent raise,' and my response is, 'here's 29 percent the first year and 65 percent over four years,' I don't have to apologize for that."

Without question, I agreed with him. If anything, the zebras work across the board would be graded C-minus, at best. With a grade like that, any salary boost should be viewed as a bonus. Bettman need not have apologized for anything.

Public relations was another story. Some NHL critics such as Steve Taub of *Financial World* magazine, complained that once the league had identified him as an unfriendly journalist, he was not provided the interview access he desired.

"Their public relations left something to be desired," said Taub. "When I wrote a story, they handled it horrendously. Once when the league had a unified press conference in New York, their p.r. people wouldn't make anyone available to talk to me. I finally interviewed Bettman at the hotel and he tried to embarass me in front of the other sportswriters; the 'all-knowing' sportswriters."

A year after Bettman had taken office, *Newsweek* magazine commented that the commissioner had not done enough. Bettman disagreed. "We've put hockey on the right path," he countered. "That includes a reorganization, hiring people like Brian Burke with in-house expertise needed for a business-like stable organization."

But ESPN ratings remained mediocre and a spate of stories about "boring" hockey blemished the NHL's image. Aging league icon, Wayne Gretzky, had lost his drawing power and Mario Lemieux, Gretzky's successor as pinup star, had become seriously ill. Marketing of the league had stumbled forward without any noticeable gains.

Bettman, of course, had the answers. "It's very nice to say you want to market, but you don't just throw a light switch and reach that market." He was right.

As vital as marketing was to the NHL's progress, it was small potatoes compared with the commissioner's most vexing challenge: a new Collective Bargaining Agreement. The NHL Players' Association contract with the league had expired on September 15, 1993, and under Bob Goodenow's baton, the stickhandlers were singing restless and angry songs.

"Hockey has the most growth potential of all the major sports," said Doug Wilson, the outgoing NHLPA president. "We believe players and owners can share in that growth in a way that is mutually beneficial."

It sounded good but the reality was more complicated and not very good after all. The arguments ahead would surround the issue of how the revenue pie should be divided and who would wield the most power. Meanwhile, Bettman had months to cultivate a relationship with his negotiating adversary, Bob Goodenow, who meanwhile had an opportunity to carefully eye the commissioner's roughing of the referees.

"Sometimes," Bettman ominously mentioned before the CBA talks began, "you have to have a strike because people's expectations are a little out of whack. And they need to be out of work to lower those expectations. Bob and I may not agree with everything, but that's what collective bargaining is all about."

Bettman's future hung on hammering out a CBA that was palatable to his owners. Goodenow, as tough an adversary as the commissioner, would provide the ultimate test. If the commissioner was lucky, he'd have a deal before the 1994 playoffs – without a strike.

"We'll have to see what the players want to do," he said. "If they want to get aggressive, that will be their call. I'm committed to getting a framework in place that will enable us to stabilize the sport and I'm always optimistic about everything."

Heading toward the conclusion of his first full season, Bettman still was enjoying more kudos than kicks. If he could pull off a new CBA, he would get an A on his report card. But as John Ziegler learned in 1992, a strike can result in an F, as in Forget-it.

"For people to think we were going to duplicate what the NBA did in a year or two years or five years is silly," Bettman concluded. "It took the NBA well in excess of a decade. David Stern was NBA commissioner three years before anyone knew who he was. I don't have apologies for what we've done."

Bettman triumphed in one sense; the 1994 playoffs were played without a hitch. But they came and went without a Collective Bargaining Agreement. Any signs of a quick agreement between Bettman and Goodenow had evaporated in a summer of charges and countercharges. The spark that would explode into hockey's Civil War was about to be ignited and there would be hell to pay.

7

··

THE FALL OF BRUCE McNALL

"I'm like a fireman. Wherever the fire is, is where I happen to be."
– Bruce McNall

Bruce McNall's name meant absolutely nothing to me when it was first mentioned during a phone conversation in the early 1980s. The fellow on the other end of the wire was Joel Bergman.

"You might want to write this name down," said Bergman, who has been The Fischler Hockey Service's west coast reporter for 15 years. "Bruce McNall. He's a big fan of yours."

He might have been talking about Joe Schlump The Midget for all I knew about Bruce McNall.

"Apart from being a fan of mine," I inquired, "who is this guy?"

Bergman went on to note that the McNall in question was a man of wealth, a devoted hockey follower and a casual friend of his. Still, it meant absolutely nothing to me until I detected a faint sense of urgency in Bergman's voice. "You really should have his number," Bergman concluded.

I wrote it down on a piece of paper and tacked it on the bulletin board behind the computer. Then, I quickly forgot about Bruce McNall.

In the early 1980s there was no reason to think about the roly-poly coin collector. The Kings were being run by Dr. Jerry Buss. Friends of mine on the NHL board of governors admired Buss in one way and chided him in another, but according to one owner, he was rarely seen at govenor's meetings.

Buss-watchers hardly were surprised by his casual disdain for the ownership meetings since Dr. Buss' passion was for basketball and his true favourites, the Los Angeles Lakers. This was the official winter glitz team of Tinseltown and was renowned for its ability to lure just about every celebrity from Jack Nicholson to Woody Allen down for a courtside seat at the NBA games. As far as his NHL colleagues were concerned, Buss' Kings were a mere afterthought, a fiscal bench-warmer, so to speak.

This could be a source of annoyance to people like McNall who lived and died with the Kings. They revelled in the halcyon years when Marcel Dionne, Charlie Simmer and Dave Taylor dominated the NHL as the Triple Crown Line and petit Rogatien Vachon punted out pucks in the Los Angeles goal.

Although it has become fashionable to declare that Los Angeles was a dead hockey town before Gretzky arrived, this hardly was the case. In 1974-75, the Kings won 42 games, lost only 17 and tied 21. They finished a vibrant second in the Norris Division, a feat they duplicated in 1980-81 when their record was a handsome 43-24-13. The Kings were respected and well-covered by the media while attracting a devoted core of followers, McNall among them.

But his name had passed from my conscious until 1986 when Bergman phoned once more. "Remember that fellow, Bruce McNall, I told you about? Well, he now owns part of the Kings."

It sounded implausible to me until I checked the papers. Sure enough, McNall bought 25 percent of the hockey club from Buss. "I don't think that's the end of it," Bergman added. "Bruce really wants to get involved."

A year later McNall owned 49 percent of the Kings. In September 1987, he was named president and in March 1988 he became the sole owner. Now I knew why there was a sense of urgency in Bergman's voice three years earlier.

I finally met Bruce McNall during one of the Kings' eastern swings. They had a date with the New York Islanders at Nassau Veterans Memorial Coliseum in Uniondale, where I broadcast the games for SportsChannel. A few hours before show time, we would hang out in the corridor near the visiting team's dressing room.

One could hardly miss the new owner. He was what my mother would have described as "pleasingly plump." McNall weighed in at about 225 pounds, wore a double-breasted navy-blue suit with a silver and white tie. That was the least conspicuous aspect of McNall. His trademark – and that which set him apart from any of the other owners – was his face. It was large and invariably was sealed with a smile.

"I think you'll like him," Bergman mentioned before our meeting.

Disarmingly affable, McNall was hard not to like. His story read like Horatio Alger and his style was right out of Dale Carnegie's "How To Win Friends And Influence People."

Before he even had complete control of the Kings, the *Los Angeles Times* profiled him with what it tritely called, "a success story." "HE HAS TWO THINGS GOING: LUCK, MONEY" noted the headline over Jerry Crowe's profile. Superficially, at least, McNall appeared to be one of the luckiest people in California. In the fall of 1987 he returned from Paris where Trempolino, a horse he co-owned, won the $1.1 million Arc de Triomphe, Europe's richest race. A full-length film, "The Sicilian," was about to be released by McNall's production company, Gladden Entertainment Corp., while his collectible-coin brokerage was discussing a deal with Merrill Lynch.

"I'm like a fireman," said McNall. "Wherever the fire is, is where I happen to be."

I learned that McNall began following hockey while a student at California's Arcadia High School in 1967 when I wrote my first book, a biography of Gordie Howe. A teenaged coin collector, McNall learned the numismatic business and soon had Los Angeles shop owners seeking him out to identify and price their coins. McNall's reward was lesser coins but he soon had the wherewithal to start his own collection and open his own store.

By the time he was 20, McNall had graduated from UCLA with a degree in ancient history and was at work on a doctorate when he decided to concentrate on his coin business. "I decided that maybe I'd make a little money first," he said. At age 24, he paid $420,000 for a 2,000-year-old Greek coin that he later sold for almost $1 million.

When the 37-year-old McNall was named head of the Kings, he claimed that his coin company, Numismatic Fine Arts, Inc., was the largest of its kind in the world. In addition Gladden Entertainment had produced a couple of hits, WarGames and Mr. Mom, while his Summa Stable, Inc. was breeding and racing thoroughbreds. McNall asserted that he owned or had interests in about 250 horses.

The Los Angeles Times reported his net worth at $34 million, but McNall corrected that to about $100 million. Now he would try to add to it by building the Kings into a respectable organization. "I want to bring the Stanley Cup to Los Angeles within the next three years," he insisted in October 1987.

It was a laudable goal. Also laughable. Nobody expected the Stanley Cup to ever reach Los Angeles. Since the Kings were born in 1967, the club never got remotely close to attaining big-league hockey's ultimate goal. While I admired McNall's enthusiasm, I dismissed his prediction as a function more of vitality than reality.

What I did appreciate in McNall was his candor and congeniality. As rich and famous as he had become, McNall was congenitally available, always willing to be interviewed and quite willing to state his mind, even if it meant challenging the establishment. More importantly, to his team, McNall was hellbent on making the Kings respectable.

"The hockey club needs help," he said. "It's something that obviously is an ailing thing. It needs something, so I've been trying to develop what the heck that is. I'm not sure what that is yet."

McNall polled his players to determine what they believed was necessary to improve the club. He became the archetypical hands-on owner, helping rookies such as Luc Robitaille and Steve Duchesne find a place to live and showing up at every game. "He's really somebody special," said Robitaille, who became one of McNall's favourites. "He really cares about the players."

He became the ultimate jock owner, savouring the liniment-smelling dressing room, courting the media and spending money to get a winner. Unlike original Kings' owner Jack Kent Cooke, who rarely was seen by the players, McNall became one of the boys. "He breathed life into the team" said veteran forward Dave Taylor.

That he did but the Kings remained on a treadmill to oblivion through his first full season as president and sole owner. They completed the 1987-88 season with a 30-42-8 record, finished fourth in the Smythe Division and actually ran through three coaches, Mike Murphy, Rogie Vachon and Robbie Ftorek.

While all this was going on, hockey's most arresting star, Wayne Gretzky, was becoming uncomfortable in his role with the Edmonton Oilers. I detected this feeling during a meeting with The Great One in Manhattan. He was accompanied by his agent, Michael Barnett, to a postseason award ceremony at the club inside Madison Square Garden. The press timing was poor and the press meeting following the ceremony was so lightly attended that we all were able to sit around a large table.

It was then that Gretzky actually stated that he was contemplating retirement. Mind you, I said contemplating. But even the mere suggestion that Gretzky was thinking of hanging up his skates was somewhere between bizarre and stupid. Obviously, he was angling for something which meant either more money from Edmonton Oilers' owner Peter Pocklington or a move out of Alberta.

Gretzky already had won four Stanley Cups and realized that his marketing potential would be better served in a larger American venue. It had become apparent on several visits that he loved New York's night life. Playing for the Rangers would have been the ideal, but then again, nobody ever expected Gretzky to leave Edmonton.

Yet there was something about Gretzky's comment that piqued my curiosity. What I didn't know was that Gretzky and McNall had become friends. "The more I got to know Bruce," said Gretzky, "the more I liked him."

Early in the summer of 1988, I received a phone call from Susan (Sam) Marchiano, then a reporter in the Los Angeles area. "Gretzky and McNall are playing golf," she said, "but I hear that it's more than a golf game. Wayne could be coming to play for the Kings." We argued the pros and cons concluding that one motivating factor was Gretzky's actress-wife, Janet Jones, who would prefer living near the studios rather than within dogsled distance to the North Pole.

"I'll bet he's coming to California," said Marchiano.

Marchiano had the same kind of urgency in her voice as Joel Bergman did when he originally told me about McNall. Shortly thereafter, there were hints that Gretzky might, in fact, leave the Oilers. They were rapidly and emphatically denied. About a week later, on August 9, 1988, McNall had completed his coup. Gretzky had become a King in an elaborate exchange that also brought

Marty McSorley and Mike Krushelnyski to Los Angeles. The cash-short Pocklington also received somewhere between $15 million and $20 million for allowing Canada's icon to pass through the border en route to Los Angeles.

I remember thinking what a monumental gamble McNall was taking because there was absolutely no guarantee that Gretzky would excel in his new surroundings. I also recall that this was a singular blow to Canadian pride and a boost for American hockey.

Until this point in time, sunny Southern California was the last place you'd expect hockey's most popular player to pitch his tent. Canadian chauvinists continued to labour under the misapprehension that hockey was "THEIR" game and had no business being expropriated by Americans.

But the Gretzky move was a benchmark. It signalled what was to be a gradual decline and fall of Canadian cities as focal points on the NHL political spectrum. When Gretzky left Northlands Coliseum, the Edmonton franchise wasn't killed but it was severely wounded.

Not that we were certain about Gretzky's ability to galvanize hockey interest in California. He no longer had Mark Messier at his side to relieve him of offensive pressure nor did he have Kevin Lowe and Grant Fuhr to anchor the defence and goaltending when the forwards were beaten. Despite the presence of McSorley the enforcer, it was quite possible that the thin Gretzky would be abused by enemy guerrillas now that he was with the weaker Kings.

I was working with Scotty Bowman on the SportsChannel America telecasts when Gretzky made his debut on October 6, 1988, at The Forum in Inglewood against the Detroit Red Wings. On his very first shot, Gretzky scored and the tone had been set for the season. Gretzky played superbly, scoring 54 goals in 78 games. He also won the Hart Trophy as the league's most valuable player.

McNall exploited Gretzky's presence in a most positive, entrepreneurial manner. He phoned Prime Ticket ensuring that the cable TV station carrying the Kings' game would provide financial support. Not only did he get Prime Ticket behind him, but also the folks handling the team's concessions and merchandising. In a trice the Kings value began spiralling upward. A year later the per-game fee for cable rose almost 50 percent and the number of regular-season games carried rose from 37 to 60. The average ticket price jumped from $18.50 to $22 and attendance from 427,721 to 547,952, an increase in average of 3,360 per game. Instead of five sellouts, there were 22.

As a hockey journalist, my relationship with McNall became naturally more intense. "Part of McNall's lure," wrote Bryan Burrough in a perceptive *Vanity Fair* profile, "is his almost child-like good humour; he may be the friendliest, most accessible and down-to-earth mogul I've ever met."

Dozens who had dealings with McNall would readily agree. If he had any knockers, they were virtually impossible to find on either side of the border. Canadians were awed by his maneuvering and Americans were impressed with his swift nurturing of the California hockey soil. If it were possible for there to be a "Mister Nice Guy" in the NHL, McNall was the man. "He's great to every-one he's worked with," said Gretzky, "the secretaries, the players – everyone."

Even cynical non-hockey journalists viewed McNall with a grudging touch of admiration. Jerry Grossman and Kirk Calhoun of Ernst and Young, the leading professional services firm which specializes in sports, noted the meaningful increase in Kings' attendance and TV viewership. "All this was not to watch the Kings win nine more games or even move from fourth to second place in the Smythe Division," said Grossman and Calhoun. "It was to see Gretzky. McNall knew that would happen. Sure, he was out to build a winner, but even if the Kings never won the Stanley Cup, his business deal would prove successful because the focus of it was on The Great One, a man guaranteed to improve revenues."

Gretzky and McNall became close friends and business partners. Their acquisitions ranged from the purchase of collectibles to the acquisition of the Toronto Argonauts professional football team from Harry Ornest. McNall encouraged Hollywood's dazzling personalities to The Forum and soon Kings games were sprinkled with the likes of Sylvester Stallone, Goldie Hawn and John Candy. "Bruce loved to bring them into the dressing room after games," said Bergman. "There were some nights when it seemed as if there were more actors in the clubhouse than players."

If McNall made a mistake – vis-a-vis his players – it was in allowing his enthusiasm to get the better of his fiscal sense. While Gretzky was worth a lot of money, McNall seemed more eager to overpay Gretzky than offer him a contract that The Great One would readily have accepted. "Bruce was the ultimate jock owner," said one of his colleagues on the NHL board of governors. "He was so tickled to get Wayne that he paid him way more than necessary. In the end he helped drive the market on salaries far, far higher than was necessary."

Peter Pocklington may have best capsulized the McNall personality when he said, "Bruce is America's oldest living teenager."

McNall's power within the league's hierarchy began increasing with the popularity of the team. When McNall annexed the Kings, the NHL was orches-trated by a triumvirate – president John Ziegler, chairman of the board of gover-nors (and owner of the Chicago Blackhawks) Bill Wirtz and the NHL Players' Association executive director Alan Eagleson. But Ziegler's power began fading after his disappearance during the 1988 Devils-Bruins playoff and was eroded to the point of no return during the 1992 players' strike.

Likewise, a spate of legal problems that continued through 1995 undermined Eagleson's leadership and led to his replacement as union boss by Bob Goodenow, a Detroit lawyer with a more hostile attitude toward management than his predecessor. Meanwhile, the political leaning of ownership began to change. Dissatisfaction with the Wirtz regime prompted a change and the affable McNall was selected board chairman in 1992.

To insiders this was a remarkable achievement. Club owners such as Philadelphia's Ed Snider and Pittsburgh's Howard Baldwin had considerable seniority on McNall, but McNall's apparent warmth and ability to bring disparate sides together cemented his appointment.

No sooner had he taken office than McNall set about to craft a more enlightened brand of big-league hockey. Unlike his secluded predecessors, McNall was open with the media and freely solicited ideas for improving the game. His power was even further enhanced with Ziegler's resignation in 1992 and the subsequent replacement by Gil Stein, who had been the league's chief legal eagle.

The McNall-Stein leadership duet seemed like a public relations dream-come-true for the previously conservative league. Stein, who had been designated interim president, immediately embarked on a league-wide goodwill tour – also interpreted by some as a barefaced attempt to become the NHL's first commissioner – and received mostly favourable reviews. Many observers hailed the breath of fresh air that permeated the league's high command. Meanwhile, McNall as chairman kicked off a search for a strong executive who would lead the NHL into the next century.

Although he coexisted well enough with Stein, McNall had his sights elsewhere. He couldn't ignore the NBA's remarkable success under its commissioner David Stern and remarked to me that he'd love to get the NBA boss over to the NHL.

Knowing that they could not lure Stern to the hockey front, NHL leaders decided to try his second in command, Russ Granik. The latter had no interest in leaving the basketball domain so McNall now eyed Gary Bettman, who was third on the NHL totem pole after Stern and Granik.

The race for the commissionership turned into a two-horse sprint between Bettman (who was virtually unknown to the inbred hockey community) and Stein. At first, Stein appeared to have the edge. He had been affiliated with the NHL since the Flyers joined the league in the big expansion of 1967-68 and then moved into a power-broker position as chief NHL counsel under Ziegler.

Stein's cross-continent tour in the spring and summer of 1992 as interim president appealed to the media at-large, but appeared to many club owners as a blatant attempt at campaigning for the newly-minted commissioner's position. It rubbed many the wrong way, but that was only one strike against Stein. Although he valiantly attempted to rebut the twitting, Stein was regarded as too old to assume the new job and not savvy enough in the area of marketing that had become an obsession with the progressive NHL element anxious to exploit areas of development.

As chairman of the league's board of governors, McNall was in an excellent position to influence key hirings. In the end, his nod toward Bettman was critical to the selection of the NHL commissioner.

By the time the 1993 NHL All-Star game was to be played at The Forum in Montreal, McNall had become hockey's top banana. His acquisition of Gretzky had turned into a gem; his Kings had overtaken the Lakers as the darlings of Los Angeles. He had emerged as the most beloved and accessible hockey leader since Red Dutton was interim NHL president during World War II.

I had an appointment to chat with McNall during his All-Star visit. It was both a heady and yet a heavy time for the man. His man Bettman was now in place, successfully wooing the media in Montreal while hockey in general seemed on an upswing ready to challenge the NBA for a larger chunk of the sports-marketing dollar.

But McNall – along with his fellow owners – also had concerns. During the latter part of the Ziegler administration, the league had been stung with a series of embarrassments. Former NHL heroes, such as Gordie Howe and Bobby Orr, had filed a lawsuit against the league over the payment of pension funds. In addition, Russ Conway's hypercritical newspaper series running in the *Lawrence Eagle-Tribune* alleged hanky-panky involving NHL Players' Association executive director Alan Eagleson.

Conway was a close friend of Orr (a blood enemy of Eagleson). Although it was never confirmed, Orr was believed by the pro-Eagleson bloc to be the direct pipeline of information to Conway. There were reports that Conway was preparing yet another series with still more substantive material damaging to the league. McNall was aware of this when we met late that Saturday morning.

Montreal was immersed in a sub-zero freeze as McNall played the telephones in his executive duplex suite in the posh Four Seasons Hotel. He was busier than the proverbial one-armed paper hanger with an itch. A day earlier he had been caught in a swirl of rumours that Gretzky wanted out of the fold. In an unprecedented move, "Cousin Brucie," as he was affectionately known to some members of the fourth estate, called a press conference in the bowels of The Forum and denounced reports of a Gretzky-McNall feud.

Whatever McNall said or did became news. Once he appeared on ESPN's "Outside The Lines" series and the subject was "The Sports of Money." An audience member noted that the Kings had once again raised their prices. "I hate to say this," the fan mentioned to McNall, "but the average fan can no longer afford a hockey ticket."

Confronted with this truism, McNall fielded the shot on the first hop and replied, "Basically, you're right. It is a business and the people who can't afford it aren't going to go to games. Unfortunately, that's the nature of the business."

Now he was planning for a high-level conference with his fellow NHL owners. A half-year in the office as board chairman, the 42-year-old clearly was hockey's ultimate power broker. It was McNall who spearheaded the drive to unseat the Bill Wirtz-led Old Guard so that the NHL could approach the 21st Century without being braked by a medieval mentality.

As I sat on the couch awaiting the chairman, I couldn't help but notice his sense of urgency. There were two phones in the suite, one on the lower level and the other above. McNall moved smartly between them and finally discovered enough quietude to pluck himself down next to me for a one-on-one. Our dialogue, which is significant in view of episodes that followed, went as follows:

STAN FISCHLER: The NHL's sudden decision to expand by two teams – Anaheim and South Florida – appears to be precipitous and unplanned.

BRUCE McNALL: Actually, it has come along very well and I'm thrilled about the two franchises. The best thing about them is the quality of the ownership. When the NHL can have a company like Disney involved in a franchise, that's really something. We're talking about one of the top dozen firms in the world. And they're not in basketball, and they're not in baseball, but they chose hockey! That's angreat, incredible statement to hockey in general and to the work that's been done in the past 75 years to make the NHL what it is today. That's why I'm proud of it. Disney is a tremendous marketing company and brings both a breath of fresh air and an air of credibility in certain areas where the NHL lacked it somewhat.

SF: But you haven't mentioned the South Florida franchise.

BM: The same thing is true of Blockbuster Video. Although they're a newer company than Disney, they are probably the most aggressive new company in the world. Again, for them to come in and put the *Good Housekeeping* stamp on the league is, once again, beyond belief. I'm thrilled about them as well.

SF: There has been talk that yet another huge corporation, Sony, was considering an NHL involvement.

BM: What you're hearing and seeing are the various entertainment companies taking a serious look at sports. I know all the people at Sony and Warner Brothers are watching what Paramount did, taking the lead in this entertainment group getting into sports. Paramount did it with the Rangers and Knickerbockers. What's happened is that they are able to merge the software that the sport creates with the hardware that the companies need. It's pretty evident that in the future more and more electronic giants like this are going to get involved with professional sports. It just makes too much sense not to.

SF: I have heard from a variety of people, that the way for the NHL to go is complete free agency. And that in the end this would be less harmful to the owners than the current system.

BM: Most important to me is to have a partnership between players and owners that makes sense in the long run. That would be instead of having a situation where all of a sudden the NHL makes a lot of money and the players get hurt; then the next minute the players are making a fortune and the owners are getting hurt. There has to be some system – if that includes free agency, if that includes a salary cap. Whatever that includes is fine with me as long as both sides understand it's a partnership that can work together moving forward.

Take the marketing areas as an example. I mean, if you can have the NHLPA along with the NHL together attack some of these issues, you're not talking about one and one equalling two. It's one and one equalling three. And it's important that we try to put together and get a true partnership scheme, whether it be free agency or some other system. Gary Bettman is pretty smart about these things. I don't have a formula of my own, but I've been talking to Gary about it. He will handle it.

SF: Why did you pick him?

BM: He's the smartest man that I've ever met; the most qualified man for this particular job. He's young, aggressive and as bright as they come; a very, very quick study; a very, very smart man. Most of all, he is a tireless worker, which is very important at this stage in our lives. He has a lot to do and he doesn't mind the hard work. He's smart and quick.

SF: Perhaps, but the skeptics say that despite all these gifts, he'll have trouble with the old guard – Bill Wirtz and his followers.

BM: All of the owners have to say, "Look, Gary, you're the CEO now. You're the guy who we hired. Lead us!" For those who feel they still want to run the league in some form and and not allow him to do his job, yes, there could be some problems. Most everybody in the league wants to have a good, strong CEO. I don't think the (old guard interference) is going to be a problem.

SF: What are your feelings about Bob Goodenow since you've had a year to study him?

BM: Bob is a very bright guy, a very qualified man and a very decent man. We've done business together with the out-of-venue games. He's been very honest and forthright. With the new breath of fresh air with Gary, we'll be able to work together and get something done. Bob has a lot of support from his players. He's a man who has command of that.

SF: Fine, but what about the concerns among some ownership types that Goodenow will bleed the league white, or, to put it another way, that the smaller markets will be badly hurt by Goodenow's potential aggression?

BM: That's Gary's most important challenge. We have to let smaller markets – the John McMullens in New Jersey; the Richard Gordons in Hartford – succeed. Even L.A. in its way is a small market, for hockey. But I think there's something we can work out that will be good for everyone concerned. I don't know what it will be or how it will play out, but Bettman and Goodenow are anxious to do something and they'll come up with something good.

SF: What about Bill Wirtz?

BM: Bill and I got along very well for a very long time. I don't think he's real pleased with some of the events that happened recently and I'm sorry about that to be honest with you. Bill probably was my biggest supporter. I've tried to do what I think he would have wanted to happen. And I'll tell you something, I honestly respect the heck out of the man, more so since I got the position than I ever did. I feel a little bad at times. I don't want to lose his support or his friendship.

SF: How will having a second team in California affect you?

BM: I hope it's a positive effect. The hockey awareness issue in California is important. This year the fans have been unbelievable – us selling out even after some terrible play on our part. Hockey has really sold in Los Angeles right now, but we have to make sure that the news and the print, TV and the fans are talking about hockey all the time. With Disney as a new owner it will be exciting. I hope we can keep up with them, both on and off the ice and hope we don't lose too many fans.

SF: Shouldn't you rethink your policy of being good friends with the players?

BM: No, it doesn't bother me too much. It's become enough of a business that it's changed in the last five years. Ever since the Gretzky trade, there's the feeling that anybody can be traded. Besides, I don't think a rapport with the players is a bad thing to have. It makes negotiations easier. It makes understanding between player and management easier. In some ways I'm not overly tight with them. We go talk business and that type of thing, but we have a decent relationship. It's not like we hang out all the time. That's not the case.

SF: Could the 1992 strike have been avoided?

BM: I thought so and I was wrong. I think Bob Goodenow had to make a statement, but I thought it was a real unfortunate thing. It really hurt some people and particularly some owners – not so much myself – but others like Mike Ilitch. I was not on the (negotiating) committee, but other people like Ron Corey put a lot of time and a huge amount of energy in their incredibly busy schedules. These are important people. Eddie Snider is another example of someone who has been good to his players, has been known to bend over backwards for them. The strike hurt them and I feel particularly bad for them.

SF: How can hockey be sold better?

BM: Exposure is an important element in selling anything in the world. We need more exposure. That's why expansion is so important because it leads to more exposure on television. More exposure will lead to more marketing by having companies like Disney and Blockbuster and our own Enterprises company to bolster our marketing aspect. The other thing is stars. The NBA has been very successful marketing its stars. It's a lot more difficult with hockey. For years Wayne was the guy and he made all the money, remarkably, for himself. We have to find a way. We have to look over the back of our stars and help ourselves out.

SF: We know the positive side of Gretzky coming to L.A. But the flip side is that you mortgaged your future in getting him.

BM: I don't think so. There is no future except today. There would be no future of hockey in Los Angeles. We would have been finished. Pack the bus! Support of hockey then, to the tune of $4 million to $5 million in losses a year? If something hadn't happened then – or you had not had a hockey nut like me buy the team – this sport wouldn't have survived in L.A. From my standpoint there is no future like today. As far as the players are concerned, what we're going to be seeing with additional players from the eastern bloc countries is that the talent pool is expanding. It will allow our team as well as others to remain strong.

SF: Your relationship with Wayne Gretzky, as a player and a business partner, has been questioned to the point of doubt that it is as strong as it once was.

BM: It's fine. We have a great relationship in many respects. We have horses together, the Argonauts together and so forth. He's a bright businessman; very smart and a great asset because he is both knowledgeable, understanding and also helpful with the business. He helps market the Argos and he does a lot of commercials.

SF: What's the most difficult aspect of your relationship with Wayne?

BM: The tough part is that he feels personally more responsible to me, toward me, than he should. He worries about things. In other words, if he's not playing well, or the team is not playing well, he'll take it all on himself.

The problem with Wayne this winter was that the team wasn't playing well and he blamed himself. He personalized it toward myself. He feels he's letting me down all the time.

SF: The media jumped all over the rumour at the All-Star Game that Wayne wanted to play for the Maple Leafs.

BM: The crazy thing came right out of the blue. First of all, Wayne was going through a lot of pressure with the hockey club. He would never speak for himself and say, "Hey, I've been out with a back injury that I shouldn't even be playing with." And he shouldn't have been playing. But Wayne says, "I know, I love this game." It's going to take him some heat, he had no condition beforehand, he was in a hospital bed, he comes out here, he has no legs, no conditioning, no timing, and he gets out on the ice and wonders, he wonders why he is not playing well at all times. What does he think? That his goal for himself is so high that he, himself, gets frustrated at times. That's tough on him.

SF: Los Angelenos view the Kings as a passing fad. Is that correct?

BM: I don't think so. I was worried about that personally, to be honest with you. When I got Gretzky, I thought, "Are people going to show up with Wayne playing and then the magic is gone, so to speak, he goes away, or the team is not performing well." What happened shockingly, was when Wayne was injured, nobody knew if he would come back or not and they still kept coming. We played poorly, we lost eight or nine home games in a row and they still kept coming. They are sold on hockey, I believe. The hockey rinks are filled with junior league kids, rollerblade teams are out there going crazy. I think we sold the sport.

And this is where the interview concluded.

It soon was apparent to me that McNall was too busy to sit still any longer, but as always, he was gracious about bidding au revoir. As I left the suite and re-entered the frigid Montreal air, I couldn't help but marvel to myself how rapid the McNall conquest of big-league hockey had been and wonder where it would go from here.

The next time I saw McNall it was at the league's annual Lester Patrick award luncheon in New York. This year the 1993 Patrick – for distinguished service to hockey in the United States – was going to Gil Stein, of all people. Coincidentally, I had just been notified by Gary Bettman of my nomination to the Hockey Hall of Fame Player Selection Committee. Bettman had phoned me with the news and, in fact, it was as high an honour as I had ever received in my professional years. Nevertheless, I was still somewhat mystified about the machination that led to my appointment.

Having been a maverick for my entire writing and television career, I certainly numbered few friends among The Establishment. I learned this years earlier when my nomination for the Lester Patrick award – annually submitted by my (late) good friend Munson Cambell – was regularly rejected.

While exchanging handshakes with the hockey people, I noticed that McNall had entered the room. I casually made my way to his corner and received the usual enthusiastic greeting. "And by the way," added McNall with noticeable emphasis, "Congratulations. I see you're on the Hall of Fame Selection Committee."

Hmmmm, I wondered, how did he know?

No more than a second was required for the answer. It was a cross between a knowing wink and a smile. Not a word was spoken, but I gathered that McNall had played a part in my nomination and I just left it at that.

The luncheon itself evolved into a retrospective sham. Stein was toasted hither and yon for his service and loyalty to the game. What wasn't mentioned was that the man who aspired to the commissionership had been nominated under questionable circumstances. In time the Stein episode would be one of the first embarrassments confronting Bettman. Eventually, Stein would exit from the league – without being admitted to the Hall.

While the Stein affair brushed McNall's administration, it was so effectively and quickly disposed of by Bettman's blue-ribbon investigation that McNall escaped virtually unscathed. In fact, he appeared to be as tall as ever in the saddle after the Kings reached the 1993 Stanley Cup finals; the first time a Los Angeles club had advanced so far in the playoffs. McNall's team was "in" in Tinseltown.

The list of celebrities glittering at ice level had now included former president Ronald Reagan, Michelle Pfeiffer and Goldie Hawn. "Bruce is one of the kindest people I know," said Hawn. "He is loyal and compassionate and as far as I'm concerned, those are the best things you can say about a person."

Others were less enthused about McNall. One, who had had business dealings with McNall, complained to me about what he perceived as McNall's potential financial problems. The businessman suggested that we hadn't heard the end of McNall's fiscal woes.

By the middle of the 1993-94 season, whatever fiscal difficulties McNall may have been encountering were temporarily overshadowed by a literary gaffe that could conservatively be termed as monstrous in terms of its damaging effect on McNall's reputation both in hockey and the business world.

The vehicle was *Vanity Fair*, an upscale American monthly magazine featuring in-depth profiles of the rich and famous. What separates the *Vanity Fair* piece from the traditional McNall article was its astonishing candor and self-inflicting damage.

Instead of accenting McNall's operation of the Kings and his ascent to the NHL hierarchy, author Bryan Burrough zeroed in on the growth of McNall's coin empire. What unfolded on the pages of *Vanity Fair* was a tale of intrigue and hanky-panky coupled with an admission by the man that his empire was about to collapse. (Nothing more prophetic could ever have been written or spoken.) No less arresting was the fact that virtually every damaging quote was spoken by McNall himself.

The piece read as if it had been prepared by McNall's worst enemy; someone determined to sabotage the owner's prestige and reputation. Burrough asserted that during a series of interviews, McNall agreed to speak candidly about art smuggling. To those who know McNall and his savoir-faire, it remains baffling why he would even think about revealing secrets of the artifact business, let alone discuss smuggling. But there it was in black and white; pages of remarkably revealing quotes that proved an instant embarrassment to the Kings and the NHL high command.

A couple of the more startling admissions that appeared in *Vanity Fair* were these:

* HIS COIN BUSINESS: "I'm f—. I will lose millions in this thing. I'm taking a big hit. This business is finished. There may come the point where I go under."
* AN 18-YEAR-OLD EXPERIENCING THE SECRET THRILL OF SMUGGLING: "I committed a crime. But I wasn't thinking then. I was a kid. I was scared at the time. I just hid the stuff and left. I knew it was wrong. But it was the norm in the industry."

Seasoned media types couldn't believe their eyes, reading and rereading McNall's words. "In the article," commented Alan Maki of the *Calgary Herald*, "McNall admitted many of his prized coins had been illegally smuggled out of foreign countries. He painted himself as a sort of Indiana Jones in search of the lost covenant. Others called him a grave robber; a dealer in stolen goods. He denied nothing and it portrayed him in an unflattering light."

Before the *Vanity Fair* article hit the stands, McNall had agreed to sell a percentage of the Kings to IDB Communications in exchange for a stake in a new 20,000-seat home for the hockey club. On May 16, 1994, IDB founder, Jeffrey Sudikoff, and former Madison Square Garden Network president Joseph Cohen, purchased 72 percent of the Kings from McNall. It was reported that the deal was made so that McNall could raise $60 million to help pay a $120 million debt with the Bank of America.

Meanwhile, whispers began spreading about McNall's deteriorating financial situation, and the tone was emphatically negative. One entrepreneur had mentioned to me more than once that he was owed a considerable sum by McNall but had not received a penny. Because of his immense wealth, the entrepreneur was able to retain his patience and keep his public silence.

The where-there's-smoke-there's-fire bromide proved valid in this case. On April 29, 1994, McNall resigned as chairman of the board of governors after it was revealed that a federal grand jury was investigating his banking practices. Finally, a blaze of headlines swept across newspapers late in the summer. On August 16, 1994, the *Los Angeles Times* reported that McNall was actively negotiating a plea agreement to resolve a criminal investigation into his banking practices.

On August 23, 1994, Joanna Orehek, a vice-president and controller of McNall Sports and Entertainment Inc., pleaded guilty to two criminal counts involving a scheme to defraud four lenders of $128 million in loans. Orehek admitted to submitting false tax returns and financial statements to the banks to borrow money, using phony coin inventories and sports memorabilia as collateral for the loans, working through a series of sham companies and shifting coin inventories among McNall companies to prevent lenders from discovering that promised collateral did not exist.

On August 25, 1994, both the *New York Times* and *Wall Street Journal* zeroed in on McNall and no longer was there any question; McNall was in big trouble. The United States Attorney's office in Los Angeles was investigating him for purportedly falsifying loan documents to borrow more than $200 million from banks, including the Bank of America. It was suggested that the charges could include bank fraud, mail fraud and conspiracy and could carry a maximum sentence of at least 20 years in prison.

Almost overnight, the NHL's executive jet was nosediving straight to the ground leaving the league in a most embarassing position. After all, what does one do when the board chairman is under investigation?

The Kings responded with Sudikoff and Cohen declaring their support with Cohen adding, "We want to make it clear to everyone that not only has Bruce been a very, very important figure to the Kings and to this game, but that he still is."

McNall put on a happy face, thanking his partners and adding, "I'm okay. You know me. I don't know what will happen, but there's nothing to do but take things as they come."

Unfortunately, they came. On September 20, 1994, Robert J. Houston, an accountant who worked for McNall, was charged with single counts of conspiracy, bank fraud and wire fraud. He followed Orehek as the second McNall associate to be charged in the U.S. government's probe of bank loans made by McNall.

Still, McNall continued to maintain his titles of president and governor of the Kings, earning $650,000 a year from Sudikoff and Cohen although he was doing little good for the club's image. Then, on November 14, 1994, felony charges that could bring up to 45 years in prison were filed against McNall. Assistant U.S. attorney Peter Spivack said it capped a probe of alleged fraud involving nearly $236 million in loans from six banks.

Not surprisingly, the media jumped all over the story. "There was always suspicion about the flamboyant nature of McNall," said Steve Simmons of the Toronto *Sun*, "but until recently, there were no charges."

By late autumn, McNall's empire was crumpling so rapidly even reporters had trouble keeping up with the breaking stories. Well before Christmas 1994, it had become apparent that he had become a liability to the NHL, if not the Kings. On December 14, 1994, he pleaded guilty to defrauding several banks of more than $236 million and to four criminal counts. McNall's plea agreement was predicated on his admission that he oversaw a decade-long scheme to defraud six lending institutions.

McNall faced maximum penalties of 45 years in prison, at least $1.75 million in fines, five years supervision by the court and restitution up to the full amount of the losses caused by his conduct.

"Bruce pleaded guilty because he is guilty," McNall's attorney, Tom Pollack said. "He's accepting full responsibility for everything that took place. There's a lot more to this story than what came out in the charges and we'll be making that clear to the courts in the coming months."

McNall had pleaded guilty to one count of conspiracy, two counts of bank fraud and one count of wire fraud. By this time six of his former associates had entered guilty pleas in the matter.

The fallen leader rested his hands on the podium, next to his attorney, and appeared unnerved as he entered guilty pleas to each of the charges levelled against him. Once McNall had entered his pleas, the assistant U.S. attorney, Peter Spivack required 30 minutes to recount McNall's illegalities over the decade.

"That was a lot that Mr. Spivack had to say," said Judge Richard Paez. "Is everything that Mr. Spivack said about you true and correct?"

"Yes it is," McNall replied.

To that point, the credit McNall had established with the press – me included – had been so substantial over the years that he escaped media criticism virtually unscathed.

My personal feelings were confused. I liked McNall. He had never let me down; be it for an interview or advice. Coming to terms with my feelings about McNall was difficult. He still was a friend but he also was a legitimate journalistic subject. Handling the matter was cerebrally wrenching so I temporarily "solved" the problem by avoidance. For weeks I simply followed the story without comment.

Others reacted differently and I could hardly blame them. One was Helene Elliott, hockey columnist for the *Los Angeles Times* and a woman who once had worked for me during her college years. Elliott had emerged as a significant NHL journalist, first with *Newsday* on Long Island and more recently with the *Times* in California. She takes the game seriously and her writing underlines that view.

On the day following McNall's guilty plea, Elliott eviscerated McNall in no uncertain terms. "We got taken in," she wrote for openers. "Played for suckers. Hoodwinked. All of us. NHL executives, fans and reporters, too. Bruce McNall fooled us, but we were willing accomplices...We thought he was the best thing to happen to hockey since frozen pucks."

She berated Cohen for suggesting that the media overemphasized the negatives in L'Affaire McNall. Elliott also chided McNall for having "yet to say the word sorry." For those, like myself, who felt pity for McNall, Elliott said, forget it!

"What the court documents don't say," Elliott concluded, "is that Bruce McNall is also guilty of betraying our trust. And there's no penance grave enough to atone for that."

A month later, while covering the NHL labour negotiations in Manhattan, I encountered Elliott and the subject of McNall emerged in the conversation. She mentioned that shortly after her column had appeared she received a heated call from McNall's lawyer criticizing her piece. Elliott told me she was unmoved by the conversation.

Other newspeople shared her opinion. Dean Chadwin, a Los Angeles freelancer who authored *Rocking the Pond – The First Season of the Mighty Ducks of Anaheim*, mentioned to me that McNall was still showing up at The Forum rooting for his Kings.

"The fans can't stand Bruce," Chadwin said. "They don't want to see him up at the glass, having a party at every game."

Enough, I decided, it was time that I offered a commentary of my own. I opened the January 30th issue of *The Fischler Report* with a headline, "TINSELTOWN TROUBLES," and followed it with the observation, "When Bruce McNall extracted a $25 million territorial indemnity fee from the NHL for permitting Disney's Mighty Ducks to invade his California turf, it was the last, best move made by Cousin Brucie."

I elaborated on the anti-McNall critiques and analyzed the state of the Kings. My conclusion: "The Mighty Ducks will rule Tinseltown on the ice and in the hearts of L.A. fans. The Kings will revert to the Jerry Buss syndrome."

A couple of days later the phone rang. Howard Baldwin was at the other end of the line. Part-owner of the Pittsburgh Penguins, Baldwin has been one of my closest pals among the NHL board members ever since he organized the New England Whalers of the World Hockey Association in 1972 and I began broadcasting their games a year later.

"Bruce was very upset over what you wrote," Baldwin said. "He thought you came down pretty hard on him."

I explained that I had been wrestling with coverage of McNall's situation for a long time and finally decided that something had to be written. Baldwin understood but added that something positive should be noted for all the good McNall had done for the game.

"Bruce is walking the coals," Baldwin added, "but let's not forget that he put Southern California on the hockey map and he cultivated Michael (Walt Disney Company) Eisner which led to a major coup when the Mighty Ducks joined the league.

"The indemnity Bruce received was chicken feed compared with the benefit to the NHL having Disney aboard. He gave the club pizzazz and turned a closet market into a great one. His mistakes were unrelated to hockey and he's paying the price, but that doesn't mean we should overlook all the positive Bruce has done."

I agreed and found it heartening that McNall's friends had not all abandoned him. A week later, I wrote six paragraphs in the newsletter pointing out that McNall deserved to be commended for all the good he had done for the NHL as well as individuals like myself.

Shortly thereafter, I phoned Bruce. We had a long, free-flowing conversation during which I explained my position vis-à-vis the McNall coverage. He seemed understanding and at no time sounded as if he was in a self-pitying mode – he certainly could have been under the circumstances – or even bitter.

"Would you be willing to do an interview for my *Hockey News* column?" I asked.

"I'd love to," he shot back as if we had been talking three years earlier without him being choked with legal entanglements. "Call me later in the week and we'll set it up."

A few days later, I phoned his office. McNall said he still was willing to do the interview but added that the legal situation was sticky enough that he had to be more careful than he normally would. "Do me a favour," he went on, "and send your list of questions to my lawyer. After he looks at them, I'm sure I'll be able to talk with you." As requested, the questions were prepared and dispatched.

I waited a week, two weeks, three weeks for a reply, but none was forthcoming. After a month had elapsed, I assumed that McNall was not interested in pursuing the interview and I forgot about it. But a few weeks later, I received a call from Joel Bergman who informed me that attorney Pollack claimed he had never received the questions.

Hmmm. That didn't seem right, but what the heck. I phoned McNall. "Do you still want to do this thing?" I asked.

"Absolutely," he replied.

We double-checked his lawyer's fax number and, once again, the questions went to Pollack; only this time I made sure that his secretary had received them. She had and, once again, I waited.

My assumption was that McNall was being extremely careful about his statements and interviews, which explains why I was stunned to learn that he would be appearing on a Canadian-produced television special devoted to his problems. Veteran broadcaster Dave Hodge emceed the two-part program called, "The Rise and Fall of Bruce McNall."

The show was noteworthy in several respects, not the least of which was McNall extemporaneously appearing before the camera and microphone. No less fascinating was the supporting cast including Gretzky and O.J. Simpson counsel – and rabid hockey fan – Robert Shapiro.

"I worry for him," said Gretzky, "in the sense that what the future holds as far as what his punishment is going to be."

Shapiro: "I am convinced this is his first and only transgression of the law. He has paid a tremendous debt, suffered great public humiliation. You got to go in there and do it and you'll come out a better person. And he will."

No less arresting was the appearance of Burrough, co-author of the best-seller *Barbarians At The Gate* and author of the *Vanity Fair* piece. Asked about McNall's admissions to him, Burrough replied, "It just kind of came gushing out of him. And as it came gushing out of him, it became like: can you top this. I'd say, 'Oh, those are smugglers and you didn't really deal with smugglers, did you? That must have been exciting.' He'd say, 'Oh, yeah! It was really exciting. Some of them got killed.' Ya know, it was like that."

Apparently, McNall reacted to the TSN interviewing crew the way he did with Burrough. The kick of being on camera was too much to resist and McNall began talking: "One day, sooner or later, I'll be able to say something. Yeah, I'm gonna write a book some time; they're out there negotiating a deal right now. It's gonna take a while. As time goes on a lot of the fact will come out. It'll be a little different from what they say now. But what can you do; you gotta stand up to the plate. In a lot of ways you feel like you let people down. You feel like, you had, you know, like you've tried to accomplish good things. And you try to do the best you can and sometimes you try to do that and you make some mistakes along the way. But basically I hang in there; everything in life is an adventure. You can't sit there and what if and all that kind of stuff. You just gotta go on with things, in my view of life."

And as he went on with things, his Kings franchise continued its nosedive. In late April 1995, coach Barry Melrose and assistant coach Cap Raeder were fired and replaced on an interim basis by Rogie Vachon, who had supplied McNall's bail money, and Dave Taylor, one of McNall's favourite Kings. Some players traced the club's disarray to the day McNall was indicted.

While awaiting the call from McNall and his attorney so we could proceed with the interview, I called someone who was owed money by the entrepreneur. He was unsparingly callous.

"Bruce was broke when he bought the Kings," the insider said. "He had the coins but not the money. Everything he did was for a public persona. Behind his ebullience is a conniving crook; but I'm not sure that he thinks he is." Through the whole ugly mess, I somehow found myself sympathizing with the indicted. Was I being naive? Perhaps. But when it comes to Bruce McNall, gut feelings run strong and, despite contrary evidence, I still liked the guy. However, when I mentioned this to a hockey acquaintance, he shot back, "Of course, he doesn't owe you any dough!"

8

••

PRELUDE TO CIVIL WAR:
THE LOCKOUT LOOMS

The scene was surrealistic, to say the least – a *Waiting For Godot* on ice.

It was the evening of October 1, 1994, supposedly the opening night of the National Hockey League season. All the 19,040 seats at Byrne Meadowlands Arena had been sold for a match between the defending Stanley Cup champion New York Rangers and the hometown New Jersey Devils.

Instead, the seats were empty and rather than a dozen players preparing for the opening face-off, five broadcasters sat on raised chairs in a semicircle at centre ice. I was one of them, along with my SportsChannel colleagues Jiggs McDonald and Ed Westfall who handled the Islanders games, as well as Mike Emrick and Peter McNab, their counterparts in New Jersey.

We were there because there was no hockey game to be played. The unthinkable had been well thought out and was happening. Major league hockey players who were making more money than they ever had in their lives – and considerably more than the average Canadian or American workingman – would not agree to an owners' offer that would hike their incomes even more.

As a result, the owners refused to launch the season. Instead, they announced a postponement of the campaign; otherwise known as a lockout. The five of us were there to examine the causes and effects of the stoppage in play and also to venture how long it would last.

Assuming that both sides would quickly come to their respective senses, some of my colleagues ventured that the lockout would be over in a week; 10 days at the most.

I wanted to agree with them but a vignette kept reappearing in my brain. It was a scene from the 1992 NHL players' strike. More specifically, a personal interpretation of union boss Bob Goodenow.

Having been a reporter for 40 years, I had developed what I call "a newsman's scent." It's based on nothing more than a feel about personalities combined with what I see in front of me. There was something about Goodenow in 1992 that remained with me in the years thereafter and it mostly had to do with his style and substance.

He had a toughness that came with playing hockey and then being involved on both sides of the fence in labour law. That would suit his union members just fine.

I believed Goodenow would tough it out. It was just a "feel," so to speak, but that was enough to prompt my prediction from center ice at Byrne Arena during a broadcast. "I'd like to think otherwise but I can see this going on into the new year," I said. "And ultimately it will all be determined by a four-legged animal with three letters in his name – FOX."

I was alluding to the FOX television network which had concluded a new deal to broadcast NHL games during the 1994-95 season and thereafter. FOX was looked upon as a major stepping stone for the NHL in its quest for TV respectability in the United States.

"FOX doesn't start broadcasting until the All-Star game months from now," I added, "so it wouldn't surprise me if nothing happened until after Christmas."

As the words blurted out, they sounded totally incongruous. How could the months of October, November and December evaporate without any major league hockey? Impossible. It had never happened before. How could it happen now?

It was happening for a lot of reasons but mostly because the peace pact of 1992 had failed miserably. It was then that owners and players had last signed their Collective Bargaining Agreement and it was then that both sides agreed to form a joint study committee to restructure the business and avoid the finacial plight that owners insisted was confronting them.

Right there in the CBA was a provision which dealt specifically with restructuring the relationship between the league and the union. But the ousting of John Ziegler and Gil Stein's subsequent preoccupation with landing the commissionership distracted NHL leaders from organizing the pivotal joint study committee which would have addressed the critical issues of the salary cup and revenue sharing.

When Gary Bettman took command, he was distracted from the joint study committee by what were perceived as more immediate problems. "Bettman's priorities were to reshape an organization which many felt was being run more like a house league than a professional sports league," commented the *Canadian Press.*

Not that Bettman wasn't trying to hammer out an agreement with Goodenow. But why would the NHLPA leader rush to a new deal? Under the old agreement his charges were luxuriating in fat and fatter contracts as never before. The longer he delayed, the better off the stickhandlers were. Not surprisingly,

Bettman found it difficult to bring Goodenow to the bargaining table during the early months of 1994.

By early summer Bettman realized that the kid-glove treatment previously applied by Ziegler wouldn't work with Goodenow so he switched to the mailed fist. In an August 1st letter to players, the league threatened to impose training camp restrictions – including the loss of $2,700 camp allowances for veterans and $55 per diem payments.

Shortly after seeing the letter Ray Bourque's agent Steve Freyer phoned me. "This looks like war," said Freyer alluding to the fact that the restrictions started with the players paying their own way to training camp and got worse after that.

Across the continent, NHLPA members bristled over Bettman's decrees. They ranged from the relatively minor – deducting training camp meal money – to the more significant such as cutting game rosters, and to the just plain irksome, like rescinding the limit practices can last.

There was a method to what unionists described as Bettman's mean-spirited moves. The commissioner wanted to galvanize the union into action. "The NHLPA refused to meet with us for five months," said Bettman, "using the fictional salary cap demand as an excuse."

Bettman's iron-fisted approach worked to the extent that he pushed Goodenow back to the bargaining table and training camps opened as scheduled at the start of September 1994. The union received a proposal from the league which included a relationship between salaries and revenues. In addition, rumours circulated that there would be a request for a rookie salary cap. Goodenow and company had insisted that they would never accept a salary cap for rookies or others.

The fact that training camps were opened and exhibition games were played was as deceptive as the calm surrounding the Normandy beachhead in the hours before D-Day, 1944. Insiders understood that talks were going nowhere, fast, and nobody knew it better than Bettman.

"I'm a deal-maker," the commissioner asserted two days before the scheduled opening night. "But when somebody doesn't want to make a deal, you've got to use all the resources that are available to you. My preference is to go quietly into a room and work things out. But that's not happening."

Then, a pause: "You're as tough as you have to be. And Bob Goodenow isn't a pussycat." That may have been the understatement of the half-century.

Not only wasn't he the purring kind, Goodenow had become a master exploiter of the circumstance. Aware that his predecessor, Alan Eagleson was under federal indictment in the United States for racketeering and was being sought by American authorities for extradition from Canada, Goodenow was able to position himself with players as the tough but squeaky-clean leader who would never allow his constituency to be intimidated by ownership.

The once mild-mannered unionists had become militant in the two years of Goodenow's stewardship and the executive director carefully surrounded himself with equally tough-minded negotiating committee members such as Marty McSorley of the Los Angeles Kings.

"The players don't look at Mr. Goodenow as being the same as Mr. Eagleson," said McSorley, an intense foe of Eagleson during the latter's reign. "They see Mr. Goodenow sitting on our side of the table this time."

It seemed not to matter to McSorley or other NHLPA members that in 1983, Goodenow was on the other – management's – side. "He stared down the teamsters in a 1983 dispute between the union and a firefighting equipment manufacturer," noted the *Los Angeles Times*. "Representing management, Goodenow kept the union out for 11 months before the teamsters gave in."

In 1992 retired teamsters' official Frank Caputo of Pittsburgh told a reporter, "There's no doubt he (Goodenow) was a union-buster. He's the most difficult man I ever dealt with."

Bettman would eventually share the same thoughts in different words. Club owners could fill in their new commissioner with horror stories from their 1992 experience. Both Blackhawks' owner Bill Wirtz – he called Goodenow unprofessional – and Flyers' owner Ed Snider were especially critical of the NHLPA executive, but Goodenow couldn't have cared less.

"The level of conflict (in a labour dispute) can get very high," said Goodenow as the September crisis crept closer to opening day. But from the viewpoint of strategy, the NHLPA was in a less desirable position than it had been two years earlier when it struck just prior to the playoffs. At that time ownership's very profitable playoffs had been at risk and the governors were sharply divided with a less-than-commanding Ziegler totally unable to unify them.

This time ownership was conspicuously together with Bettman providing a surprising amount of cement to avoid any cracking. Furthermore, the timing of the anticipated lockout meant that the players figured to suffer more than the governors. After all, the stickhandlers had not been paid since spring and they would miss an October paycheque if they were not playing.

"We're negotiating with a bit of a gun to our head," complained NHLPA president Mike Gartner of the Toronto Maple Leafs.

Perhaps, but then again, perhaps not. Gartner, for one, had become one of the wealthiest players in NHL history; and without ever having been on a Stanley Cup-winning team. Likewise, other players of even lesser abilities were demanding – and receiving – fabulous amounts of money for little value in return.

To underline its case, ownership did not have to look beyond the September 7, 1994, signing of Benoit Hogue by the New York Islanders. A productive performer in his first two seasons on Long Island, Hogue began slipping in 1993-94 and was a total bust in the four-game playoff sweep at the hands of the Rangers. Furthermore, Hogue consistently bedevilled the coaching staff with often indolent play that belied his natural ability. He was, as they say in the dressing rooms, "a floater" who came to play when the spirit moved him.

Yet Hogue, after missing the first three days of training camp after playing out his option the previous season, signed a new contract for an estimated $1.2 million and then proceeded to stink out the joint.

Think about it for a moment: $1.2 million for a performer whose dependability quotient out of a possible 10 was somewhere around four! "I've been here for three years," said Hogue, "and this is where I want to play." (But, before the season was over Hogue was traded to Toronto after whispers were heard that he couldn't wait to leave Long Island.) Not surprisingly, he was a bust as a Maple Leaf.

It was Hogue, like so many other players, who was figuratively holding a gun to his manager's head over a contract signing. And, as had been the case ever since Wayne Gretzky was wildly overpaid by Bruce McNall in 1988, it was the player who forced management to blink and come up with the big bucks.

Moreover, it was because of such contract inflation that Bettman was sought to impose a system that would firmly put the brakes on runaway salaries. "We need a salary cap," said New Jersey Devils' owner John McMullen, echoing the thoughts of many colleagues.

Which is precisely why Bettman had been hired. The NBA was raking in huge profits and doing so with a salary cap in place. Bettman was the NBA's cap architect. Goodenow knew it all too well and never stopped telling his constituency that the cap was analogous to a noose. And since the joint study committee never was formed, Goodenow figured there was no longer any need to include the salary cap in any discussions and that put Bettman right on the spot.

"Bettman is so determined to get a cap because it's going to mean his job," said Blackhawks' ace Jeremy Roenick. "It's almost like where he promised the owners he was going to get them a salary cap. Now he's under the gun and it seems as though he's pressing. He's very, very proud of quote end quote authoring the NBA cap – he takes credit for that, which is great for him; it gives him a good name. So now he comes to the NHL owners and says, 'Hey, I got a salary cap for the NBA owners, I can get one for you.' Now it seems if he doesn't get it, he's out the door. That's why he's pushing hard and very, very fast to get this done.

"Bettman also wants to be the guy who wants to turn this league around. And that is great; I hope he turns this around. But he's not going to do it with a salary cap."

While Roenick was uttering those words, teammate Gary Suter, who had played only 41 games in the previous season, came to terms with the Hawks on a four-year, $6.5-million contract. The fiscal oppression of the players was difficult to discern, yet extraordinarily well-paid stickhandlers such as McSorley were behaving as if they were being treated like peons. "If we're put to the wall," said McSorley, whose annual income surpassed $1 million, "you always know that the tiger is most dangerous when it is cornered."

A week before opening night, I refused to believe that cooler heads wouldn't prevail. Then, I spoke with Steve Freyer and the intensity in his voice changed my mind within a half-minute. "I would be close to wagering my first-born male child on there being a lockout on October 1st," Freyer asserted. "I hope I'm wrong, but this time, I'm almost sure I'm right."

Player after player seconded Freyer's motion although there were some surprising cracks in the NHLPA wall of unity. Kelly Buchberger of the Edmonton Oilers suggested that one way of resolving the argument was to put a cap on first-year players' salaries.

"When I broke into the league," said Buchberger, "I made $60,000, now they (rookies) are making millions. I mean, what do they want?"

Buchberger's sensible observation was exactly what Goodenow didn't want to hear, but the Oilers' tough winger made sense. "There are some guys coming in that are making millions of dollars a year and they haven't even proven themselves. You have to sympathize with the owners that it just might not be fair."

Significantly, Buchberger's orations were no longer heard for the duration. Goodenow was. "A rookie cap is not in the cards," he said putting a period at the end of the thought.

Always, Goodenow had ammunition from previous battles to recycle and use against Bettman. If it wasn't the time-tested Eagleson horror stories, there were fresh tales about the new commissioner. During the officials' strike, NHLPA observers had studied the National Hockey League's techniques for future use. Just days before the lockout, McSorley argued that "Bettman really put it to the refs."

A day or so later in Tampa Bay, the Lightning's player representative Danton Cole met privately with the club's general manager Phil Esposito. When Cole emerged from the conference and walked into the locker room, coach Terry Crisp eyed his forward carefully and said, "No marks on you. That's good!"

They both smiled.

It would be the last time any levity would be shared between management and labour for some time. On Saturday night, October 1st, 1994, I walked out of Byrne Arena with Ed Westfall, Mike Emrick, Jiggs McDonald and Peter McNab.

"Who would have dreamed it would have come to this?" I said to nobody in particular.

"None of us," said Emrick, speaking for the group.

We headed to our automobiles and as I crossed the parking lot, I felt an overwhelming surge of anxiety. The NHL's Civil War had begun and none of us had any idea when it would end, nor the extent of the destruction it would wreak on professional ice hockey.

9

•••

THE GUNS OF OCTOBER:
WAR BEGINS IN EARNEST

If ever there was a bittersweet athletic gathering the setting was Lee Mazzilli's Manhattan sports bar in the autumn of 1994. A group of broadcasters and writers had gathered for a luncheon press conference launching a new SportsChannel show called "Game Time."

Normally this would be a time for upbeat chatter about the NHL season, the Rangers' bid for a second Stanley Cup, the Islanders' new coach Lorne Henning and New Jersey's tremendous prospects. But the pleasurable talk was counterbalanced by angst over the impending NHL lockout and the fear that a 2 p.m. press conference called by the union in Toronto would merely reaffirm that the players were preparing a long battle with ownership.

As I chatted with colleagues Jiggs McDonald, Ed Westfall, Mike Emrick and Peter McNab, we wondered whether some miraculous move could be made that would calm the conflict. At precisely 2 p.m. the chatter ceased as all hands gathered in front of the television screen.

NHLPA executive director Bob Goodenow was doing what he does so well; wearing a solemn face. He declared that the union was willing to return to the ice and launch the season as scheduled. However, he added that it would do so under terms of the former contract which expired September 15, 1993, but was renewed for one season by mutual agreement.

Goodenow's air of piety seemed to impact on some of the listeners. "You'd have to say the union is doing everything it can," said Emrick. "Goodenow seems earnest and concerned. Everything would be back to where it was last year, only now the fan interest in hockey is higher."

The union boss went on to criticize his foe, suggesting that "the approach by the NHL has been confrontational."

To which one wag at the bar added, "Well, it takes one to know one!"

Goodenow went on to righteously proclaim that his proposal "would allow the game to go on" with a no-strike pledge through the playoffs in return for an end to Bettman's lockout which would start the next day.

"He put it back on the commissioner's plate," said McDonald. "How can the owners turn it down?"

Westfall added, "It would be embarrassing if Bettman doesn't accept it."

Everyone seemed caught up in the euphoria of hockey's new boom which was accelerated by the Rangers' 1994 Stanley Cup triumph. The fact that Major League Baseball was on strike led most onlookers to believe that hockey now had a window of opportunity that it couldn't ignore.

"Now," said Emrick, "it's a question of how much Bettman wants to stick to the principle of not starting the season without an agreement."

I was taken in by Goodenow's performance. His well-studied earnestness and the no-strike offer seemed like a deal that would be hard to refuse. As the group of broadcasters walked out to the sunlight of West 71st Street and Broadway, the rays from above seemed to signal a possible settlement.

Emrick mentioned that this simply was not the right time for a self-imposed NHL drought. "People who might have been won over to hockey for the first time or don't know much about hockey will be turned off," he warned. "The timing is worse than ever because the popularity of hockey is so much greater."

Westfall estimated that we'd have the NHL's answer by nightfall which, by sheer coincidence, was when we were scheduled to meet again at another sports gathering. During the intervening hours, I felt buoyant, actually believing that the Goodenow offer would be virtually impossible to refuse. Obviously, I wasn't thinking like a realist.

Frank Brown of the *New York Daily News* – and a onetime intern of mine – thought otherwise. We chatted later in the afternoon and he pointed out that Bettman had been hired by the owners to introduce a salary cap. A one-season delay under the status quo was not something the owners would approve. Still, I remained hopeful, as did many others, when we convened for the evening festivities.

Westfall excused himself to make a phone call. He didn't say who he was calling but the feeling among others was that it was either an NHL official or a club owner. When he returned a few minutes later, Westfall turned his thumbs down.

"They won't go for it," was all he would say.

After careful analysis, I found it difficult to see why ownership would accept a return to status quo. After all, they were attempting a major overhaul of a sick fiscal system. By granting the union a reprieve, they were merely delaying the inevitable.

"The league collectively is losing money," said Boston Bruins' owner Jeremy Jacobs.

Wealthier than ever, the unionists refused to listen to Bettman, who correctly asserted, "This is not about holding salaries down. This is about the mechanism to make this sport stronger so revenues and players' salaries can grow."

The guns blazed as never before; a salvo from one side, a counterattack from the other. Ownership emphasized what it charged was Goodenow's lack of good bargaining faith; that he would not negotiate from the time he received the league's proposals in January 1994 until late summer.

"He didn't come to the table until Mr. Bettman had implemented his 19 points," complained Winnipeg Jets' president Barry Shenkarow. "And Mr. Bettman had notified him of the rollbacks a month earlier and Mr. Goodenow still didn't respond."

This point was reiterated over and over again with validity by management types who long ago had become accustomed to Goodenow's negotiating style of frustration at every turn. "The enemy," said Boston Bruins' general manager Harry Sinden, "is the same as it is for the players; as it is for the owners; as it is for the fans; as it is for this great sport of hockey."

He was talking about Bob Goodenow.

The union boss had crafted a simple, workable strategy; turn the salary cap into the bête noire of the NHLPA. This was easily done. By avoiding meaningful negotiations with Bettman from January through August, Goodenow had considerable time to crank up an anti-cap propaganda program so that the mere mention of the term would cause a negative knee-jerk reaction among his constituency.

When asked why he permitted a five-month delay before reopening negotiations with the league, Goodenow replied that there was no five-month delay at all. "We received the league's system proposals on January 12 (1994). These proposals contained in black and white, salary cap proposals relative to an NBA format, an NFL format, or a salary-pyramid format. We told them, repeatedly after that time, that we would not negotiate a cap on salaries.

"I told Gary that as long as this is your initial point to begin with, that I didn't see how fruitful negotiations can be conducted. Clearly, we've always said, all along, we were not prepared to negotiate a cap."

Yet the union, under Goodenow, had made a moral commitment to work toward a partnership agreement with club owners that would have included a salary cap and revenue sharing. It was in black and white from the memorandum of understanding that settled the April 1992 players' strike.

Under the title "Restructuring," the provision read as follows:

"During the recently concluded Collective Bargaining negotiations, the clubs have stressed, because of their tenuous financial condition, that there is a vital need for a commitment from the NHLPA for cooperative restructuring of their relationship in the direction of partnership sharing. During these negotiations, the parties discussed restructuring. Based on NHL economic studies and projections, the League and its Member Clubs believe that a continuation of the current system would have a serious negative impact on the business of hockey and hence the parties. Accordingly, the NHL clubs have expressed an intent to develop and submit to the NHLPA as promptly as possible a proposal for restructuring with a Salary Cap and revenue sharing concept along the lines of the NBA system. The NHLPA commits that, as soon as reasonably practicable after the Joint Study Committee report issues, it will begin bargaining in good faith with the Clubs in an effort to reach agreement regarding restructuring by September 15, 1993."

Goodenow's sudden claim that discussion of a salary cap was now a taboo upset NHL officials who regarded his position as different from the earlier stance.

Nor was this the only example of Goodenow being challenged on his word. Edmonton Oilers' general manager Glen Sather charged that "Goodenow has told me time and time again, if teams in Canada can't survive, they should move. That has bothered me from the first time he said it. I'm sure he regrets saying it, but I've never forgotten it."

Goodenow: "I did not make that statement."

Sather: "Goodenow also told me that he was the guy who negotiated Brett Hull's first contract in St. Louis and he (boasted) that all he did was keep saying no, and he kept getting better and better offers. Those two situations seem to say a lot about what's going on in hockey now – i.e. players laughing at the owners' stupidity, and the owners continuing to be stupid."

As usual, Sather had an excellent grasp of the core issue. So did Sinden. Goodenow, of course, disagreed. "I think Harry's comments are very slanted," the union head concluded, "and possibly misguided."

Considering such rhetoric, it was difficult to imagine that the sides would come to an agreement in time to start the season on October 15, 1994, as suggested by Bettman. If Goodenow was correct in any of his promises it was that the league and the union were in for "a long, nasty and dirty fight."

The dirt, however, was hurled with unprecedented intensity by the unionists at their commissioner.

10

• •

THE DIRT FLIES AND
THE IMPASSE HARDENS

Respect for the National Hockey League's office of the president had traditionally been high among players. Through the administrations of Frank Calder, Red Dutton, Clarence Campbell and John Ziegler, criticism of the NHL leader was muted at worst and inaudible at best. Even when Campbell suspended Montreal hero Maurice (The Rocket) Richard for the final week of the 1954-55 season and the entire Stanley Cup playoffs for pushing linesman Cliff Thompson, Richard's verbal assaults were relatively subdued.

But as hockey players became richer, more independent and uncontrollable, their deportment vis-à-vis the chief executive began to change. By the autumn of 1994 it had become downright onerous – if not scandalous – and nobody in the union expressed himself more distastefully than Blackhawks' defenceman Chris Chelios.

In some of the most inflammatory language ever directed at a big-league hockey official, Chelios said:"If I was Gary Bettman, I'd be worried about my family, about my well-being right now. Some crazed fan or even a player, who knows, might take it into his own hands...

"The main thing is, he doesn't know anything about hockey. That's obvious. He doesn't recognize players like Jeremy Roenick and Brendan Shanahan at the meetings. Maybe it's the little man syndrome. He's the problem."

Chelios had been as respected for his defensive skills as he had been notorious for his short fuse on the ice. But this time the defenseman had trespassed far beyond the line of impropriety and the reaction throughout the continent was negative.

"OPEN MOUTH, INSERT PUCK" shouted a headline in *New York Newsday*. Nationally read columnist Mike Lupica observed that Chelios "sounded like the kind of punk who sometimes makes fans hate all athletes. He sounded like someone who had made a career out of stopping pucks with his forehead. He is another athlete who thinks the world will be turned upside down if he misses a paycheque.

"Chelios brought Bettman's wife and children into a dispute between hockey players and owners about money, and acted like just another hockey goon in the process, carelessly using words instead of his stick. It is where an apology from him does not do the job here."

The apology, however, appeared half-baked. It went through union boss Bob Goodenow who insisted it was the stress of a labour crisis that provoked it. Goodenow said that Chelios called the league office to say he was sorry. Conspicuous by its absence was a vehement denunciation of Chelios by Goodenow. His response was meaningfully tepid and, interestingly, then followed by a continuation of anti-Bettman actions by other players.

Montreal Canadiens' defenceman Mathieu Schneider taped a large piece of white adhesive to his helmet and scrawled the message "BETTMAN SUCKS" so clearly that it became a photo opportunity that could not be refused. The Schneider helmet appeared in newspapers throughout Canada and the United States.

Instead of quiet in the wake of L'Affaire Chelios, players in almost every NHL city seemed choreographed to utter something disparaging about the commissioner. In Quebec City, Nordiques' captain Joe Sakic ridiculed Bettman. In New York, Rangers' goalie Glenn Healy suggested that the commissioner didn't care if the games were played.

In one of the more obtuse utterances of the year, Healy – like Chelios – felt obliged to haul Bettman's family into the dispute. "From what I understand," said the goaltender, "his wife doesn't enjoy the games anyway, at least not Ranger games. Maybe she should take the opportunity to go shopping."

Veteran defenceman Jay Wells, who should have known better, called Bettman a "punk" in an inflammatory statement that almost reached the top of the Chelios scale. "He (Bettman) will get his someday," said Wells. "Some punk (Bettman) comes in who never played the game a day in his life, probably never sweated a day in his life, trying to revamp the league."

Even students of rudimentary propaganda could detect a pattern among the NHLPA attacks: a. Bettman was foreign to the sport; b. He never played the game; c. There will be retribution somewhere down the line.

Similar anti-Bettman observations were made in the media on both sides of the border, but none were more consistently strident than columns written by Al Strachan, of the *Toronto Sun*. A persistent critic of John Ziegler, Strachan would become even more virulent in his attacks on Bettman.

Among the columnist's most frequent twists was the reference to Bettman as a "New York lawyer." To some sensitive souls at the NHL's Manhattan office, Strachan was conveniently omitting one word – Jewish – as in "New York Jewish lawyer," and it smelled bad.

Bettman is Jewish but never made an issue of it nor public reference to it, (not that there was any reason to do so) since taking office. However, Jewish journalists including myself, Steve Simmons of the *Toronto Sun*, Jeff Klein of New York's *Village Voice* and Jason Kay of *The Hockey News* seriously wondered whether the assaults on the commissioner did, in fact, have an anti-Semitic taint to them.

Moreover, there was a pointed suggestion that at least one NHLPA member betrayed the brand of redneck thinking that one associated with skinheads or neo-Nazi groups.

"The reference was made the other day in an off-the-record conversation with an NHL player," Simmons wrote in opening a column on October 19, 1994. "The reference can no longer be ignored. He called league commissioner Gary Bettman a 'Jew.'

"He did so with a sense of malice.

"The matter becomes more important now because of a nasty sequence of events that has surfaced in the backdrop to the labour wars of the National Hockey League.

"Almost predictably, and somewhat dangerously, anti-Semitism has become an issue in a controversy that has nothing to do with either race or religion."

Obviously, it meant something to some writers, one of whom described Bettman as a "nebbish." (Leo Rosten, author of *The Joys of Yiddish*, describes a nebbish as either: 1. a weak sister; 2. a born loser; a very unlucky person; 3. a small, thin unimpressive sort; 4. a nonentity ; 5. a namby-pamby.)

But why use *nebbish* in the first place unless there was a pointed need to isolate Bettman as a Jew?

The Jewish references continued at both ends of the continent. A columnist guessed that the players would not return to the ice until Passover, an important Jewish holiday which takes place around Easter. Why mention Passover in the first place since Vancouver's Jewish population is relatively small? Obviously to introduce Bettman's Jewishness into the issue. (Ignorant of Jewish holidays, the writer actually meant Hanukkah, which takes place in December.)

"He could have easily used Christmas," noted Simmons. "But the inference was both clear and unnecessary. The holiday was Jewish."

Bettman pointedly avoided any entrance into the anti-Semitic arena but his deputy, Brian Burke, charged that the commissioner was subject to a battering from unnamed members in the Toronto press who Burke felt were anti-Semitic.

"In my mind," said Burke, "a couple of writers are clearly influenced in their coverage by the fact that Gary Bettman and much of the league hierarchy are American and that Gary Bettman and some of the other league higher-ups are Jewish."

The league's vice-president and director of hockey operations added, "It's scary in 1994 to think that someone would be that ignorant. For me to state that I feel it's a factor, I have to feel very strongly that it is, but to level that charge against any one writer I'd have to be able to support it."

Boston Herald hockey columnist Joe Gordon wrote on October 23, 1994, that perhaps Chris Chelios' "statements helped foster the anti-Semitism Burke believes exists."

While Simmons contended that the "New York lawyer" allusion was not equated with being a Jew, others disagreed, me included. So did Will Exton, writing in the October 11, 1994, edition of the *Village Voice*. "To allow anti-Semitic codes to creep in at this critical moment can only poison the game's atmosphere far worse than any economic impasse," commented Exton.

Still, Strachan's repeated "New York lawyer" tweaks throughout the lockout bothered me enough to phone a mutual friend, Harry Ornest. The former Blues' owner, now an official of Hollywood Park Race Track, was as intensely proud of his Jewish background as any sportsman I knew. From time to time, Ornest would send me clippings alluding to the Holocaust and similar issues related to our past.

I pointedly asked Ornest whether he thought Strachan was anti-Semitic and he emphatically rejected the suggestion and offered a few thoughts to reinforce his point. Ornest was very persuasive about the anti-Semitism issue and it was enough to convince me.

What remained perplexing, however, was Strachan's obsession with New York and his incessant reference to the "New York lawyer" routine. I had hoped at some point to confront him on the issue, but quite frankly, never expected to get the opportunity on television.

As it happened, one day in mid-winter I received a phone call from a producer of the "Inside Sports" TV show hosted by Dave Hodge. Over the years I had done several segments with Hodge, a respected Canadian sportscaster, but most of them had either been one-on-one interviews, whereas this would be different.

The subject was the media and the lockout; how the confrontation was being covered and what to expect. Instead of the one-on-one, Hodge would have a third guest and, what do you know, it would be Strachan.

Never having done a show of this type with him before, I was uncertain what to expect so I decided in advance that I would keep it low-key and reasonably respectful – unless he indicated that he was getting out of hand. Then, I decided, I would let him have it.

The program opened on a fairly calm note and remained that way for a few minutes until Strachan went off on his anti-New York kick. I wouldn't say that my blood boiled, but it certainly did stir and that's when I launched my counter-attack. Here's how the dialogue unfolded on the air:

Strachan: "I think what's happened is that we're in an unusual situation here because most of the people who have covered hockey, and have covered it for many years, we've become fairly comfortable, we know the people in the game, we know who's telling the truth and who isn't. But we're in a situation where the game is being run by a bunch of New York lawyers who are extremely professional in what they do. I don't think anybody really likes them, but they have to give them credit for being very good. They leak stories when it's suited them to leak them, the rest of the time they had a total news blackout. Gary Bettman, the NHL's commissioner or business manager, whichever you prefer, managed to get a bylaw through or rule, whatever, last summer that empowered him to levy six-figure fines to anyone who spoke out of turn, so there was very few leaks and we're used to getting those kind of leaks, so it was an unusual situation for the media and I think that's why we got misled sometimes. My sources say that (unintelligible) situation was a direct leak from the New York NHL office in the hopes of putting pressure on the players, and that's the kind of things they've been doing.

Hodge: Stan, have people been used here?

Fischler: Well, first of all, I disagree with Al completely. First of all, Al likes to use this New York lawyer thing like there's a distinction between a New York lawyer, a Detroit lawyer and a Toronto lawyer. And I'd like to know the difference between a New York lawyer and a Toronto lawyer.

Strachan: Well, a Toronto lawyer knows hockey, basically.

Fischler: I mean if it leaks, it leaks all over the place. Talk about leaks, I'm sure you could get information on how Bob Goodenow and his henchman have choreographed certain players. I mean you got that whole flak about how Bettman is this and Bettman is that and it all happened at once. You have a series of players who are always the ones they go back to, you always hear a Larry Murphy, this is certainly a choreographed situation coming out of the NHLPA. So I would submit that the amount of propaganda coming out from both sides, whether they're New York lawyers or Toronto lawyers or whoever these guys are, Goodenow has done an excellent job in one respect – he has managed to keep the dissidence quiet, I mean this whole booshwah about voting 26 to nothing. I just talked to people who told me several players who dissented – it wasn't 26 to nothing. But that's the way Goodenow presented it, and another thing I haven't read in any of the papers, I don't know if anybody in Canada wrote about it, but how come nobody in the media other than Keith have in the Detroit paper? Why hasn't the union put it to a popular vote? I mean, why is it this Goodenow-politburo that decides everything?

Hodge: Let me suggest this, that Al, you probably, if forced to name a villain in this, would say Gary Bettman. Stan, if forced to name a villain, you'd probably say Bob Goodenow.

Fischler: No probably, no probably.

Hodge: You already have.

Fischler: Yes.

Hodge: How easy is it for people to understand this when they get it from polarized sides? We say Al, is it easy to sit on the side you've been painted on and still try to be responsible and still try independently to figure out what's going on?

Strachan: It is at a paper like the *Sun* where we had a number of people who are covering the event. We have four guys at least who write on it on a regular basis, and I'm a columnist, they pay me to take a stance, not sit on a fence. We have our newswriters – Dave Fuller, Lance Hornby – who have done an excellent job of covering the day-to-day negotiations. They give you the nuts and bolts and I try and give you an opinion, I don't think that's a big problem. And referring to what we were talking about earlier, I think the difference between a New York lawyer and a Toronto lawyer is that Toronto lawyers go to hockey games and they understand hockey. And the other thing that is interesting to note, that Stan mentioned certain players whose names keep popping up all the time as sources. Larry Murphy you mentioned, that's true, but who do you ever hear from the league? Because they don't, they just weasel stuff out from under the table that they tell selected players, selected writers. But they don't come out and say, "this is my opinion."

Hodge: Stan, you take a crack about how easy this is to analyze from one side of the post to the other.

Fischler: Well, once again – I disagree again – to say New York lawyers don't go to hockey games is stupid. I mean it's a generalization, it doesn't mean anything. I mean these guys, tons of New York lawyers, subscribe to Ranger games. So that's meaningless. The weaseling it out, I mean there's been so much weaseling on the union side it's ridiculous. Some of the statements are so absurd, I mean you take a guy like Glenn Healy, who played about 25 games tops – the guy's getting $800,000 and the guy's beeping about his deal. I don't see anybody taking shots at guys like Healy. They just accept his quotes and leave it at that. But obviously the average reader is having a tough time and the average fan is having a tough time because it's complicated for the average hockey fan to figure out all these deals, and the Group I, Group II, Group III, I mean the fans got sick and tired of that stuff a long time ago. I mean, it's very difficult for anyone in the media to keep the fans apprised so the fans don't lose interest. I think a lot of the writing, and I don't mean this as an insult to anyone, but a lot of the writing has gone over the head of the fan. The fan wants it resolved one way or the other.

We had run out of time but not out of venom. The lockout certainly had not run out of time. It lasted through Christmas 1994 and into 1995.

For the first time, I began to question whether we would see NHL hockey again in the 1994-95 season.

John Ziegler succeeded
Clarence Campbell as
NHL president and led
the league through the
1992 players' strike
which ultimately
proved his undoing.

The author with former
NHL union boss Alan
Eagleson at a time when
The Eagle was a top
power broker.

Yellow Sunday. The day NHL officials walked out on the Bruins-Devils playoff in 1988 only to be replaced by an amateur referee and linesmen.

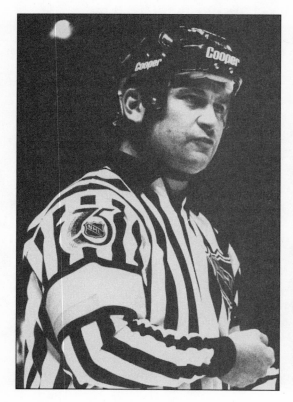

Referee Don Koharski's fiery exchange with Devils' coach Jim Schoenfeld during the 1988 Bruins-New Jersey playoff was the spark leading to the NHL's first walkout of officials.

Fielding a call from President Bill Clinton, Mike Keenan accepts congratulations for the Rangers' 1994 Stanley Cup triumph.

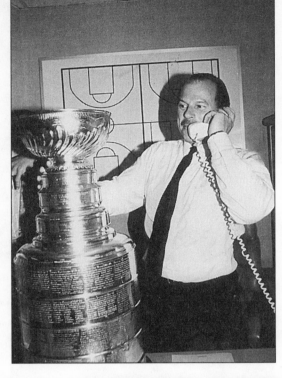

Once two of the NHL's most powerful figures, former chairman-of-the-board Bruce McNall (left) and NHL chief counsel Gil Stein; both left the league under clouds of controversy.

Ex-union leader Al Eagleson talks business with the NHL's first commissioner
Gary Bettman

Gary Bettman was
somewhat of an anomaly
when chosen NHL
commissioner. He was an
NBA executive with no
hockey background.

By the mid-1990s Bob Goodenow's appearance in NHL dressing rooms became commonplace. Goodenow in 1992 was the catalyst behind the first NHL player walkout of modern times.

NHL players haul their equipment out of arenas across the continent at the start of the 1994 NHL Lockout.

Members of the NHL Board of Governors meet the press during The Lockout of 1994-95.

NHL vice-president Brian O'Neill took over the league administration during the 1988 Boston-Devils playoffs when President John Ziegler was "missing in action."

11

....

GETTING HAIRY:
DIGGING IN FOR THE LONG HAUL

The empty feeling I experienced in the pit of my stomach whenever I glanced at the sports pages was similarly being shared by many friends and acquaintances who made a living out of hockey. People in the publishing business were hurting big-time because fans weren't buying hockey books without hockey on TV. Arena workers, from hot dog vendors to icemakers, were all laid off and many teams already began furloughing employees in their public relations and marketing departments.

I was among the lucky ones. Although SportsChannel had lost its usual slate of Islanders and Devils games, the cable television company with which I had been affiliated for almost two decades did not eliminate its broadcasters' salaries. Instead, it made a deal with the American Hockey League Albany River Rats for a slate of games to be broadcast. Because the Rats are the Devils' AHL farm team, the New Jersey broadcast team, including Mike Emrick, Peter McNab and I, was assigned to the Rats' telecasts.

To say I was tickled would be an understatement. Albany had been a second home to me since I was a kid and I liked New York's state capital. Knickerbocker Arena was a relatively new, handsome building of major league proportions; a good place to work and the Rats' staff, from president Doug Birch on down to marketing ace, Eric Servetah – a former intern of mine – were A-1 people with whom to work.

Then there were the players themselves. As hockey players go, the Rats were a journalist's dream come true. They were thoroughly without pretension, eager to do interviews and cooperative at every turn. "They haven't been affected by the big money yet," said one of the Rats' staffers. "Every one of them is down-to-earth, regular."

Our first televised game of the season was against the Hershey Bears. I arrived at the rink in the late afternoon and drifted down to the dressing-room area. Instinctively, I walked toward the ice and stopped at the visitors' bench. A tall figure had one foot up on the bench with his head tilted upward staring toward the balcony. I decided to share his hockey reverie and rubbed shoulders with Jay Leach, Hershey's coach.

We had known each other from his days as an aide to the Whalers. We pumped hands and then asked each other the inevitable question: how long will this lockout go on?

I mentioned to him that Canucks' assistant general manager George McPhee had assured me that a deal would be cut within 10 days of the season opener. "They'll do a little posturing and then work something out," said McPhee. "Both sides have too much to lose by letting it run long."

But the 10 days had turned into two weeks and there were those, Wayne Gretzky among the most prominent, who ominously predicted that the lockout could extend into (perish the thought!) 1995. When I mentioned that to Leach, he shook his head doubtfully.

"I don't see it going *that* long," he said. "Those players have mouths to feed and mortgages to pay. Once they miss that first paycheque you'll see a lot of pressure being put on the union to make a settlement."

Theoretically it made sense, but practically, no. Hockey players have the "team" philosophy so ingrained in their heads by the time they reach the NHL that they would instinctively back their union leader – even if it became apparent that Bob Goodenow had his own agenda and was engaged in an ego battle with Gary Bettman even more than he was crusading for players' rights. Which, not so incidentally, were at their optimal point in late 1994.

In fact the players seemed totally mesmerized by Goodenow. He had a Svengali effect on their Trilby and those who earlier had challenged the NHLPA position – Kelly Buchberger, Patrick Roy, among others – were mystifyingly, quickly and effectively silenced.

I learned this first-hand after appearing on a Minneapolis all-sports radio station to discuss the labour issues. At the conclusion of the interview, I mentioned to the host that it seemed fruitless just to have me on when my anti-Goodenow position was left unchallenged.

"Why don't you get a player or two or Goodenow, himself?" I suggested.

"Okay," the host replied. "We'll try for Brett Hull. And if we can't get him perhaps Dennis Vaske or Tommy Kurvers."

"And I say you won't get any of them because Goodenow won't let them appear in a discussion," I insisted.

"We'll try," said the other.

That sounded good. I knew Hull from dozens of interviews and was even friendlier with Vaske and Kurvers from their days on Long Island. I was told that we'd probably have the on-air confrontation in a week and that they would get back to me. But a week went by and no call. Then, two weeks and still no call. Finally, Minneapolis all-sports was on the phone.

"Would you still be willing to discuss the lockout?" he asked.

"Did you get Hull?"

"No."

"Vaske?"

"No."

"Kurvers?"

"No."

"And you didn't get Goodenow either; so who did you get?"

"How would you feel about coming on with Brian Lawton? He's an agent based here and he handles some of those players."

Lawton and I were pals dating back to his season with the Rangers. He was a good guy and we had a frank discussion on the air with plenty of give-and-take. My point was that the players never had it so good; they were offered an even better deal overall; and that by not agreeing to the owners' offer, they were not only jeopardizing small-market teams but their own careers. Lawton countered that owners make more money than they let on; that they were responsible for escalating salaries, not the players; and that abuses of the past had to be rectified.

Lawton was a worthy debating opponent but not the one I had wanted. I still was hoping to go head-to-head with Goodenow and finally thought that moment had come when New York sportscaster Howie Rose invited me to his WFAN studio for a discussion of the lockout. It was now early December 1994, positions on both sides had hardened and just about everyone had dug in for what appeared to be a lost season.

Rose's producer had told me he expected Goodenow to be on simultaneously with me and the inference was quite clear that fireworks would be the order of the day. Frankly, I wasn't so much looking for fireworks as I was an explanation from Goodenow about how he had agreed to include the salary cap in the discussion with the league as part of the 1992 Collective Bargaining Agreement, but now would not talk cap, no matter what.

When I arrived at the studio, Rose's producer was at the door. "Are we all set for Goodenow?" I asked.

"I'm afraid not," he replied. "We had him on already about an hour ago."

"But I thought we'd be on together."

"So did we, but he said he had to do the show earlier and there was nothing we could do about it."

These interviews were growing redundantly tiresome and frustrating since it appeared that neither side would crack. Ownership maintained a surprisingly united front as did the union, although there were dissenters on both sides. Players seemed willing and able to withstand the economic hardship of missed paycheques while owners, aware that the International Hockey League might attempt to sign NHL players en masse, talked openly about a non-1994-95 season.

"I learned my lesson from baseball," Devils' owner John McMullen told me one afternoon. Having owned the Houston Astros, McMullen knew whereof he spoke. He had studied the machinations of baseball union boss Donald Fehr and was convinced that Fehr was orchestrating Goodenow's moves. (He may have been right!) "We can't let happen to hockey what's happened to baseball," McMullen went on. "And if we have to kill the season, so be it."

It was difficult to find an objective observer when it came to analyzing the lockout, but the individual who appealed to me most for that particular role was Mike Milbury.

When Alan Eagleson was king of the union and hockey's premier power broker, Milbury was the only player to challenge him both face-to-face and in print. I wrote several *Hockey News* columns about Milbury's courageous pro-union stance and knew full well how deeply he felt about improving player conditions. But Milbury also was aware of the management side. He had been an assistant general manager of the Bruins before becoming an analyst for ESPN late in 1994. In my estimation, nobody could more objectively articulate the subject than Milbury, especially since he once had been a player representative when he was patrolling the Boston blue line.

Milbury was unequivocal. Goodenow was wrong. He asserted that if he had been a player in 1994, he would have urged his union to go back to work. Remember, this is the man who once charged that Eagleson was too soft with ownership and who nearly was run out of the NHLPA for being too liberal – nay, too radical – in challenging the administration.

"If the players are guaranteed the same money is being spent," said Milbury, "and the benefits are the same, I'm back working. The players seem extremely hung up on the doctrine involved. I spouted the same stuff when the average salary was $60,000, not $600,000. Guys have to realize they are never going to make this money up.

"Some guys are blowing $80,000 cheques each month. The owners will pay whatever the total payrolls are, plus a cost of living and that's the floor. If I were the Bruins in the union, I'd be beating down the door to play. If you're a 32-year-old guy and you give up the money now, you're never going to get it back. You need that for your future."

Players seemed to be oblivious to the fact that there had been a remarkable escalation in salaries, that their average paycheque was soaring through the roof and that there had to be an end to ownership's ability to continue hiking payrolls.

"The owners are having serious problems," Milbury added. "A majority of teams are losing money, and when that's true, you're in trouble. Based on their actions, the owners are giving a signficant signal they need help. They're not trying to fight with the players, they're trying to tell them something."

Milbury acknowledged that Goodenow had wrought gains for his constituency but noted that, "Anyone coming after Alan Eagleson would have made progress." Milbury expressed a sensitivity to the issue and an understanding that the players never had it so good.

"If the players have to slow down and suck it up for a couple of years at what they've been getting paid, that's not so bad. Even if they have to take a five percent pay cut, no one is saying this is forever. I don't think Gary Bettman is trying to stiff players. How could you say that when you look at where salaries have gone?

"If I was playing and I knew the same general revenues would be going out to pay players, I'd find it damn tough not to go back. When you talk about principles, people get stubborn, but the practicalities of the situation don't merit their stance."

As autumn moved closer to winter, there were suggestions that a deal could be done by early December and, following a brief retraining camp, the players could be back on the ice by Christmas. But no deal was hammered out by the end of November and purveyors of doom and gloom took centre stage. One exception was my *Hockey News* editor Steve Dryden who steadfastly maintained that a deal eventually would be cut. Finally, in mid-December some faint, hopeful signs were heard and a week before Christmas the *New York Post* boldly announced that the union had capitulated and a deal was in the offing. According to the newspaper, the owners had won the battle, big-time.

This was the most hopeful sign we had since the lockout began on October lst. I vividly recall picking up the *Post* at my corner newsstand that December morning and reading the headline on the back page along with a photo accompanied by a dubbed-in white flag of surrender carried by the players. I said to myself that this was too good to be true; that something would happen to screw up the apparent peace overtures.

But a follow-up story the next day reiterated that only a week or so would be needed to tidy up the loose ends; that the owners had won a clear-cut victory and that the season would begin after the holiday. If so, this was a major breakthrough and I arranged to have a SportsChannel camera crew meet me at the NHL office near Rockefeller Centre where I would interview NHL vice-president Brian Burke on the subject.

Armed with the *New York Post* stories proclaiming that the battle was over, I sat down with Burke to discern precisely how the armistice would be handled. To my astonishment, the stories had no relation to what he was about to tell me and, in a sense, the interview was one of the most fascinating and frustrating that I've ever conducted.

It opened with my feeling of elation that a deal was near and followed with the crushing news that I was experiencing a false euphoria. Here's how it went:

STAN: How close is a deal?
BRIAN: Not close at all.
STAN: Can you amplify this?
BRIAN: We have major differences really in just about every area as far as I'm concerned. We're a long ways away from making a deal.

STAN: That doesn't jive with stories in the papers. Why would they suggest the end is close?

BRIAN: Well, I haven't seen the newspaper, but I don't know the answer to the question why there are stories like that. We do not have a deal. We are not close to a deal. We don't have any talks scheduled. So I don't know how anyone could conclude we are close to a deal.

I think the union told the players, given the position they're in, that we have to be close to a deal, that if they move on one or two points we're going to have a deal. That's just not the case.

STAN: What are the main stumbling blocks right now?

BRIAN: Well, we've supposedly been discussing a deal with a tax and discussing a deal without a tax; that is not accurate either. We have never proposed a deal which does not include a tax. Players are trying to negotiate a deal. Fine, put enough on the table that a tax would not be part of the deal, would not be necessary whatever. That hasn't happened as far as we're concerned. So that would be the starting point?

I think that the players hope to negotiate a deal that doesn't include a tax. And we can't see that happening at this point. Beyond that we have differences on entry-level systems, we have differences on Group I, the old Group I. We have differences on Group II. We have differences on Group III. But other than that we're close.

STAN: What is the drop-dead date?

BRIAN: It changes daily. In my mind we're already past the drop-dead date, in terms of the training camp. In order to have the right product on the ice and reduce the risk of injury, we have to have a training camp of a duration that's probably already impossible. So I think if someone is waiting for the clock to stop ticking on the final hour, in my mind, we're already in that time now.

STAN: What would be the latest start date with 45 games?

BRIAN: I don't know that date. It changes constantly because we get a date here and there. Like, someone calls today and says Motley Crue cancelled and we got the building. Or the circus cancelled three performances in Boston, we got the building. The schedule of available dates changes daily. I don't know the answer to the question with the day this date would be and we could play 45 games.

STAN: Can the league play a 45-game season?

BRIAN: Not if it's up to me.

STAN: What's the minimum?

BRIAN: In my mind the minimum is 50; anything less than that, where you jeopardize the potential for 28 playoff games to determine the Stanley Cup champion, makes no sense.

STAN: If it was a 50-game season, what is the latest date to start?

BRIAN: If you're talking about a 14-day training camp, you're into the period now, where I think there should be a training camp. The latest date you would have to start playing subject to dates being made available, is somewhere in the first week of January.

STAN: When will the talks resume?

BRIAN: Good question. I don't know. We have not heard from the union as far as another meeting, and I don't know when they will resume.

STAN: How do you explain that you haven't heard from the union at such a critical time?

BRIAN: There is no question now we should be looking for common ground and not pointing fingers and not throwing grenades. On that one issue, the pace of bargaining, the intensity of bargaining, the frequency of bargaining, what the union has done in my mind is indefensible. It's very frustrating to me personally because we're not playing, in my opinion, in large part because the union has not bargained. They have not made the proper commitment to this. I've said it before, lock the doors; let's make a deal.

We've begged for a quicker timetable. We've said, "Bob, what do you mean you'll call us? Why can't we meet tomorrow?" He'll say, "Well, I'll call you." So why don't we meet the next day? So, on that one issue, the players and union have absolutely no defence to the fan's question: "Why aren't you meeting?" We're not meeting because the union won't meet.

STAN: What do you think their motive is?

BRIAN: I have no idea. I assume there is a plan. Bob Goodenow is not a stupid individual. I assume there's a plan, but we can't discern what it is. He's bragged that he is a last-minute negotiator. He's bragged he'll make the best deal at the 11th hour now.

STAN: If meetings resume next week, could a deal be made before the new year?

BRIAN: If you're talking possibility, sure. Do I think that it's going to happen? No.

STAN: Is it safe to say Brian Burke does not think there is going to be a season?

BRIAN: I'm very pessimistic at this point. I've been optimistic since we began this process. My belief in life generally is if you don't have dreams you have nightmares. I believe you've got to have aspirations of greatness. You've got to have dreams of success to be successful. Based on the last couple of days, I'm no longer optimistic, I'm pessimistic.

STAN: There has been talk the owners would drop the tax.

BRIAN: Not from our perspective, and it's certainly not anything we've discussed. The players have said to us they want to put as much on the table as they can, in hopes that that's enough to not have a tax. In my mind, arbitration is clearly inflationary and not necessary. They don't have it in football; they don't have it in basketball. Inflation is one part of the problem that I don't think eliminating arbitration will solve.

The basic problem is: how does the league compete, when you have individual player contract negotiations, but teams with widely-dispersed revenue bases? They've solved that in two sports with a cap. Our players don't want a cap. We've proposed a tax. I don't think eliminating arbitration does it. That would be the owners' call if and when we get to them. That has not been proposed, nor do I anticipate it will be proposed by the players.

STAN: What influence has baseball had on the hockey situation?

BRIAN: We're fearful of a significant influence. We don't know the extent. The union has denied there is a link, yet the catcher of the Blue Jays allegedly asked a reporter what was going on in hockey and the guy said why do you care? The catcher said, "Well, I know that our guy (union head) and your guy talk all the time."

We're nervous about that. We fear there is an influence. We fear that to a large extent our players are involved in this dispute, indirectly. Maybe they're hostages. Maybe part of the position the NHL Players' Association has taken in large part is to reinforce the baseball players. But we have no concrete evidence of that. It's just a fear on our part.

STAN: What about Stephane Richer's comment (basically, that there were many players who wanted to play and to bolt the unified union position)?

BRIAN: I give Stephane Richer great credit for integrity and courage to speak out, speak his mind publicly at this time. We have reason to believe, based on comments made to us by agents and by players to GMs, that he is not alone. That's not an isolated viewpoint. There are many players who believe that Richer spoke the truth for a large group of players. The union makes it difficult, calling guys to a room and having a pep rally and shouting down dissenters. But we have concrete evidence. It's not a belief. It's clear many players share Stephane's sentiments. But at this point there's obviously not enough of them; not enough who are courageous enough to go public.

STAN: Has the league made its last, best offer?

BRIAN: No, but we're not far from it. What we'd be prepared to accept to go back to work would not be, from our perspective, far from what we have on the table. We have attempted to negotiate in good faith and get a deal done. We don't have any magic trick to pull at the last minute to make a deal. We're close; we've tried to get to where we have to be.

STAN: The fans are hurt. What's the message to fans?

BRIAN: I guess the first thing I'd say to a fan is, be patient. This, too, shall pass, as they say. What we're going through is not unique to hockey. They went through six, seven years of litigation and work stoppages in football before they arrived at a system that made sense. Basketball is going to have its day of reckoning in the future. Baseball is a mess right now. What we're going through here is resolving and defining what the labour relationship's going to be in pro sports in the 90s. We know our fans miss hockey. I miss hockey. But I think it's a fight we have to have if we want the league to survive, if we want the smaller market teams to have a chance. This is a fight we have to have now, unfortunately, but in many ways it comes at the worst possible time.

STAN: The league and players have taken a financial beating. Can it be defined in numbers?

BRIAN: I've seen the figures tossed around in terms of the actual monetary losses the owners will sustain, the actual monetary losses the players will sustain by not playing. It's in many millions of dollars. It's certainly an unattractive prospect in terms of the total player payroll, if there's no season at all.

STAN: If something is worked out, how long will it take the league to regain momentum?

BRIAN: Well, you've seen great resiliency in other sports after a work stoppage. The fan base, loyal fans recover quickly. They forget quickly. I'm not sure how quickly. We have the best fans in pro sports, in my opinion. The surveys, different statistical bases, indicate that a season ticket holder to an NHL team goes to more games on a percentage basis than a season ticket holder to an NBA team. We have great fans. Very loyal fans.

How quickly they come back, the marginal fan, the fan that has been turned off by this? I don't know. How quickly they forget? I don't know. We think we have the greatest product in the world and the greatest athletes in the world and we think we can get it back on track. What kind of scars you have left? I don't know. We haven't been through a work stoppage of this duration. I think the damage caused by work stoppage is directly proportional to the length of the stoppage and the acrimony of the dispute. This has been a professional dispute for the most part, with the notable exceptions of some nasty personal attacks and a few fairly ignorant comments by a couple of players. Other than that it's been professional.

STAN: Goodenow said the league has a plan that there will be no hockey 'til January.

BRIAN: I marvel when I hear a statement that ignorant. I'm mystified by it and I marvel at it. Someone explain to me what percentage we would have to gain by chopping 30-plus games off the schedule, or 40 games off the schedule; hurting the new television deal, hurting the new commercial sponsorship relationship with Busch and Nike to do this.

Sure, that's right; that was our plan all along! That might be the single, dumbest comment ever made in the history of labour negotiations in this country.

STAN: How important is the FOX deal to inspire a settlement?

BRIAN: In terms of the labour negotiations, I don't think it's a factor. We are very pleased with our relationship with FOX. We think of it as a tremendous, long-term benefit for the league. We think it can make us more of a 50-state sport, in terms of enthusiasm and viewership and everything. We think it's a tremendous partnership. But in terms of getting this deal done it's really not an issue.

STAN: What about the threat of the players forming their own league?

BRIAN: This is a case where you're talking about comments your own players make, and you don't want to ever insult your own players. That's our theory. They're a product. We think they're great guys. I see comments by players, "We're going to start our own league. We're going to do this." It's incredibly naive to suggest or to assume that it's a simple undertaking, starting a new league.

Worse, I see journalists egging them on. Saying well, we have 20 corporate sponsors. I mean, you're talking player payrolls of $25 million and they're talking teams' corporate sponsors. What's wrong with this picture? Someone's going to put up millions and I ask, what corporation, looking at our industry, is not going to insist on some type of salary structure, some type of economic system going in. I mean, there's a new baseball league plan that's got a salary cap; that's what the owners are trying to get right now in Major League Baseball. I say to the players, there's a lot more involved in that than you think.

STAN: Players have been hypnotized by Goodenow to reject a pretty good deal. How can they not see it? Has the league failed in its attempt?

BRIAN: Well, I don't know if conned is a fair word. Hypnotized maybe. I've used this phrase publicly. One agent told me about a month ago that when he heard the reaction to the tax: no tax, no tax, no tax. And, how is it possible to have a philosophical objection to a system without evaluating the merits of that system? It doesn't make sense at this point in time. It's easy to confuse the players, when you distort the facts.

Have we done a good job of getting our message across? I don't know. We have not gotten a deal on that basis; so I'd say no, we haven't done a good job. However, where there are big barriers built up to your message before you get your message there, I'm not sure how you can succeed. I think the players take whatever we say with a grain of salt. I think there's no question this labour negotiation is a legacy of past abuses. I think there is, with a great respect for true rape victims, I think there is a rape-victim mentality here; that our players mistrust the owners, mistrust us. I think there is an historical basis for that. And we're trying unsuccessfully, as of yet, to get the players to realize it's a new day out there. Whatever abuse you feel you've suffered in the past, it's a new day.

STAN: The essence of the dispute is money. You offered to show them the books. Why haven't they looked?

BRIAN: I think they're afraid to look. We've offered not only to show them the information we've assembled, but we've offered to submit this to a Big Six accounting firm for audit purposes. We are fearless when it comes to the numbers. We're not worried about turning these numbers over to an accounting firm and demonstrating that this is an industry that's in grave danger. Why has the union refused to look at the data? In my opinion, it is because they are afraid of the results. They're afraid the owners are telling the truth. They think if they look at the numbers they're going to see an industry on life-support.

STAN: Is Goodenow the chief problem?

BRIAN: I have no interest in getting into name calling. It's not going to help get a deal done now. So I'm not going to answer that question. He's not alone in his position. He's got support with his negotiating committee and with the executive committee in the union.

STAN: Since October 1, it has been a roller coaster. Can we possibly have one more climb that's the real one?

BRIAN: After one early meeting, I came out and said to a reporter that I was optimistic, that we had had a real good day, the fact we were in here. And in my opinion, I showed great inexperience. We came out of the meeting and I said to Gary, "You're not as upbeat as I am." Gary Bettman's comment was, "Well, I've been through this before. I'm not going to get sucked in again." I blame myself for being inexperienced in collective bargaining and reading it the wrong way. I was hopeful and then the next day everything ground to a screeching halt.

I'm not getting sucked in again. I'm not going to display any elation or emotion or optimism until I see someone picking up a pen.

STAN: I've been disappointed in two groups. One is the fact that agents have not helped and two is Wayne Gretzky.

BRIAN: Well, the agents, what troubles me about the agents as a group is I don't understand the mixed message we're getting from them. Privately, they're telling GMs and they're telling me there's a deal being made there with the tax. They feel the tax we've proposed is not outrageous or restrictive. They're telling me that; then publicly there is no such comment from them. Nor do I discern any pressure on the union from them. And I'm troubled by that, I'm puzzled by that. Either they're not telling me the truth or they're not willing to stand up to the union. They're either not telling me the truth, or our GMs the truth, or for some reason, they're intimidated.

As far as Wayne goes, Wayne's a great player. He's done tremendous things for the game of hockey. Nobody in hockey, myself included, wants a public dispute with Wayne Gretzky because of our respect for him. I'll leave that to the agents and to the journalists, as far as their view of his role, the player tour and everything else. No one in hockey wants to fight with Wayne Gretzky. He's done too much for this game and we prefer to negotiate with the union.

STAN: Based on our conversation, the realistic chances of a season are 5-1 against.

BRIAN: I don't know if it's 5-1 against; I'm not a mathematician. But I'm not optimistic. I think there is tremendous doubt whether we will be able to play at all.

STAN: If no season, where do we go from here?

BRIAN: I don't know. I mean, there's no plan B. We don't have a plan B. We have one plan, which is to negotiate a deal with our players and take this sport to where it should be in the U.S. Grow it. Make it bigger, better. Gary Bettman has demonstrated he has the ability to do that. But we need a partner. You can't dance by yourself. We need someone who wants to dance. We think we can make a deal with the players and grow the sport; start making up ground and catching up to some of the other sports going by, making a better sport for the year 2000 and beyond.

STAN: Was this lockout, or a strike, inevitable?

BRIAN: No. Absolutely not. When historians look at this they're going to marvel that we had this work stoppage. They are going to marvel that we had to have it.

STAN: The biggest sin is that the union didn't start talking in January, February, March 1994.

BRIAN: We didn't meet for almost five months as you mentioned. We have missed days and hours and weeks. We have had huge breaks in the negotiation. We're not meeting today. We have no scheduled meetings. I'm really frustrated by that. On that one issue alone, as I said before, has no defence, to us, to our fans, to sponsor-members. The lack of pace, intensity and commitment to this negotiation is shocking. There is no other word for it. There has not been the proper attention paid to this negotiation. From an intensity standpoint, from a time commitment, or preparation, it's bizarre.

STAN: The union claims it was the NHL who pulled the plug on the season in October.

BRIAN: I think our fans have seen through that. We have not gotten any backlash about why we're not playing in terms of the no-strike pledge. We think the whole thing was very well done. It was a charade. We got called at 11:00 or 12:00 the day the players announced their no-strike pledge. The press conference was at 1:00. At that point Marty McSorley and Wayne Gretzky had been on a plane all night from L.A. They knew we could not continue under the old system. Now why wouldn't we play five more years with the way revenues are being distributed? The fans have seen through that, although some of the media bought into it.

We truly want to solve the problems facing the industry. Our fans understand that. Hopefully we'll get a deal made and get everyone back to playing and get the fans back in the buildings.

STAN: Who do you think the fans sided with?

BRIAN: Oh there is no question about that. There is very little sympathy for the players' position from a fan's standpoint. The mail we're getting, the coverage in Canada. The coverage in the U.S. markets has been very clear. You'll get a different answer, though, from someone in the union.

There is no question in my mind where the support is, and not just in hockey, but in the other sports as well. I think the average fan can't understand why, with an average salary last year of $560,000 or whatever it was, that's not enough. When is it enough? There is no question where the public opinion is on this; it's with the owners.

STAN: A mediator wouldn't have helped?

BRIAN: No.

STAN: Why?

BRIAN: A mediator is designated to help parties talk. We're talking with the union just fine. When we're together, we communicate well. We understand the issues, we understand their viewpoint. They understand ours. Negotiations are professional. They're amicable. I've been in negotiations before where if you didn't know how to swim when it started you sure as hell knew how to swim when it was over. That's not the case here. I don't think a mediator would be of any value at all at this point.

STAN: The best case scenario for settlement.

BRIAN: I don't know what is next, partly because I haven't done a lot of collective bargaining, partly because I don't understand the union's position on some of the issues, partly because I don't understand the union's timetable. I do think it's very bizarre that we're going into a Christmas holiday with no meetings scheduled. I think it's bizarre that there has been very little contact or communication at all, recently. I don't sense any urgency on the part of the union. Frankly, I'm mystified by the entire process at this point.

STAN: Anything to fans?

BRIAN: I'd like to wish our fans a merry Christmas, a happy holiday season and a happy New Year. It is our intention to get this problem solved and get our boys back on the ice and get playing. We regret the inconvenience and the loss of hockey. Everyone misses it terribly, but we're determined to get this industry back to where it can grow, to where it can be healthy.

As we packed the television equipment following the interview, I looked out of the skyscraper window toward the circular building that was Madison Square Garden. It was a cold and gloomy morning, consonant with hockey's dismal state of affairs. For the first time, I primed myself for a complete season without NHL hockey and wondered when we would ever see an Eric Lindros, Stephane Richer and Mark Messier again.

12

•••

A DEAL IS MADE:
THE 1995 SEASON BEGINS

It was a half-hour before midnight, New Year's Eve, December 31, 1994. Rain mixed with sleet coated the New York State Thruway near Albany as SportsChannel's hockey television crew drove toward the Plattekill Rest Stop.

The miserable conditions mirrored the feelings of both the talent and technical staff. Big-league hockey's longest work stoppage had now run through the Christmas holiday without a significant sign of a breakthrough. We had telecast a half-dozen American League River Rats games, but now there was a question in our minds whether the station would continue doing them in 1995.

And if the NHL season was cancelled – as many believed likely – what long-term effect would it have on us? Would the International Hockey League move into the vacuum as it had threatened and become a second major league? Could the NHL actually go down the tubes, as some extremists within the media actually had articulated?

Almost abandoned, the rest stop only had one of its six sales areas open. It was a McDonald's and the cocoa was hot and tasty as was the conversation. My colleague, Peter McNab, his father Max, Roland Dratch our producer, as well as statisticians Dave Katz and Mark Topaz stretched out and together we knifed our way through cole slaw, potato salad and hamburgers.

"Do you still think there's time for a settlement?" I asked Peter McNab.

"It's getting tight," he shot back. "There's only so many games you can play between the middle of January and the start of summer. And they'll have to factor in a mini-training camp. But the big thing is there's still no settlement."

The clock struck midnight. The new year had arrived and, significantly, not a horn was blown, nor a whistle heard inside the rest stop. It could well have been the middle of July for all the lack of festive evidence. We acknowledged 1995 in the simplest of manners; shaking hands and wishing each other well, but there was a distinct lack of conviction behind the back-pats because nobody knew quite what to expect either short-term or long-term.

"We got a lot of hoping to do," cracked Dratch. "And let's start hoping that Bettman and Goodenow start talking again."

The sides had not held full negotiations since December 6th and were fast approaching the lockout's 100th day. Finally, the talks resumed after the new year with intense pressure on both sides to make a deal. Many agents with whom I had been in constant contact were becoming more antsy. Steve Freger in Boston had a standard opening when I'd phone: "Suicide Central." None of the agents actually would go on the record as being critical of Bob Goodenow. He had succeeded in keeping the reps in tow, at least superficially. But several confided privately to me that they were unhappy with his performance.

Likewise, owners maintained their united front, but the liberal wing, headed by Howard Baldwin, kept pressing for an end to the lockout. In a conversation with the Islanders' executive Steve Walsh, I was told that it still was possible to cut a deal, but with a January 16th deadline, time was running short.

Nothing in the constitution said that the NHL commissioner and the union boss had to like each other. The more I talked with Gary Bettman, the more I got the feeling that he did not consider Goodenow his favourite person. This had nothing to do with issues and everything to do with style, personality and any other trait that leads to a turnoff. To me, this meant that the possibility of a settlement was less likely than if the adversaries were fond of each other.

Fortunately for the wheels of progress, there were others on both sides who could add lubricants, namely Bettman's top legal whiz Jeff Pash, Brian Burke and union lawyers John McCambridge and Bob Riley. By January 3rd, the league had agreed to drop its tax proposal which had been so onerous to the players.

For Bettman to forsake the payroll tax was a major concession on the part of ownership and would require equally significant moves on the other side. Management was seeking concessions such as a virtual wipeout of arbitration and free agency as well as the addition of a rookie salary cap, the likes of which had once seemed out of the question to Goodenow.

Personally, I was torn. As much as I enjoyed broadcasting the Albany River Rats games, I sorely missed the NHL. I was concerned about how a full season without either Devils or Islanders games would affect my employer, SportsChannel, which already had lost considerable baseball coverage because of the Major League Baseball Players' Association strike.

But I also was concerned about the NHL's long-range welfare. Unlike many of my colleagues, I believed that ownership had a very solid case; that the salary cap – payroll tax, call it what you will – was vital to overall league fiscal sanity. It seemed to me especially important to smaller market teams such as the Quebec Nordiques, Winnipeg Jets, Hartford Whalers, Washington Capitals and Edmonton Oilers.

Then, there was the possible loss of face for Bettman. Had he not been hired by the governors on the premise that he would impose a cap, or payroll tax, on salaries? Goodenow supposedly pledged to his constituency that he would resign rather than accept a cap. But if the NHLPA director accepted a rookie cap, wasn't he losing face as well?

"They'd better make a deal or they'll both be out of work," said one angry general manager. "All this time lost, and one side gets no tax or cap and the other gets no free agency. What a waste."

I had January 16th marked off on my 1995 calendar. Either I'd be preparing for Islanders and Devils telecasts or I'd be rewriting *Uptown, Downtown*, my history of the New York City subway system. Passionately, I hoped that it would not be the latter.

The break came in a phone call; an assignment. The NHL board of governors would be meeting in the offices of the league's Manhattan law firm. This would be followed by a news conference at a Times Square hotel. I was to head for the Marriott Marquis Hotel and meet our SportsChannel camera crew. We then would wait, along with a phalanx of reporters and television journalists, for Bettman to render his decision: hockey or no hockey.

Joe Lapointe, the *New York Times* reporter whose writing throughout the lockout tilted towards labour, predicted that there would be a settlement. Others argued against. Ownership was considering what was purported to be the players' last offer and, if refused, the season was over.

For me it was déjà vu – a repeat of the 1992 strike watch, only this time Goodenow was up against a more formidable foe. How formidable would only be determined by the final outcome.

Ownership's meeting consumed seven hours during which I spent six exchanging ideas with everyone from Lapointe to Frank Brown of the *Daily News*. Howard Berger, covering for *The Fan* radio station in Toronto, persuaded me to take him for a walk to Eighth Avenue and 49th Street, a block away, for a tour of the old Madison Square Garden site. The wind blowing off the Hudson River pierced our coats as we bent our heads westward toward the corner.

"Hockey sure has changed since you worked the old Garden, hasn't it?" asked Berger, who knew that I began working professionally there in 1954.

"Yeah," I replied, "in those days you didn't have to worry about unions and strikes. Just whether or not the Rangers made the playoffs. Which they usually didn't."

By the time Berger and I had returned to the warmth of the pressroom, it was buzzing with reports that Bettman soon would arrive. Somehow there's always someone among the journalists who gets a tip on such things and, usually, they are correct, as was the case this time.

The commissioner was unusually somber when he took his seat at the podium. He had come from a divided governorship, with some owners warning that if the season was cancelled they would face financial ruin. (Both Howard

Baldwin and Steve Walsh had independently told me that they felt the season should be resumed.) Others, such as John McMullen, believed that the NHL should not make the same mistake as Major League Baseball.

Owners voted 19-7 to reject the players' offer. That was the bad news. The good news was that negotiations were not dead. Governors had then proposed by a vote of 20-6 to offer a counterproposal.

Instead of resorting to gobbledygook or p.r. speech, Bettman candidly allowed that the ranks hardly were united. "There was a free, open, candid discussion because of the importance and significance of the issues at stake," said the commissioner, "possibly the cancellation of the season. It was at times emotional. There were some owners who wanted to play regardless of what the offer was, although it was only a handful. They were vocal, they were passionate and they were adamant. There are two sides to that equation and we debated it."

Once Bettman finished the question-and-answer period, I began lining up interviews for SportsChannel. I was especially interested in Hartford owner Pete Karmanos who had been relatively new to the NHL, but had a long hockey involvement with his Compuware teams in Detroit. I liked Karmanos as much as McMullen, particularly since Karmanos was virtually unwavering in his demand for a salary cap.

"There are a few people with a lot at stake," said Karmanos who looked more like a lumberjack in his plaid shirt. "They wanted to make their point that they were not willing to take that risk."

Perhaps most amazing of all were the high number of leaks to the media. One governor insisted to me that an executive for one of the Canadian teams was one of the tipsters and claimed to have caught him in the act of feeding information to Goodenow.

"I'm amazed we have people walking out of the meeting and describing blow-by-blow what happened inside for the media," said Brian Burke.

One of the best day-by-day descriptions was provided by the *Post*'s Larry Brooks, who set a new standard for New York-Metropolitan Area hockey journalism. Brooks' pipeline was far better than any of his competition from start to finish.

Ironically, the finish line still appeared out of sight as late as Tuesday night, January 10, 1995. I had camped out at the pressroom early in the day awaiting word from the NHL's propaganda minister, Arthur Pincus. The hope was that the two sides were close enough to an agreement for a pact to be completed by the end of the day.

That night, SportsChannel was hosting its annual Leukemia Society dinner across town near Grand Central Terminal. It was a fete that I never missed, but the 102-day hockey lockout seemed so close to resolution one way or the other there was no way I could afford to leave the now-gloomy pressroom.

The hard-line NHL owners were pushing for still more concessions from Goodenow and there was a fear that the deal – so near to completion – could blow up in the hawks' faces. With that in mind, I remained with the press-gang through the afternoon and into early evening. At about 7 p.m. Pincus walked from the press office into the room, suddenly inspiring hope that something – anything – was about to develop. Instead, he reported that nothing was imminent.

I walked out onto Broadway and then east along 42nd Street to the Grand Hyatt Hotel. It was a 10-minute jaunt, but enough for me to mull over the possibilities; mostly that we now genuinely faced the loss of the season. When I arrived at the ballroom, my colleague Jiggs McDonald was chatting with some SportsChannel friends.

"It doesn't look good," I said.

"Nawww," said McDonald, shaking his head. "They'll settle in a day. You wait and see."

Mike Richter, the Rangers' goalie, was the honoured guest. Richter had permanently earned his way into our family's hearts with his visit to Simon, my son, in the hospital during our 1993 crisis. Yet when he walked up to the podium for his award, I experienced point-counterpoint emotions. Yes, I was tickled for Richter, a genuinely good guy who proved his sensitivity with the trip to Columbia-Presbyterian Hospital. But I felt no empathy for the goaltender who was earning in the neighbourhood of $1 million a year and still was complaining about his lot.

I kept thinking about remarks made by some of the 1970 Stanley Cup champion Bruins, who now owned their own businesses, and frankly couldn't understand what the 1995 players were beefing about. "I feel for the owners now," said Fred Stanfield, "because they aren't making any money. I'm not taking anything away from the players, but I think now it's too much, the salaries are high enough."

Former teammate Don Awrey added, "Hey, I own a business and it's no one's business what I make. (Hockey players know what each earns.) I put up the initial investment, start up the business and do it. These guys are asking for the world here.

"Okay, so an owner puts up $50 million or $100 million to buy a team. He has to make a percentage on his investment, right? So, what if he makes 30 percent or 40 percent? He's the guy who stuck his neck out in the first place. If he makes money, good for him. He has all the employees, he's the guy paying everybody and, as a player, all you should care about is, 'Am I being paid a fair salary?' Now they want us to understand when they say, 'We have principles, and we aren't going to back down.' Come on, something's wrong."

Awrey was impeccably accurate. The owners were not going to back down anymore. They presented what Harry Sinden described as "the final, final, final, final offer" to Goodenow. I returned to the pressroom at 10 p.m. after subwaying crosstown only to discover that it was practically empty. One straggler mentioned that nothing further would take place that evening.

I then went home still expecting the cancellation of the campaign, but that night Bettman received assurances from both the Devils and Canucks that they would reverse earlier negative votes and would support a new Collective Bargaining Agreement.

When I arrived at the newsstand the next morning, the *New York Post* proclaimed that Bettman had reasserted his control over the governors. Now it was a matter of whether the union would remain obstinate or agree to ownership's "final, final, final, final offer."

The fact that the sides still were in communication was the best news. That we were down to the eleventh-and-a-half hour was the negative side of the picture. Except that when I walked into the Marriott Marquis for the umpteenth time, that optimistic buzz was in the air – again. Steve Dryden reminded me that he was about to win the bet (a dinner) he had made with me and that a settlement was about to be announced. Before noon one of the radio people was reporting, unofficially, that the union was accepting the owners' offer. Bit by bit, the news began to filter through; Goodenow had advised Bettman that the players' negotiating committee was recommending to the rank and file that the league's contract proposal be accepted.

I can't say that I felt an ecstatic surge when I learned that the peace pact was official. Rather, it was like the relief – and exhaustion – one feels after completing a marathon. Nor could I feel satisfied that the 103-day lockout really was worth the cost. To me, it was imperative to have a salary cap for everyone, not merely rookies. While other journalists instantly proclaimed ownership the winner, I took the other view. Sure, there were a few fiscal brakes on the union here and there, but essentially, salaries would continue to spiral upward and players would earn more than ever before.

Sure enough, before the ink had dried on the new pact, Mark Messier signed a $6 million a year contract with the Rangers, which was about twice the price I thought he deserved. One by one, other players followed suit with such remarkably good deals that one never would have known ownership had "won" the battle.

However, NHL governors such as Steve Walsh assured me that he could operate responsibly within the new CBA parameters. "Sound business practices could make it work," Walsh insisted.

He almost had me convinced; but not quite. Not when the Islanders already had committed a small fortune for completely untried Brett Lindros and were being prodded by Steve Thomas for a contract far in excess of $1 million.

But that would come later.

We had NHL hockey again; I was heading for Hartford for the Devils' season opener with the Whalers and, for the moment at least, all was right with the world.

13

·····································

GAME ON:
THE STRANGE SEASON

Dale Hunter, the irritating Washington Capitals' veteran, is not one to smile very often on the ice, but this day was different.

His club, like the 25 other NHL teams, had ratified the new Collective Bargaining Agreement and had returned to scrimmage at Piney Orchard practice rink in Maryland.

"My nine-year-old is all pumped up," said the Washington captain. "He wants to see some hockey."

My sixteen-year-old, Simon, was equally energized. He had fretted on and off for eight months about his favourite hockey club, the New York Islanders, and their hasty exit from the playoffs in 1984. The lockout baffled him, as it did millions of fans in two countries. He had difficulty understanding why Steve Thomas, who was earning more than $800,000 a year, sounded terribly unhappy about playing another season at his abysmally "low" salary.

But, most of all, Simon couldn't wait for opening night and neither could I, although already some disturbing sounds were assailing my ears. I had heard that members of the Jets had decided to boycott *Winnipeg Free Press* columnist Scott Taylor, who had taken ownership's side during the lockout. Taylor had supported ownership's contention that a salary cap was necessary to preserve clubs like the Jets. When Taylor walked into the club's dressing room following the settlement, the Jets, to a man, refused to talk to him. This set me wondering how members of the Islanders and Devils would react to yours truly since my pro-management stance was as vocal as anyone's.

I'd find out soon enough since I was scheduled to interview New Jersey captain Scott Stevens between the first and second periods of the Devils-Whalers game; not to mention Geoff Sanderson of Hartford and possibly even one other Devil if they won the game.

According to standard operating procedures, my request for the interview had to be made through Devils' public relations director Mike Levine who then would pass along the information to Stevens. I had never been rejected for an interview by Stevens, which meant that if he turned me down this time, it must be related to the lockout .

Within minutes, Levine returned and said, "No problem," whereupon I quietly sighed with considerable relief. The other cause for concern was the game itself; or to put it more accurately, the games.

The season had been shortened to 48 games spread over 100 days. If you believed the party line, it would be monstrously exciting. "This season won't be as good as a normal season," said Dale Hunter. "It's going to be better."

Perhaps, but just about everyone agreed that the one-week conditioning period was absurdly short and likely would result in injury. "You can't condition yourself in a week," said Capitals' coach Jim Schoenfeld. "If you try, you'll have injuries all over the place."

Nevertheless, the Devils-Whalers game did have a positive spark to it. A healthy crowd almost filled Hartford's Civic Center and they responded enthusiastically to a club that took the body to the favoured Jerseyites. I kept expecting the Devils to take over the game, but it was not to be. Their play bordered between interested and lethargic, leaving me to rationalize that the boys still weren't in shape.

Stevens, who appeared with me between the first and second periods, voiced the expected platitudes about wanting to get off to a good start; how every game would be a four-pointer and the importance of playing within coach Jacques Lemaire's system.

I couldn't tell whether it was me, the strange new season or something involving the club, but Stevens was conspicuously brief and aloof. I chalked it up to the new season and was quite pleased when Sanderson came aboard for the second period and sparkled in conversation about his trip to Finland during the lockout.

Both owners and players were concerned about fan reaction, particularly in Canada where there seemed to be more resentment toward the players than in the United States. "I don't think people are bitter," said Capitals' coach Jim Schoenfeld, "but no one really knows how this will play out."

It played out badly in Vancouver, Winnipeg, Quebec City and Edmonton where crowds were noticeably weaker than they had been in 1993-94. This was particularly galling to the Canucks' management whose team had reached the seventh game of the Stanley Cup finals in the spring of 1994. Likewise, the Nordiques' general staff had expected sellouts for an exciting team that featured Wendel Clark, Peter Forsberg, Joe Sakic and other aces who had catapulted Quebec to the top of the Northeast Division. Instead, the crowds at Le Colisée were conspicuously below capacity and remained that way throughout the season.

I had no difficulty understanding the fans' unhappiness. Vancouverites remembered how superstar Pavel Bure allegedly held the Canucks hostage during the 1994 Stanley Cup finals with the Rangers so that he could obtain a fabulous new contract. Others had watched players' union advocate Ken Baumgartner filibuster throughout the lockout as if he were getting a raw deal. Baumgartner, who on any given night would have been a fourth-stringer on the Anaheim Mighty Ducks, was earning $370,000 (U.S.) before the lockout and received a sizeable increase after it had ended. This for a part-time goon with little artistic value.

A few days after the Devils-Whalers game, I was at Nassau Coliseum for the opening night telecast of the Islanders home season. I was especially interested in the crowd reaction here because of the Isles dismal finish the previous year and the fact that the hated Rangers now owned the Stanley Cup.

I was pleased to note that the arena was filled just short of capacity and that the audience was as intensely behind the home club as ever before. As was the case with New Jersey, I had suspected that some of the more militant unionists among the Islanders would, perhaps, boycott me the way the Jets did columnist Scott Taylor. But when I ambled down the dressing-room corridor for a chat with coach Lorne Henning prior to the game, every player to a man was as cordial as he had been in the pre-lockout days. (Interestingly, not a single player voiced a word of displeasure from that point on through to the end of the Stanley Cup round in June.)

Way back in the summer of 1994, I had written my annual NHL prediction piece for *Inside Sports* magazine. As always, I ventured a guess as to the Stanley Cup champion in 1995 and decided upon the Devils who had lost to the Rangers in double overtime of the seventh game of the 1994 semifinals.

After watching New Jersey in the first weeks of the abbreviated campaign, I began suffering second thoughts about my choice. The Devils opened with several road games before returning to Byrne Meadowlands Arena and were depressingly lacklustre. Scott Stevens, who now was among the league's highest-paid performers, appeared distracted and nothing like the player who had been runner-up to Raymond Bourque for the Norris Trophy in 1994. Even goalie Martin Brodeur, who won rookie-of-the-year honours, seemed mortal as his club dog-paddled its way around a playoff berth, barely keeping its collective head above water.

There was no end to the explanations.

One had it that the players, as a group, were angry with owner John McMullen who was among the more militant owners. Another suggested that the Devils had overachieved in 1993-94 and now had slipped to a more realistic level; a theory which I believed may have had some merit. Others lamented the loss of Bernie Nicholls to the Chicago Blackhawks and the fact that his replacement, Jim Dowd, had suffered a recurrence of his shoulder injury.

Ironically, the player who was supposed to be the major problem for New Jersey turned out to be the Devils' major asset. Stephane Richer had been projected to be a physical target of every enemy player who had been angered by his comments made during the lockout.

The way it was written at the time, Richer sounded as if he was criticizing the NHLPA. He supposedly had said that if a secret vote was taken of all the players, the majority would have accepted the owners' proposal and returned to the ice. Richer had become a dirty word to union membership and talk of retaliatory action led me to think that it would have a terribly negative effect on the Devils' most skilled – and often dominating – forward.

Whether it was because they were a cohesive team or whether they chose to forgive Richer on grounds of free speech, the Devils welcomed their sharpshooter as if he had said nothing. Nor did the opposition appear especially vindictive at any time. For his part, Richer reacted with the verve and self-confidence of one who has courageously spoken his mind and now was in effect daring anyone to do something about it.

While other Devils floundered in an attempt to regain their momentum of yesteryear, Richer literally and figuratively moved full speed ahead. His scoring kept the club in the playoff hunt and his frankness arrested the attention of media types, some of whom had regarded him as a flake.

"What I said," Richer explained one day, "was that I don't see any human being liking to lose money and being in this situation. What I was saying was that if you took a vote of the players, everybody would like to go back on the ice and play the game. But it came out as something else when somebody picked out one quote and it got into the newspapers in New York.

"I wasn't talking about whether the deal was good or not. I was saying that I don't see anybody in the NHL being rich enough to say I have enough money to sit out a full year. On the other side, I said that if some guys have businesses and they know what business is all about, maybe they will understand the owners a little more because I have a business and I know what I'm talking about."

Other players had other reactions and a spate of lockout stories began spreading from locker room to locker room. While this one may be apocryphal, it did gain considerable circulation.

According to the tale published in the Montreal *Gazette*, union members were on a conference call to consider management's final offer. Line by line, the proposal was considered by Penguins' defenceman Larry Murphy who had been an NHLPA mainstay.

"Hey, that doesn't sound so bad," said Murphy, "why don't we take it?"

Marty McSorley, among the hardest of the union hardliners, took exception to Murphy's position.

"Hey, Murph," snapped McSorley, "where's your balls?"

To which Murphy purportedly shot back, "I don't think with my balls!"

If there was any bitterness engendered by the lockout, it was evident by the smaller crowds in some Canadian cities as well as hostility generated by those whose incomes were directly affected by the work stoppage. In some cases, teams released workers for the duration of the lockout and then rehired them. Some were never rehired.

The NHL furloughed Michael Berger, who had the title, "general manager, publishing." A key public relations and publishing staffer during the Ziegler administration, Berger was among many Zieglerites affected by the lockout. However, he was luckier than most; he was retained as an editorial consultant as well as a consultant to the FOX Network which began producing the weekly NHL games of the week. John Halligan, who had enormous public relations skills and friendship with every significant sports newsperson, was also given a leave but returned to the league compound after the lockout.

Simple wage earners across the spectrum were affected. "The strike put a hurtin' on me," said Jamie Gibson, one of two regular Zamboni drivers at USAir Arena, home of the Washington Capitals. "We don't get the overtime like we used to before the lockout." He estimated that the lockout had cost him 100 over-time hours.

"And," he added, "it has affected morale more than anything. There was nothing going on there for a long time. It was no fun."

An estimated 250 part-timers – food-service workers, parking attendants, cleaning personnel – were directly affected by the lockout at USAir Arena. "It hurt them a whole lot," said one of the workers. "It was devastating."

Chris Chelios' outrageous suggestion – that commissioner Gary Bettman and/or members of his family had a good chance of ending up on a hit list if the lockout persisted – could have had a devastating effect on the defenceman's career. However the NHL boss discreetly but firmly handled the matter. Chelios was flown to New York for a 45-minute conference with the commissioner and then was asked to sign a written apology. Bettman refused some critics' demands that he suspend Chelios.

"But," noted *Montreal Gazette* sports editor Red Fisher, "all is not forgiven. It never will be. The next time Chelly acts up on or off the ice, he can expect the book to be thrown at him. What he shouldn't expect for now and, perhaps forever, are telephone calls from the business arm of the league inviting him to appear in rich commercials."

With the new, abbreviated season, Chelios was on uncharacteristically good behaviour although the quality of his play hardly deteriorated. The same could not be said for other superstars. Wayne Gretzky, who orchestrated a questionable European tour during the lockout, supposedly would be in such excellent condition, he would lead Los Angeles to the top of the Pacific Division. Instead, The Great One stumbled at the gate, lost his gait and became a non-factor – along with his team – throughout the condensed campaign.

Doug Gilmour performed in a similar depressing style for the Toronto Maple Leafs, as did Pavel Bure in Vancouver. But nowhere was lockout fallout more deplorable than on Broadway where the 1994 Stanley Cup champion Rangers attempted to defend their title under new head coach Colin Campbell.

Although captain Mark Messier played to his capabilities, a number of Rangers – particularly Brian Leetch, winner of the 1994 Conn Smythe Trophy –

appeared to treat the season as one long sabbatical. My theory was that the Rangers collectively were suffering from a post-Cup hangover. They were still, figuratively at least, swilling the victory champagne. Among the league's highest-priced clubs, the Rangers disgraced themselves with desultory performances which were alibied away week by week until the Broadway Blueshirts almost missed a playoff berth.

If nothing else, the Rangers' disaster eloquently proved a point that had been made over and over by fiscally prudent owners such as John McMullen in New Jersey and Jeremy Jacobs in Boston: that lavish spending on players' salaries is not necessarily the key to success. McMullen, who was forced to overpay defenceman Scott Stevens, had long maintained that the Rangers had bought the 1994 Stanley Cup. Jacobs insisted over and over again that it was irresponsible to exceed one's reasonable budget.

"Our number one objective with this organization is to win," said Jacobs. "But I am not in business to lose money. I want winning teams and teams that make money. There is absolutely no correlation between spending money and having a consistent winner. None.

"The highest-paid team in the National Hockey League in 1994-95 was the Los Angeles Kings. They were also one of the worst. They didn't even make the playoffs. They stunk on the ice and they lost a ton of money. And they have also put themselves in a hole with those contracts that they won't be able to dig out of for quite a while.

"One of the highest-paid teams in the league was Buffalo. What did they win? They lost a ton of money. A lot of money.

"When you spend enormous amounts of money on a player's contract, you are taking a tremendous risk. Look at Pittsburgh. They have a fine team. They built most of it through the draft. But with the contract they have to pay [Mario] Lemieux and with him not playing, they are really in a bind for the future.

"Our philosophy with the Bruins is this: we will spend whatever it takes to win as long as it makes sense. I don't want Harry Sinden to spend just to spend. That's silly. But we will spend for value. If Harry tells me this is what we need to get the job done on a certain player, then he will get it. But fortunately for me, he doesn't want to do anything stupid, either.

"What you pay doesn't necessarily mean you win. A year ago, the New Jersey Devils had a lower payroll than us and they beat us in the playoffs. This year they had a higher payroll than us and they beat us in the playoffs. The difference was one player's contract from last year to this: Scott Stevens'. He had some things kick into his contract that put their payroll higher than ours. In the NHL, you can move several spots up or down on the payroll scale with just a few player contracts changing each year. For the most part, we have always been about in the middle of the league."

Jacobs was precisely on target.

The "Jacobs' Theory" was seriously considered by the New York Islanders' general manager Don Maloney whose club was torpedoed in 1994-95 by an inordinate spate of injuries that left the club vainly groping for a playoff berth. One of Maloney's most perplexing challenges centred around right wing Steve Thomas.

Earning $877,000 a year, Thomas had been one of the most productive and popular Islanders during the 1993-94 season. When his club ousted Florida from a playoff berth in the final week of that campaign, it was Thomas who provided both goals in a 2-0 clinching triumph over the Lightning at the Thunderdome.

In the eyes of many observers – not to mention lunchpail-carrying fans – Thomas was exceptionally well-paid for his efforts, but he didn't think so. Following the 1993-94 season Thomas began telling friends that he expected a significant increase and the talk continued through training camp, only to be temporarily halted during the lockout.

At least one friend of Thomas with connections to the team complained to me that Thomas' attitude was exceptionally negative and could contaminate the locker room. And when Thomas regrouped with his teammates in mid-January, Islanders' watchers kept a close eye on the forward to evaluate his performance.

What I saw was a well-paid athlete needlessly distracted by contract negotiations – not to mention wild demands – that were having a catastrophic effect on his game. Steve's one-timers that normally would be converted into goals were going off the heel of his stick, checks were missed and overall Thomas seemed out of synch.

What's more, Thomas was the first to admit it. Throughout what was becoming a keenly disappointing season, Thomas consistently underachieved when the Islanders most needed his contributions. His linemate, Pierre Turgeon, whose annual salary was $2.25 million, was no bargain either. Turgeon, who never seemed to have fully recovered from the behind-the-back clobbering administered by Dale Hunter in the 1993 playoffs, constantly disappointed and added to the club's demise.

As was the case with so many clubs, the salary issue directly and disturbingly impinged on performance. The same was true in New Jersey as it was on Long Island where Thomas continually disappointed. Across the Hudson River, you could substitute Claude Lemieux's name for Thomas' and get virtually the same result for almost the same reason: money.

Represented by my pal, Steve Freyer, Lemieux had emerged from ugly divorce proceedings and, according to the lawyer, was significantly strapped for cash. At $825,000 a year, Lemieux would have seemed to be well-paid by an objective outsider who would point out that Lemieux's salary was far, far above the national average. But Lemieux had seen teammate John MacLean's pact climb above $1.5 million so it was natural for Lemieux – and his agent – to press for a similar deal.

Freyer engaged Devils' president-general manager Lou Lamoriello in talks which got nowhere through the first half of the season. Lemieux's desultory performance was noticeable and troubling although he addressed the problem with only partially successful results. A preseason favourite to reach the Stanley Cup finals, the Devils stumbled through most of the campaign; their performance partially reflecting Lemieux's distraction over his contract.

A theory evolved that the poisonous relationship between the front offices of some teams and their players during the lockout would have a bitter aftereffect. This theory was best tested in Boston where Harry Sinden was the most visible and vocal member of management in the war against Bob Goodenow.

To a man, the Bruins had good reason to be angry at their boss. During the lockout, Sinden dismissed one NHLPA contract with the observation, "It was like giving a canoe to an Arab."

Shortly after the work stoppage began, Sinden recalled three players from his AHL team in Providence. Although none of them had figured in the Bruins' plans, Sinden now did not have to pay them. "Once the season started," noted David Shoalts in the *Globe and Mail* of Toronto, "no one would have been overly surprised to see the Bruins implode because of the strained relationships."

Yet the Brian Sutter-coached Bruins immediately secured a position in playoff range and remained competitive thereafter. If friction between Sinden and his employees existed, it was well-concealed.

"My players haven't shown me they're angry," said Sinden.

In fact, Sinden's post-lockout anger was betrayed on several occasions as he disgustedly observed colleagues overpaying their stickhandlers as if no lessons were learned from the labour crisis. One which Sinden found particularly galling was the Vancouver Canucks' decision to sign defenceman Jeff Brown to a four-year pact worth $7.8 million.

By any stretch of the imagination, the figure made no sense at all. Brown's skills placed him in the average-to-slightly-above-average category. At best, he seemed worth no more than a Curtis Leschyshyn or Sylvain Lefebvre, each of whom was earning $600,000.

"Although the Canucks had a lousy year," said Sinden, "they ended up getting to the Stanley Cup finals (1994). They didn't make any money doing it, but now they've signed a player for more money than Ray Bourque who's won 15 All-Star berths. How can I have sympathy any more? I give up."

Sinden's well-taken exasperation not only was directed at Pat Quinn, his Vancouver fraternity brother, but other free spenders such as the Rangers' Neil Smith and the Blues' chairman Michael Shanahan. "We go through a 105-day lockout and I don't see any signs that we've accomplished anything," said Sinden. Nothing. And the losing clubs, in terms of money, are the biggest culprits. It's their business. It's none of my business how they run their hockey clubs, but I can't listen to their crying anymore."

The temptation among media critics was to dismiss Sinden as some right-wing kook, when in fact, his points all were perfectly valid. In many ways, the lockout was a waste as agents and players pretended that management had merely been joking about their fiscal dilemma. But they knew that professional hockey had become a player's market. Several cities were clamouring for NHL franchises while minor league hockey was undergoing an unprecedented boom.

Under the aegis of Bob Ufer, the International Hockey League loomed as a distinct threat to the NHL had the lockout not been settled. Ray Bourque, for one, was negotiating to move to the IHL's Denver Grizzlies a week before the NHL-NHLPA deal was brokered.

But "The I," as it is affectionately known, remained a thorn in the NHL's side. Without asking Gary Bettman's permission, it brazenly opened its own franchises in such NHL strongholds as Detroit, Chicago, Los Angeles and San Francisco. IHL markets included top-rated cities like Houston, Kansas City, Minneapolis-St. Paul, Cleveland and Las Vegas. Before the NHL could establish a viable European base, Ufer declared that his outfit would install a division on the continent.

While all this was going on, Bettman Inc. struggled through its makeshift 1995 season. Lockout anger notwithstanding, attendance remained remarkably robust in many areas, especially relatively new territories such as Anaheim, Miami and San Jose where sellouts were the norm despite teams of modest talent.

Some critics denigrated the 48-game schedule as insulting to the fans and claimed that it was the cause for erratic play. Nevertheless, with its "Game On" theme, it allowed big-league hockey an opportunity to regenerate itself and I personally was fascinated by the homestretch, particularly as it affected the Islanders, Devils and defending champion Rangers.

Despite an unconscionable number of injuries, the Islanders remained within sight of a playoff berth and actually pulled off a monstrous win that could have catapulted them into contention. The aftermath, however, demonstrated to me precisely what was wrong with the game in terms of IQ (as in Intensity Quotient).

The episode began with a typically heated game between the Rangers and Islanders at Nassau Coliseum. Oozing with talent the visitors appeared capable of demolishing the home team on this night and from the opening face-off penetrated the Isles' defence and tested goalie Tommy Soderstrom. It would be an understatement to report that Soderstrom made a dozen truly difficult saves over two periods, protecting his crease. Having one goal with which to work, he dazzled throughout the third, robbing Rangers such as Mark Messier and Adam Graves through the final 20 minutes.

During my post-game interview with Soderstrom, I mentioned that in all my years of covering the NHL, his performance this night was among the 10 best I had ever seen. Perhaps even among the five best.

The win was an enriching one for the floundering Isles and the kind which should have launched them to a galvanic performance in their next contest on Saturday afternoon at Hartford; a game we were televising back to New York. Although we broadcasters technically are not supposed to get overly excited about such things, I was looking forward to the Whalers match with considerable enthusiasm.

Hartford was a beatable club running neck and neck with the Islanders for a playoff spot. The victory over the Rangers should have provided the Isles with the tonic to skate the Whalers right off the ice. At least that's what I was thinking. After all, the better the team plays, the more magnetic our broadcast is likely to be.

But my fellow announcers Jiggs McDonald and Ed Westfall opened the show with a cautionary note. Time and again the underdog Isles had beaten a superior Rangers' team and, inevitably, they then would take on a lesser club and play like losers. It was the classic build-up-to-a-letdown and one we hoped would not happen again.

An hour before game-time I examined notes in our TV studio which just happened to adjoin the visitors' dressing room. A few of the Islanders walked in to tape their sticks and shoot the breeze. One of them was Travis Green, a curly-haired centre whose potential had remained unfulfilled for two years.

I liked Green as a character. He was amiable, occasionally funny and always available. He was the kind of kid you wanted to make good although management kept whispering that he was a chronic underachiever. But on Thursday night against the Rangers, he was dominating and capped the evening by winning the final face-off from Mark Messier.

"Win this and the club could be on its way," I mentioned.

Green nodded his approval but added little more encouragement. No matter. As long as he worked his tail off on the ice, all would be well. Or, so I hoped.

Soon after the opening face-off, I walked down to my ice-level location near the visitors' dressing room. The Civic Center was nearly packed and its crowd bellowed as the home team immediately bisected the Islanders' defence and forced a face-off in the New York end. Hartford had just obtained Glenn Featherstone from the Rangers in a deal for Pat Verbeek – a deal that evoked Harry Sinden's priceless comment: "Verbeek is made for the Rangers; he's overpaid!"

Featherstone is a rugged defenceman known for his bulk, not his scoring ability. But on this play, as he patrolled the right point, the puck skimmed to him and he took a 60-foot shot at Soderstrom. I watched the puck meander through the air toward an unscreened Soderstrom before it passed the goalie into the net. This same Soderstrom had stopped shots 50 times as difficult in the previous game and now this!

It was excruciating to watch the Islanders from this point on to the conclusion some 58 minutes of play later. They alternately seemed disinterested, distracted and disillusioned (perhaps by Soderstrom's erratic goaltending), so it was hardly a surprise that the game ended with a Whalers' rout. Green, from whom I had expected more, was virtually invisible all game although he had considerable company.

On the drive home with my producer, Kevin Meininger, I lamented the sorry effort they generated. "You've seen the Islanders' season end with this game," I mentioned.

"I can't argue with that," said Meininger turning the car into a McDonald's driveway near the Connecticut Turnpike so that we could drown our sorrows in root beer and Big Macs.

For all intents and purposes it was the end. Periodically, Thomas would complain about his salary distractions and Soderstrom would rediscover his magic, but the Islanders never could put enough wins together to make a serious run. Shortly before the trade deadline they shipped Pierre Turgeon and Vladimir Malakhov to the Canadiens for Mathieu Schneider, Kirk Muller and Chris Darby.

It was a blockbuster deal and big stuff for us, especially since we had a game with the Rangers at Madison Square Garden on the next night. While many in the crew were fond of Turgeon as a person and artist, we were just as delighted to see him move on to Montreal. The same could be said for Malakhov. The tall Russian had always been aloof off the ice and thoroughly unpredictable on the pond.

One night he would execute a spectacular foray from end to end and another night he would mindlessly pass the puck to an obvious opponent who then would score. To have him replaced by a superior Manhattan-born defenceman of Jewish extraction was almost too good to be true.

The corridors outside the Islanders' dressing room at Madison Square Garden buzzed with that special excitement of a just-completed trade two hours before the game with the Rangers. Wearing his oversized smile, Schneider arrived with Darby and we exchanged hellos. Schneider's father, Sam, is one of the world's best talkers and he was due to arrive later for the game – and a between-periods interview with me.

However, the TV gang sensed that something was missing when the Islanders' press aides turned their grins to frowns and began pacing the corridor. "Muller isn't here," Jiggs McDonald whispered, "and it doesn't look like he's showing up."

"Any reason?" I wondered.

"Good question," said McDonald.

Muller, supposedly the ultimate team player, was nowhere to be found. Finally general manager Don Maloney revealed that Muller would not be playing that night. Apparently the trade was sufficiently shocking that he couldn't get himself to jet down to New York and join his new employer.

Cynics among the press corps guessed that Muller's absence had as much to do about money as it did about the trauma of leaving the team he had captained. I grilled Muller about it when he finally did arrive on Long Island a few days later. He insisted that the emotional upheaval was too much to take at the time. Money, according to Muller, was not the object of his brief but unpleasant absence. (The Islanders beat the Rangers without Muller, but with him in the lineup, they faded out of playoff contention.) Even after he had become a regular, Muller dropped hints that he might not remain with the club after the season; that he might demand a trade or whatever.

I found this terribly disconcerting, especially since he had been sought as a potential captain of the hockey club. After the season had ended, an Islanders' official confided that money was the object. Muller had been paid $1.7 million but in Canadian funds. He wanted the sum converted to American currency, which would be substantially more than its Canadian counterpart. Not surprisingly, the general staff agreed to the request. Some observers argued that the Isles had no choice. Others within the NHL high command winced and deplored the runaway inflation.

"Nobody wants to hear it," said Flyers' general manager Bob Clarke, "but we're paying too much for salaries. That's the whole bottom line. If we're smart enough and tough enough to hold the line on salaries until we get our revenues up, we'll be all right, but the big money is not there right now. And it may not be until the next generation of players comes along.

"We don't know when it's going to come, or if it will. We're all hoping that with the FOX TV contract and all the stuff we're doing that things will go well, but you don't know.

"Obviously, the lockout was the start of putting the brakes on salaries. Now we've got to see what the finished product of collective bargaining leads to; see how we all do."

Based on events during the homestretch, ownership was not doing well. Wherever I turned, as the shortened season rushed to a close, money stories took precedence over game stories. Dale Hawerchuk declared that he would leave Buffalo because he was unhappy with a $1.3 million annual salary; Trevor Linden was despairing over his $1 million a year pay in Vancouver; Jeremy Roenick couldn't abide $1.1 million in Chicago; and so it went to the abject disgust of fans who somehow remained more interested in the hockey than the haggling.

But, as the citizens of Quebec, Winnipeg and New Jersey would learn – as if they didn't already know – the name of the game was money. Big money. And that's why each venue would undergo a terrible catharsis in the spring of 1995. As it happened, I found myself in the midst of one of them.

14

....

FROM QUEBEC TO DENVER:
THE AMERICANIZATION AND POSSIBLE DEATH OF HOCKEY AS WE KNOW IT

There never has been a more hockey-minded city than the capital of La Belle Province de Québec.

Quebec City abounds with outdoor rinks, has a rich history with the ice game dating back to an NHL franchise called the Quebec Bulldogs and has celebrated many local heroes – Jean Beliveau, Camille Henry and more recently Joe Sakic – as fervently as any metropolis on the continent.

By any stretch of logic, Quebec City should have been able to support a major league team. For most of the franchise's life its arena, Le Colisée, was virtually filled to capacity for nearly every home game of the Nordiques and the team dominated the local media, both print and electronic.

"Hockey talk was the main topic of conversation," said longtime sports columnist Claude Larochelle of *Le Soleil*. "It should have stayed that way."

In 1980, it would have. But this was 1995, the dawning of Bettman Inc., a swing toward Disney-type ownership, the divine right of FOX Network TV and the NBA-ing of the NHL. For any who expected an easy, hockey-loving ambience of yesteryear, all bets were off.

To say the least, I found this somewhat disconcerting as old values – some of which were truly valuable – seemed to be discarded as quickly as Eric Lindros banged bodies. But anyone who studied the evolutionary process at the NHL bunker on Sixth Avenue and 50th Street understood that big money took precedence over anything else on the priority list.

"Gary Bettman's plan was simple to understand," said a former NHL employee who had studied Bettman's transition from the Gil Stein era. "His agenda calls for him to make the owners as rich as possible."

But to do so, Bettman also has had to be politically correct. He learned early in his administration that Canadians were hypersensitive about their hockey.

Beware, Bettman, beware. Any suggestion that small markets such as Winnipeg, Quebec or Edmonton had no place in the greater NHL only served to invite the wrath of power brokers north of the border. But in terms of the league's future, Winnipeg, Quebec and Edmonton – or at least one or two of them – had to go. Where, when and how was another story to be addressed whenever possible.

As the abridged season unfolded in mid-winter 1995, I began to sense that a Bettman plan was unfolding. It appeared to be broad in range and pegged to the premise that sooner or later every NHL arena had to be upgraded to whatever he deemed big-league standards through the next century. Replacement of old rinks such as Boston Garden, Buffalo's Aud and Chicago Stadium became an imperative, not an option.

Corporate boxes became a major revenue source where once they had been an afterthought. On visits to Winnipeg and Quebec City, Bettman began hinting more broadly that new arenas – or vastly refurbished older ones – were an absolute must if the franchises were to remain operative in the NHL. The hint was that these franchises could easily be transferred to eagerly awaiting American cities which coveted big-league hockey.

"I don't view this as blackmail," said the commissioner. "My discussions with the mayors of Quebec and Winnipeg have pointed out that if they want to have a sports franchise in the 21st century, they must appropriately house them. If they choose not to, that doesn't make it a bad city. The cities are simply making a business decision on whether it's worth having a sports franchise."

Remember the secret words, "business decision." The two words would underscore the bottom line for virtually every move made by Bettman Inc. As a result, I couldn't help sense that his NBA orientation was playing a bigger and bigger part in his NHL planning. For one whose roots were deeply planted in hockey, I couldn't help feel somewhat awed by the increasing numbers of non-hockey people who were added to his staff, some coming over from the National Football League and some from Major League Baseball.

These were big market people with neither cultural nor historic ties to the Winnipegs and Quebecs of the world. When they looked at the league and its future, they could see Canada's decline in many areas or an Americanization of the league. To wit:

*   The Vancouver Canucks' team was purchased by a Seattle billionaire, John McCaw, whose controlling interest dwarfed that of the Canadian Griffiths family which previously ran the club.
*   Canadian currency more and more was being regarded by Americans as if it were as valueless as "money" in the game of Monopoly.
*   Bettman centralized league operations in New York, leaving Montreal and Toronto NHL offices as distant outposts of no consequence.
*   The number of Americans and Europeans in the league was increasing while the number of Canadians was dwindling.

*   Formerly run by Canadian-born Alan Eagleson, the NHL Players'
      Association was now orchestrated by an American, Bob Goodenow,
      who had no special urge to favour Canada.

Goodenow's players couldn't care less whether they played north or south
of the 49th parallel as long as the money was big. "If you had a choice between
an ideal situation in Canada and an ideal situation in the States," said Kirk Muller
when he still played in Montreal, "90 percent of the guys in this room would be
out of here. Just like my friends who have businesses in Kingston, Ontario. A lot
of them are trying to move 35 miles over the border because it's cheaper to function in the States."

During the late 1960s, I had befriended an aspiring Canadian-born play-
wright who had moved to Manhattan and lived near our Upper West Side apartment. Rick Salutin was as ardent a hockey fan as any artist I have ever encountered and eventually (1977) wrote a play about his favourite team, Les
Canadiens. In his preface he noted that to Canadians hockey was "the sole assur-
ance we have a culture." In conversations with Salutin – and in my encounters in
Canada – this was as accurate a representation as one could get.

Nearly two decades after he began writing his play, Salutin could view the
Americanization of hockey from a more cynical perspective. "Canadians aren't
sure if it's the War of 1812 again or whether it's simply the octopus quality of
business, the tentacles clutching the game.

"The lockout hit Canadians more than Americans because the elements of
national culture and mythology are more fragile in Canada than in the United
States. In the U.S. they have baseball, but they also have lots of other stuff. In a
general sense hockey is one of the few things that makes this place coherent. In
the U.S. there's no worry the country will cease to exist.

"Here, there's a sense the country is falling apart. With free trade, the threat
of Quebec separation, issues of national sovereignty, hockey assumes a sense of
national loss."

That sense became more evident to me as the Jets were being wooed to
Minnesota and the Nordiques to Atlanta or Denver since both cities were vying
for Marcel Aubut's club. Phoenix was not far behind, along with Houston and
Portland, to name a few contenders.

I had held the false hope – primarily based on misleading headlines based on
misleading quotes – that the so-called "ownership victory" in the CBA war would
have strengthened the smaller markets. And when Bettman hired Bortz and
Company, a Denver consulting outfit, to devise a plan to help the have-nots, I
actually thought some sort of revenue-sharing program would solve the problem.

Naturally, I should have known better. The "have" teams such as Boston,
Chicago, Detroit, New York Rangers and Toronto wanted no part of anything like
a 60-40 home-visitor split used by the NFL. "I thought communism died," barked
Harry Sinden of the wealthy Bruins. "You won't see it revived in the NHL."

As I watched the Nordiques inch closer and closer to a transfer and the Jets high command regularly confer with Minneapolis suitors, I felt a concern. They were, however, distant partners with no direct effect on my good and welfare; or so I thought.

But then, one day late in the season, I found myself slowly slipping into the fiscal whirlpool. It seemed like the most preposterous of all scenarios, but there it was in black and white. The city of Nashville, Tennessee, was courting *our* New Jersey Devils. My stomach felt as if it had been hit with a pile-driver.

15

••

McMULLEN AND THE MICKEY MOUSE CLUB:
THE DEVILS STRIVE FOR RESPECT

When a huge, white, state-of-the-art arena took shape on swampland in the Meadowlands of New Jersey within view of Manhattan's skyscrapers, it seemed a logical home for a National Hockey League team. Madison Square Garden invariably was sold out for New York Rangers home games while in the early 1980s the SRO sign usually was hung at Nassau Coliseum where the New York Islanders were in the midst of a four-year Stanley Cup run.

With a seating capacity of 19,040 for hockey, the Meadowlands Arena seemed a natural for an expansion team, a point that was underlined when the Philadelphia Flyers and Rangers played an exhibition game there and filled the place. If two non-Jersey teams could do so splendidly, imagine how much better the state's first major league club in any sport would fare.

I wasn't so sure about the answer to that question and in 1982 I expressed my opinions in an article, "Can The Metropolitan Area Support Three NHL Teams?"

My doubts were rooted in the fact that the NHL never had a situation where there had been three clubs in one greater urban community. I pointed out that Montreal once boasted the Maroons, favoured by the English-speaking fans, and the Canadiens, representing the Francophones. Prior to World War II New York featured both the Americans and Rangers playing out of Madison Square Garden. Both the Maroons and Americans were victims of the Great Depression and disappeared despite a loyal following.

But Dr. John J. McMullen, a shipping tycoon and owner of the Houston Astros baseball team, had been sold a bill of goods by the New Jersey Sports and Exposition Authority, the NHL and some of his personal friends, including then governor Brendan Byrne.

"The governor came down to training camp with me when I had the Astros," McMullen recalled. "He asked me if I could help bring a sports franchise to the new building and said he'd appreciate if I did so. I've lived in New Jersey all my life and I thought it would be good for the state if it had its own big-league team. Without trying to over-glorify it, that was the reason I bought the Colorado Rockies."

The purchase date was June 30, 1982. Having failed to win sufficient fan support in Denver, the Rockies were sold to McMullen and John C. Whitehead, a leading investment banker who would become U.S. Deputy Secretary of State during the Ronald Reagan Administration. Byrne was the third man in the tri-umvirate and even had the Meadowlands Arena named after him.

Soon after he took command of his team – renamed the New Jersey Devils – McMullen read my article questioning the ability of Greater New York-New Jersey to successfully embrace three NHL teams. "At the time," he later told me over dinner, "I didn't believe you. Everybody was telling me that I'd sell out every game."

It was the beginning of more than a decade of disillusionment that soon would be compounded by the neighbouring Rangers, Flyers and Islanders, each of whom demanded territorial indemnity. In 1982 McMullen agreed to pay the Rangers $9.2 million, the Islanders $8 million and the Flyers $2.5 million for invading their protected territory. With league approval, the Devils suspended payments within five seasons, leaving a considerable outstanding balance. But the disappointment, which eventually led McMullen in 1995 to consider an unlikely move to Nashville, was only beginning.

From the start, he mistakenly assumed that the Sports Authority was both partner and friend, as it should have been in a partnership such as this. Instead, McMullen discovered that Authority boss Bob Mulcahy was hardly the pal that he thought he would be and, perhaps, was quite the opposite.

"I brought Mulcahy to every meeting with the NHL prior to the transaction," McMullen elaborated, "fully expecting that the Authority would be helpful and cooperative. And from the minute I committed myself, the administration had changed and they brought a new chairman in and I suddenly walked into a very confrontational and difficult management at the Sports Authority.

"At that point, I should have said, 'Look, let's go back to Denver.' I made a serious mistake and I acknowledge it. But it's a mistake. I think that is understandable. First of all, all the publicity surrounding it. Then I had already committed and paid, I think $8.5 million to Peter Gilbert (for the Rockies) and had already agreed on things. I should not have completed the transaction."

But he did and thus began a rather rocky relationship between McMullen, the NHL and, of course, the Sports Authority. Within the league hierarchy, McMullen was part of a small but very thoughtful minority which included St. Louis Blues' owner Harry Ornest. At one preseason meet-the-press breakfast at the Meadowlands Arena, McMullen mentioned to me how frustrated he was with

John Ziegler's administration by select committee and how Blackhawks' owner Bill Wirtz was helping command the league through his league chairmanship.

What impressed me most about the man was his brash candor. Also the fact that he was a Navy man meant a lot. My father had served in the U.S. Navy on a minelayer in the North Sea during World War I. A graduate of the Naval Academy, McMullen had been an officer during World War II and remained a key figure in the Navy for many years thereafter. His pugnacity was evident from the moment he joined the NHL fraternity especially after the notorious Gretzky affair.

It was bad enough that he had been stuck with an inadequate team and was playing in the shadow of the championship Islanders and fat-cat Rangers, but his club almost instantly became the subject of ridicule; and from the unlikeliest source, hockey's foremost player spokesman.

Wayne Gretzky had become king of the NHL by the time McMullen bought the Devils, but he was a benevolent despot in his role as hockey's ultimate performer; an ambassador of goodwill, so to speak. But on November 19th, 1983, that all changed. McMullen's Devils limped into Northlands Coliseum with a 2-17-0 record – four points in 19 games.

New Jersey's general manager-coach Billy MacMillan started Ron Low in goal, knowing that Low had tended goal for the Oilers over four seasons. Armed with the hardest shooters in the NHL, the Oilers peppered their old teammate unmercifully and emerged with a 13-4 victory. It was the largest score ever run up against the hapless Devils. Gretzky, who had eight points on three goals and five assists, held court after the game.

It must be remembered that The Great One had been a close friend of the Devils' victimized goaltender and felt for Low's predicament. Also noteworthy is the fact that reporters traditionally bait athletes into answers they might not otherwise want to give. And so it was with Gretzky on this night.

He was asked about the Devils' performance and delivered a peroration that would have reverberations right into McMullen's heart. "It got to a point where it wasn't even funny," said Gretzky. "How long has it been for them? Three years? Five? Seven? Probably closer to nine. Well, it's time they got their act together. They're ruining the whole league.

"They had better stop running a Mickey Mouse operation and put somebody on ice. It's not a question of not working. It's a question of talent. I feel sorry for Ronnie and New Jersey. The 37 shots we took were all good shots. They struggled in Kansas City; they were awful in Colorado and now look what is happening."

For about eight hours it appeared that Gretzky's comments would be lost in the mountain of weekend sports stories. I had been covering an Islanders game that night and listened to the Edmonton rout on the radio returning from Long Island to Manhattan. But the next day, which was Sunday, the sh— hit the fan. Someone phoned and asked whether I'd heard Gretzky's remarks which then were read to me. On Monday the headlines roared, "GRETZKY TAKES SLAP

AT DEVILS' ORGANIZATION." That was in *USA Today*. The *New York Post* put it another way. "GRETZKY: DEVILS ARE MICKEY MOUSE TEAM."

Naturally, the quotes reached McMullen's office and he reacted with appropriate fury. He dispatched letters of protest, but it was too late to alter the image. The Devils were equated with Mickey Mouse and that was that. What's more the label stuck for years as McMullen vainly attempted to construct a winner.

McMullen fired MacMillan shortly after the Gretzky affair and hired Max McNab as general manager while Tom McVie was brought in as head coach. Marshall Johnston was named director of player personnel. McMullen's Devils hardly transformed into playoff contenders, but they showed more life under McVie and, perhaps, they showed too much in the eyes of some cynics.

It was at this point in time when I came to appreciate McMullen's innate sense of honesty. This was early in 1984, the year that Mario Lemieux was the outstanding Junior performer on the continent. Every sane hockey person understood that Lemieux would be the first player selected in the next draft and would automatically become a franchise cornerstone for the next decade. The Devils, because of their ineptitude, were in excellent position to finish last and thereby draft Lemieux.

One other team had a crack at Lemieux and that was Pittsburgh, but on the basis of roster quality the Penguins should have finished ahead of New Jersey by at least five or six points and thereby miss Lemieux.

But Pittsburgh wanted Lemieux badly, very badly. Several commentators and insiders held the view that the Penguins were so desperate for Lemieux they would ensure that they finished last. To do so, they would lose hockey games they ordinarily might have won. Naturally, there never has been anyone who would publicly articulate this view, although it has been commonly shared by many journalists and NHL insiders, amid broad hints. Benching regulars and inserting untried rookies, the Penguins continued losing and supporting the cynics' view. When the issue was raised, the Penguin general staff emphatically denied it.

At this point, McMullen could very well have instructed McVie to do likewise, but as much as the Devils coveted Lemieux, McMullen refused to follow suit. "We're here to win hockey games," said McVie, echoing his owner's philosophy. "It's the honourable thing to do."

McMullen's Devils then won games on March 6th over the Penguins and March 17th against Boston, ensuring a fifth-place finish for themselves and Lemieux for Pittsburgh. McMullen's pick was Kirk Muller, a tenacious, hard-driving centre who eventually would become captain of the team.

In the meantime, the Devils' owner continued suffering the embarrassment of non-playoff teams as coach after coach came and went. I attended just about every announcement always made at the restaurant adjoining the club offices – inappropriately named Winners – for the usual optimistic party line.

McMullen always was there and we began to get chummy as the seasons went along. His general manager, Max McNab, had become a good friend and confidant and it bothered me that McNab couldn't seem to deliver a winner. His coach Doug Carpenter came close a couple of times, but by 1987, the boss decided that a change was in order. Club president Bob Butera was released and McNab was bumped up to a vice-presidency. With that decision, McMullen made the most significant move in his franchise's history. He hired Providence College's athletic director Lou Lamoriello to run his club.

A former hockey coach, Lamoriello was not your run-of-the-mill manager. The native of Providence was out of the traditional GM loop and a major gamble for McMullen.

To me, Lamoriello was an intriguing choice; an American with no NHL experience, but one who I had known through the hockey grapevine. We had spoken a few times when he still was at Providence and had come to know each other through *The Hockey News*.

A few days after he took over the reins, Lamoriello and I had lunch. We exchanged views on the team, its coaching, public relations, just about everything. Being a part of the SportsChannel Devils' broadcasting team – which I was at that time – I wanted to see the club do well. After all, the better the team, the more fun it – usually, but not always – is to broadcast.

Lamoriello retained Carpenter as coach, but after a humiliating 9-3 loss to the Rangers at Madison Square Garden on December 16, 1987, I sensed that Carpenter's goose was cooked. The McMullen-Garden rivalry had been growing by the year with the Devils' boss facing the fact that so many metropolitan area fans rooted for the New York club. "It's like they all have Ranger genes when they're born," he lamented.

On the morning of January 26, 1988, I received a hurried phone call from Dave Freed, one of the Devils' publicists. "Press conference at noon!"

That could mean only one thing; and it was – a new coach. Carpenter had been fired and replaced by Jim Schoenfeld, the ebullient, redheaded, former defenceman. Frankly, I don't get overly excited about press conferences, but this one had a genuinely upbeat air about it.

Carpenter, for his many virtues – and he did have many – betrayed a negative charisma quotient. Part of it may have been a result of the team he coached, but the other part simply had to do with his severe personality. By contrast, Schoenfeld bubbled like a just-opened seltzer bottle and would become the catalyst for one of the NHL's most gripping stretch runs.

Apparently out of a playoff berth for the umpteenth time, the Devils scored two short-handed goals in Washington to defeat the Capitals, 4-2. From that point on, they sprinted forward thanks to the sensational goaltending of Sean Burke. Still, as they approached the final weekend of the season, they still trailed the hated Rangers for the final playoff berth. It came down to a pair of games on Sunday night: Quebec at New York and the Devils at Chicago.

Even if the Rangers won – the game at Madison Square Garden was an hour earlier – New Jersey could clinch with a win against the Blackhawks. That night I was a guest on New York's "Channel 5 News" with Bill Mazer. Prior to the telecast, I watched the Rangers blank the Nordiques, 3-0, and then switched to the Devils game.

As it happened New Jersey rallied to tie the game late in the third period, forcing overtime. A tie would do them no good; it was win or they were out of it.

Before the overtime began, Mazer had to go up to his set since the show was almost ready to begin. Hockey was going to be the main topic which is why I was there for commentary. He wanted to make sure we got the Devils' score in, even if it meant doing it in the middle of the news.

What Mazer did was assign a runner to watch the game in the studio. The runner was to come up to tell us if anyone scored and relate the final outcome. I remember being there a long time without hearing a word and I assumed that was bad news for the Devils. I thought that the game would end in a tie and the whole season would go up in smoke. So, I waited and waited and waited. Finally, the runner walked onto the fringe of Mazer's "Sports Extra" set with a huge piece of cardboard and the writing: JOHN MACLEAN – 2:21 OF OVERTIME.

I did a doubletake. It was as if I had to see the cardboard over and over to realize that it was for real. After the show, I was still shaking my head. I went to the bar down the block and gulped two Bloody Marys.

So, it was onto the playoffs for me, the Devils and our SportsChannel broadcasts. In the opening round, the Devils upset the Islanders and then went up against Washington, a heavy favourite to beat the upstarts. But once again, the Devils would not fold. They pushed the Capitals to a seventh game and won it on a late goal by MacLean.

The lockerroom scene was straight out of Bedlam with McMullen excitedly pumping the hands of his players. Watching him, I sensed that he felt more like a kid than some of the young fans who were following his hockey club. He walked over to me, grabbed my paw and said, "This is some hockey team, isn't it?"

That it was, especially after extending Boston to another seven-game set before capitulating. More importantly, in the political sense, was McMullen's bold decision to challenge the NHL – meaning president John Ziegler, chairman of the board Bill Wirtz and the officials – and go to court.

McMullen's defiance was both unprecedented and infuriating to the Establishment; which is why I was so tickled with his brash response. He believed in his cause and simply would not be pushed around; not even by a Wirtz. And if it meant going before a judge to prove his point, so be it.

"Why they wanted me to violate a court order and put the NHL in contempt of court – it's very embarrassing," said Wirtz. "I don't think at the time they (McMullen and Lamoriello) realized what they were doing. That was not a nice thing to do."

But Wirtz, whose hand was forced by McMullen, had to give the order to play the game with backup officials since president Ziegler was nowhere to be found.

After New Jersey lost Game Seven to Boston, it was freely predicted that McMullen's daring move would have repercussions. In fact, McMullen's own comment proved to be most prophetic: "This is not finished," he exclaimed.

The statement was open to considerable interpretation, including my own. I felt the statement had to do with the extraordinarily tight fraternity comprised of referees and linesmen. Travelling alone from city to city, the zebras lead a life of partial solitude, often feeling paranoid about criticism from players, coaches, managers and the media. Insult one referee and, in a sense, you insult them all.

With that in mind, it hardly was surprising that in my opinion, the Devils were subconsciously targeted by the zebras in the 1988-89 season. The officials were going to avenge Koharski and McMullen's Devils would pay the price. In game after game, they illogically got the short end of the officiating and – with some help from their own ineptitude and overconfidence – missed the playoffs.

In time Schoenfeld would be fired and replaced by John Cunniff, who in turn was replaced by Tom McVie who was replaced by Herb Brooks. From time to time the Devils would make headway, but their failure to exploit the 1988 miracle finish with a second straight playoff berth did irreparable damage and severely curtailed their fan growth at a time when the Rangers continued to be a major attraction and competitor.

Meanwhile, McMullen and I gradually were becoming closer friends, as was the case with Lamoriello. My wife, Shirley, and I had dinner with Lamoriello once a year. There was plenty of hockey talk but all off-the-record. By this time Lamoriello had been developing an iron-fisted image, although it wasn't apparent away from the rink. Those who knew him from his Providence days and had dealt with him on hockey matters reiterated that he was one of the most misunderstood characters in the business and that was the feeling that we shared.

Because McMullen continued to be the iconoclast, I found myself constantly in his corner. While NHL traditionalists scoffed at the idea of Russians playing in the majors, the Devils' owner told his staff as early as 1983 that they should draft Soviet players, presuming good ones became available.

"My feeling was that changes in the European political situation could come about and bring an easing of relations between East and West," said McMullen. "If that happened, we might be able to lure a couple of players to the Devils. At least it was worth a try."

At the June 1983 draft, the Devils' eighth round pick was a defenceman named Viacheslav Fetisov of the Soviet Union. By 1988, Lamoriello was pressing the search and on July 7, 1989, I attended another milestone press conference at the Winners Club. Fetisov and Sergei Starikov, another defenceman, were signed to New Jersey contracts. "It was a long battle," said Dr. McMullen, "but better late than never."

McMullen cornered me after the press conference dissolved. It was obvious he was pleased with himself and he had every right to be. However, it also was evident that he wished that the event had happened six years earlier when Fetisov was in his prime. "I'm glad I made the move," he said, chuckling in his inimitable way. "You can see he's a quality person."

The good doctor expected quality from his personnel as well as loyalty. The loyalty theme – something that was rooted in his youth and naval days – was among McMullen's most powerful and laudable traits. I noticed this for the first time when Pat Verbeek talked his way into hot water with management.

Verbeek, who had played on a line with Kirk Muller and Aaron Broten, had been a star of the 1988 playoffs, but slipped noticeably the following year. He developed a reputation as a whiner and soon lost favour with Lamoriello because of his contract demands. He was dealt to Hartford for Sylvain Turgeon in 1989.

It was a significant deal in more than one respect, but most of all it underlined the point that sedition – or disloyalty as viewed by management – would not be tolerated on a McMullen team. This philosophy would be emphasized even more two years later after the Devils had once again become an attractive playoff team.

By now Muller had become the captain and symbol of the team. Tenacious, effervescent and productive, Muller epitomized the lunchpail, hard-working style that appealed to many fans who preferred that brand of hockey over the more artistic kind delivered by the Rangers. Captain Kirk, as he was affectionately known around Byrne Arena, was reaching the prime of his playing career and the Devils looked better than ever as they led the Penguins, three games to two, in the best-of-seven opening round.

In Game Six at the Meadowlands, New Jersey scored a quick goal against substitute goalie Frank Pieterangelo, then fell behind only to tie the score on a tip-in by Laurie Boschman. However, the long-running referee's curse struck again. Despite a video replay that clearly indicated otherwise, a goal was waved off by the zebra. Eventually the Devils lost Game Six and then Game Seven in Pittsburgh.

Muller was a monstrous disappointment. He did not score a goal and collected a mere two assists over the seven games. Had he played to his potential, the Devils surely would have beaten Pittsburgh and moved closer to the Stanley Cup. This did not elude McMullen's notice nor did he ignore Muller's walk-out during the September training camp. In McMullen's eyes this was a deplorable move for a captain. Before the 1991-92 season began Muller was traded to Montreal for Stephane Richer and Tom Chorske. If ever an owner was directly conveying a message to a player – not to mention his team – about loyalty, this was it.

McMullen's loyalty extended to his general manager, Lou Lamoriello, who was the target of imbalanced reporting. When the Devils did well, he received scant credit and when they lost he was overwhelmingly blasted. As one reporter who covered the team mentioned (on condition of anonymity), "The guys on the beat were all Rangers' fans and couldn't wait to rip Lou. They were fans first and reporters second."

What piqued McMullen more than anything was what appeared to be the treatment he received from New Jersey's biggest-selling newspaper, the *Star-Ledger*. Instead of giving the local team an advantage in coverage, the *Ledger* played it even or sometimes favoured the rival Rangers from Manhattan. It would be difficult to imagine a tilt toward an out-of-town team by a local newspaper in any other community.

As for McMullen, the more time I spent with him, the more I enjoyed his abrasive yet amusing personality. One day I decided to do something unusual; I phoned him and invited the tycoon and his wife, Jackie, to dinner. I told him it was a payback for a dinner he had invited Shirley and I to at Monmouth College where he was honoured for his contributions to New Jersey education.

We met at The Meadowlands, where I interviewed him for about a half-hour. The focus was on the NHL's future and specifically its labour problems. He made it clear that a basketball-type salary cap was an imperative in the NHL's next Collective Bargaining Agreement. Until that moment, I hadn't even thought about it, but McMullen spelled out the details and how important it was for big-league hockey's fiscal well-being.

Then we drove to an Italian restaurant in Hoboken and he spun yarns about his youth in New Jersey. We talked about the poor contract the NHL had cut with ESPN and the state of the game. His wife, Jackie, met us for dinner on the restaurant's rooftop. A wisp of a breeze put just the right topper on a balmy summer evening as the subject drifted from sports to politics. After telling me how destructive baseball had become and how much happier he was in hockey, McMullen began talking about a New Jersey politician whose name hardly made an impression on me.

"You'll be hearing a lot about Christie Whitman," Mrs. McMullen promised. There was a note of intensity in her voice that caused me to register the name. "She's *very* bright and has terrific ideas. Watch for her." (A few years later, with McMullen's backing, Whitman became the Republican governor of New Jersey.) We also talked about Lamoriello and Mac left absolutely no doubt that he believed implicitly in his general manager and, furthermore, couldn't imagine a harder worker nor one who could better balance a budget.

From time to time beat writers would question Lamoriello's stewardship of the club, particularly after he dismissed Tom McVie, replacing him with Herb Brooks, and then dismissed Brooks after the 1992-93 season. Shirley and I had dinner with Lamoriello early in June 1993 at Borelli's, an Italian restaurant near The Meadowlands. After discussing the season – in which he admitted erring in the selection of Brooks – Lamoriello winked and then said he had a surprise for us.

"I'm not going to tell you," he went on, "until it's certain, but I think you'll like it."

We hadn't a clue and wouldn't know until the morning of June 28, 1993, when the media was summoned to Winners for yet another press conference. Never before had such an effective veil of secrecy been placed on a hockey appointment. There were no hints, not a single forecast in the media.

I was sitting at a table on the aisle with a couple of reporters awaiting the new coach's arrival when I felt a tap on my shoulder. Before I could wheel around to see who it was, the person was past me heading for the dais. He wore a sly smile when he turned back and looked at me. Jacques Lemaire realized that his appointment was a surprise to everyone.

After the introductions, McMullen and I huddled as we had done many times before. "We had to get permission from (Canadiens' general manager) Serge Savard and (president) Ron Corey," said McMullen, "but we think it's well worth it. Jacques is a class act and I guarantee things are going to be different around here."

I wanted to believe Mac – that was what everyone called him in his native Montclair, New Jersey – but it was difficult considering the Brooks disappointment. There was no doubt in my mind that Lemaire and I would hit it off and I had planned to dine with him shortly after he had settled in, but Simon's heart failure and subsequent hospitalization intervened. More than two months passed before we met again, this time at a preseason Devils' breakfast, emceed by publicist Dave Freed.

Curiously, Lamoriello was not present although McMullen, his son Peter, who worked in the club's front office, Lemaire and new assistant coach Larry Robinson all were there. There was an obvious edge to the questioning with some of the writers putting Lamoriello on the spot in absentia. The coaching turnover was mentioned as well as the playoff failures. McMullen defended his GM and eventually the hostility was defused by Lemaire's upbeat presence.

But when the media headed for the exits, a few of the journalists ventured that Lemaire was Lamoriello's last hope. If the new Devils' coach didn't deliver, McMullen would clean house top to bottom and send Lamoriello packing. Which set me wondering about Lemaire and his potential.

The *Times'* man covering the press conference quoted *Montreal Gazette* columnist Red Fisher who denigrated Lemaire. (He later learned that Lemaire and Fisher had feuded when Lemaire worked for Les Canadiens. There was no way that Fisher would endorse the new coach.) Others took a wait-and-see attitude and so did I since I would be sharing a "Coaches Corner" segment with Lemaire on the SportsChannel pregame show before every home game.

Having done the same routine the previous year with Brooks, I had cause for concern. Beset with personality problems within the dressing room, Brooks often would be late for interviews – or rush for an early interview – or have one of his assistants do the show himself. I had no problem with that although it unnerved my producer. A coach's job comes first and interviews are secondary; which is why I wondered whether Lemaire would be similarly unpredictable and moody.

Not so. Lemaire was unfailingly on time; regularly amusing, relaxed, amiable and most of all insightful. The conversations were more like fireside chats than uneasy third-degrees and it was obvious after about a month that we had good chemistry between us.

The same could be said for Lemaire and the Devils. A team that previously had been rent by discord suddenly had united behind an exceptionally down-to-earth, no-frills, leader. What you see is what you get with Lemaire, and the Devils liked what they saw, bought into his system and finished with the best record in the team's history.

Nevertheless, there was something disturbing about the scene. A legacy of disappointments seemed to have dulled the fans' enthusiasm while a legacy of perceived mistreatment by both the New Jersey Sports Authority and the NHL left McMullen wondering whether he should keep his team at Byrne Arena.

These feelings crystallized after his Devils had defeated Buffalo four games to three in the opening round of the 1994 playoffs. It had been a stirring series, topped by a marathon overtime (sixth) game in Buffalo won by the Sabres followed by the Devils' clincher at home on a Friday night.

Catering to its U.S. network audience, the NHL scheduled the next round (Devils vs. Bruins) to begin less than two days later on Sunday afternoon. This did not allow the Devils to promote the match and do the usual ticket-selling job. Furthermore, it turned out to be the first absolutely magnificent Sunday of spring, the kind of day that any right-thinking New Jerseyite would consider ideal for lawn-mowing, barbecuing, golfing, biking or hiking but certainly not for attending an indoor hockey game whose date was not even touted a day ahead; especially when said game was available on free local television.

The result was appalling to the horde of visiting journalists. Gaps of empty seats pockmarked every level of the arena, suggesting – though incorrectly – that Jerseyites simply didn't care about their Devils. It was difficult to refute, particularly after the home team was defeated and feeling lousy afterward.

Reporters began grilling Devils about the attendance and always voluble Bernie Nicholls publicly criticized the lack of support while other Devils echoed his thoughts but with less vigour. A much larger crowd nearly filled the arena for Game Two but again New Jersey lost and it appeared that the Devils could be eliminated in four straight.

I was worried about the team and its future in East Rutherford, especially since it would impinge on my broadcasting career. Thanks to Lemaire's coaching and Lamoriello's player selection, I had come to really enjoy this club which was in marked contrast – competitively, at least – to my other assignment on Long Island where the Isles were wiped out in four straight games by the Rangers.

While waiting for our plane at Newark Airport, I discussed the Devils' situation with my colleague Peter McNab. Although considerably younger than myself, McNab had an avuncular quality that was very comforting in such stressful times. Living in Maplewood, New Jersey, McNab had developed a keen feel for the state, its fans and their interest in the Devils.

To my astonishment, he pointed out that the Devils Fan Club was the largest of any such organization in the 26-team league. He told me how the team's fan base was growing and how the first generation of Devils' rooters was attaining maturity. "Fans who normally would have turned to the Rangers," said Peter, "are now growing up pulling for New Jersey. This group is only going to get bigger."

Still, I couldn't shake the thought that a cloud hung over the franchise's future although as Lemaire's club rallied to win four straight over Boston, I began concentrating more on the playoffs than the box office. The strong finish produced robust crowds which remained strong through the semifinal series with the Rangers, one of the most arresting in memory.

The loss to New York stuck in the craw for several reasons, not the least of which was officiating. The Curse of Koharski still was potent six years after the 1988 series. With the score tied in Game Six, Esa Tikkanen continually fouled Scott Neidermayer with impunity. When the young Devils' defenceman finally retaliated, he was penalized along with the Rangers.

New York was gifted with a four-on-four situation, which was precisely to the Rangers' liking and they proceeded to score and retain the lead through game's end. In the decisive Game Seven, two egregious officiating sins cost New Jersey the game and the series.

With seven seconds remaining in the third period Valeri Zelepukin tied the score at 1-1 for New Jersey with a shot from the lip of the goal crease. Rangers' goalie Mike Richter then charged referee Bill McCreary, bodying the official into the end boards. Such blatant abuse of a zebra should have resulted in a game misconduct or, at the very least, two minutes for unsportsmanlike conduct. McCreary called nothing.

The game was incorrectly decided in the second sudden-death period when Stephane Matteau banked the rubber off goalie Martin Brodeur's pads after an around-the-net excursion. Had McCreary been sharp – or had he cared to check with the video replay official – he would have waved off the goal since Tikkanen clearly was standing in the crease.

Still, the Devils were toasted from coast-to-coast for their invigorating performance and even though New York won the Stanley Cup, McMullen's club had earned a large measure of respect.

It also was clear to those who cared – and especially to the Devils' owner – that there was a wide discrepancy between the Rangers' payroll and that of the Jerseyites. With an unlimited budget, New York plucked players other teams simply would not touch and once again Mac was on target when he asserted that the Rangers had "the best team money could buy."

Noting that his team's payroll was somewhere in the vicinity of $13 million while the Rangers was about twice that amount, McMullen added the perfect squelch: "It cost them $13 million for one goal!"

16

·····································

THE NHL IN THE LATE 1990s:
NEW JERSEY VERSUS NASHVILLE

When Gary Bettman became commissioner of the NHL, all bets were off in terms of the power balance among ownership. In conversations I had with Bettman, he kept insisting that he was having no problems with old-guard power broker Bill Wirtz. "As a matter of fact," Bettman told me, "I haven't had a problem with any of them."

There was an easy explanation; as the new ice boss of bosses, Bettman would not allow rule by committee nor would he permit a group of owners – as in Norris-Wirtz in the Clarence Campbell days, or Wirtz-Green-Jacobs in more recent times – to take over any meaningful committees and thereby gain as much power as the president.

In fact, Bettman quietly allowed the board chairmanship to become powerless. Once a board chairman such as Bill Wirtz exercised as much power as president John Ziegler, but this no longer was the case under the league's first commissioner. Bettman enjoyed unprecedented power and also was open to new ideas and allies. For the first time since he bought the New Jersey Devils in 1982, John McMullen would become a major player in the ownership group and a force working with Bettman in the Collective Bargaining negotiations during the lockout of 1994-95.

"Gary Bettman is the best-prepared and most-balanced person that I've ever seen to date in my experiences in this league business," McMullen said. "Maybe there's somebody better out there, but I haven't seen one."

His fellow owners had grown to know McMullen as a fiercely opinionated leader and, as one friend put it, "an old-fashioned conservative." He added, "John is the smartest guy I've ever known with an education that rivals anybody's. But unless you know him, he can turn you off with the way he'll say something. He's never been a PR guy, that's for sure."

Bob Goodenow learned this from the get-go. When talks broke down in October 1994, McMullen withered the union boss with invective, suggesting that he knew nothing about negotiations. At another time during the talks, McMullen was widely quoted after he supposedly alluded to Edmonton, Hartford, Quebec and Winnipeg, saying, "To hell with the small markets!"

While fellow owners such as Howard Baldwin took a more fraternal approach to their players, McMullen was typically blunt. "Some semblance of common sense has to enter into all this," he snapped when talks reached an impasse. "Every single player on my team has gotten more money from this team than I have. I haven't gotten a dime. I'm not complaining, but for every dollar we make in revenue we spend a dollar-and-a-half.

"I see where the union wants to remain status quo and allow things to go the way they're going. Well, they've hit a wall with all the franchises. All of them. Unless something is done, we may never be able to recover.

"An element of fairness is not being recognized. No one is trying to take anything away from anyone. What we're trying to do is stop the ever-increasing cost of operating the league. We have no intention of limiting the salary of any individual. What we're talking about is a fair distribution of the total gross revenues that go toward player salaries."

McMullen was justifiably furious. His anger with the Blues stemmed from one particular move made by the St. Louis team. An outrageously high $17.05 million four-year offer sheet was tendered to Devils' defenceman Scott Stevens, a player who had yet to win a Stanley Cup or a Norris Trophy. This was far in excess of what Norris Trophy winner Raymond Bourque was receiving, and it was considered to be totally unrealistic and, more to the point, vindictive on the Blues' part.

McMullen had no choice but to sign Stevens and make the best of it. "From a financial standpoint it was a mistake," McMullen admitted. "But if you're walking down the street and a thug mugs you, what are you going to do? Let him take everything you've got? No, you defend yourself. We defended ourselves the best way we could in the interest of the franchise. But that is why the whole system needs correction. It was a fault of the system and the lack of fiscal responsibility of one team (the Blues)."

McMullen wasn't kidding. During several conversations with me he revealed his displeasure over the Blues' handling of the Stevens' situation and at being pushed into a corner over the contract. He was absolutely right.

I had no doubt that McMullen was assessing the lay of the sporting land with 20-20 foresight as well as hindsight. He understood the NHL's problem: the combination of soaring salaries and relatively small television incomes combined with public hostility toward outrageous ticket prices threatened many franchises.

Newark Star-Ledger columnist Sid Dorfman said it best, "The problem is mathematical; a lot of markets got too small only when salaries got too big."

McMullen's fan base in New Jersey was growing, but the club could not sustain the higher and higher salaries on income from tickets alone without decent

TV revenue. "It may take a severe scaling down of salaries to correct all this," said Dorfman, "and it will come."

Which explains why McMullen urged Bettman to maintain a hard line during the lockout. As the dispute moved past Christmas, he made it clear to me that he was ready to scuttle the entire season if ownership couldn't get what he regarded as a satisfactory deal with Goodenow.

He wasn't kidding either. McMullen teamed up with Capitals' owner Abe Pollin, Peter Pocklington of Edmonton and Quebec's Marcel Aubut to overrule Bettman on the night of January 10, 1995, rejecting – by a vote of 14-12 – a deal Bettman had negotiated with the NHLPA. In effect the ownership group forced the commissioner to revise his proposal. Had Goodenow rejected the new offer, the season could very well have been cancelled. McMullen believed in his cause and, along with his colleagues, eventually won the day. Goodenow capitulated to the extent that he accepted the new deal and Bettman, in the end, emerged as strong as he had been when he entered the fray.

Throughout the negotiations, I wondered – and worried – about the health of both the Islanders' and Devils' franchises. How would each hold up if the lockout extended through the entire season? Would McMullen, in disgust, simply decide to chuck it all and get out of hockey? They were legitimate questions and some were answered by the participants.

Steve Walsh, co-chairman and chief executive officer of the Islanders, who had maintained a more optimistic air than most through the talks, told me that he was pressing for a deal. He believed that through prudent management his club could live with the deal on the table preceding the final round of negotiations. He wanted the abridged season to be salvaged.

McMullen was farther to the right but told me that the deal was the best the league could get at the time and he, too, believed that it was better to play a 48-game schedule than none at all. When the 15-week lockout finally ended, there was no angry fallout among the Islanders vis-à-vis Walsh, but there was on the other side of the Hudson River.

Before the shortened season began, I had heard whispers that some Devils were furious over their owner's hard-line stance. Furthermore, they didn't appreciate his 11th-hour maneuvering when he, Pollin and others demanded a deal that took away two more years of unrestricted free agency for players at age 31.

Devils' defenceman Ken Daneyko, a stand-up individual, had been extremely close to McMullen. He said he felt that the relationship would continue to be positive after the lockout. "Maybe I'm wrong and naive," said Daneyko, "but these guys in management, if they want to win a Stanley Cup, will take care of the guys they need."

McMullen did take care of his players. Slowly but surely, they shaped up and many received significant contract increases right up until playoff time in the spring of 1995. I watched the team lurch forward, stop, fall backwards and lurch forward again during late winter and early spring, wondering whether they would even have enough energy, motivation and talent to reach a playoff berth.

Despite the disappointing season, attendance was surprisingly high. The Devils were averaging more than 16,000 per game – among the top half in the NHL – and the foundation of fans appeared to be growing. Anyone taking a superficial view of the club's future would have to be optimistic.

But I never got that feeling in my chats with McMullen. He sounded very unhappy about his situation in East Rutherford and would lament his ongoing battles with the New Jersey Sports Authority. One of the most grating episodes occurred during the lockout when the Authority formally suspended the Devils' lease on Byrne Arena.

This development, which occurred on December 22, 1994, was overshadowed by the labour dispute, but did not go unnoticed by McMullen. It infuriated him and prompted the team's management to question its relationship with the Authority. "This was quite a Christmas present," said a member of the club hierarchy. "It caused the team great concern."

McMullen promptly demanded an audit to find out "how much the Devils may or may not be owed by the Authority." Even more infuriating to McMullen was the fact that the Devils were the only NHL club to have its lease suspended because of the lockout. Meanwhile the team alleged 13 specific breaches of the team's lease by the Authority.

I had no idea about these episodes when I chatted with McMullen as his club headed into the homestretch of the 1994-95 season. On one occasion, I was in Philadelphia for a SportsChannel telecast from The Spectrum. I caught a ride home with *New York Post* hockey writer Larry Brooks who once had been a vice-president of the Devils. He knew as much about the club's inner workings as anyone and we began the drive with a discussion about the loss to the Flyers.

That done, we switched to other topics including the fiscal state of the league. Out of left field, Brooks dropped a bomb: "I wouldn't be surprised if McMullen pulls the club out of New Jersey in a couple of years," Brooks declared.

Because of Brooks' knowledge, I found the prediction disturbing, but I listened without comment and said nothing because I wanted this story to go away. After all, over the past six years, I had heard a number of rumours about the Devils' imminent departure – once for Hamilton, Ontario, another time for an American city – but they eventually evaporated and we went on with the business of telecasting and enjoying the team.

Brooks told me he was researching a piece about the move and I wondered about the impact once his story eventually made print.

I didn't have to wait as long as I had expected. Late in the season – once Daneyko returned to the lineup after a long injury – the Devils got their act together and earned themselves a playoff berth. Their opponents in the first Stanley Cup round were the Bruins, which meant that our SportsChannel broadcast would open on the road at Boston Garden.

This was exciting stuff, the playoffs. I could hear the positive tension in my producer Roland Dratch's voice when he phoned and said, "Stan, baby, we're gonna rock 'n roll!" Sure, I'd been through playoff coverage as a journalist since 1955, but 40 years later the adrenalin still was flowing as briskly as it had when I broke into the business.

I couldn't wait to grab the shuttle for Beantown until the phone rang a few minutes later. It was another SportsChannel colleague, Dave Katz, who once had been my intern. "Did you hear about the story out of Nashville?" he asked.

"What story?"

"Down in Tennessee they're saying that the Devils are going to move to Nashville. It appeared in one of the business papers down there."

Nashville. How could an NHL team move to Nashville. The city was too small, couldn't even support an East Coast League club and wouldn't have an arena for at least another two years. It didn't make sense and I tried to laugh it off, but Nashville stuck in my craw and wouldn't go away.

For reassurance, I phoned my pal Harry Ornest who was a longtime pal of McMullen. "I don't think he's moving," said Ornest.

That felt better. When others called, I pointed out the ridiculousness of Nashville until I had given myself a cerebral enema. Then it was off to Boston and the playoffs. The Devils were sharp and easily dispatched the Bruins in Game One at The Garden.

Prior to Game Two, I reported to our SportsChannel TV truck adjacent to the arena. It was time for a staff meeting to lay out the night's show, but instead of production talk, the gang was discussing Nashville. An hour later, after I had walked out of The Garden, I overheard Mark Czerwinski of the *New Jersey Record* telling a colleague that his paper was running a major story on the Nashville situation.

I wanted Nashville to go away, but it was obvious that there was something to the rumours that McMullen and the Nashville-based Gaylord Entertainment outfit actually had been talking about the Devils leaving New Jersey for Tennessee. Like reproducing amoeba, the headlines multiplied. "McMULLEN REACHING OUT TO NASHVILLE GROUP. NHL IN DARK OVER NASHVILLE MOVE."

It reached a point where we at SportsChannel no longer could ignore the story. When we returned to New Jersey for Game Three on May 10, 1995, Dratch decided that Mike Emrick, Peter McNab and myself should conduct a roundtable discussion of the Nashville issue.

Both Emrick and McNab were fervently pro-New Jersey and so was I. "The New Jersey Sports Authority was created to keep teams, not lose them," I said. "I certainly think if the Authority is trying to woo the Yankees from the Bronx they should spend a lot of effort to keep the Devils at Meadowlands Arena.

"Nashville seems like a ridiculous place to put a hockey team right now because first of all it is a small city of 500,000. It has absolutely no hockey heritage. They have an East Coast League there and they averaged only 2,200 for the playoffs. So we're not talking about a hockey hotbed."

Now I was angry. The more I thought about Nashville, the more absurd it sounded to me, especially since New Jersey Governor Christie Whitman, her husband John and children were avid hockey fans. Whitman was a regular at home games; a rooter who was there for the opening face-off and remained until the final buzzer. Being at Byrne Arena far transcended politics for her.

I remembered how the McMullens had touted Whitman to me over dinner a few years earlier and I couldn't understand why she wouldn't be more supportive of her friend McMullen. My next move was to get the governor on camera with me during a playoff game. This should not be difficult, I figured, since Whitman had appeared with me several times over the years.

Sure enough, she came down to the studio between periods – flanked by bodyguards and press agents – and did a no-holds-barred interview. She allowed that the issue was emotional as well as fiscal; said she was bringing her husband in as a mediator, emphasized that the Devils had a lease to honour and pressed home the point that she would do everything possible to keep the club in New Jersey.

We got terrific mileage out of the interview. The *New York Times* built an entire story around it including Whitman's statement to me, "There are a lot of things that would make the deal to move a lot less attractive than it appears on the surface." Bill Pennington's column in *The Record* featured our telecast as well as other dailies.

By now the Nashville story had become as newsworthy as the Devils' irrepressible march through the playoffs. They disposed of Boston in five games and moved on to Pittsburgh for the second round against a team filled with stars such as Jaromir Jagr, Kevin Stevens, Luc Robitaille and Ron Francis.

Yet, the Devils were growing stronger both individually and collectively. They were buying into coach Jacques Lemaire's game plan, growing more confident by the game. Even though they lost the opening game at Civic Arena, the Devils looked good enough to rebound, which they did in Game Two.

Enthusiasm for the club was reaching record proportions in the New Jersey-New York metropolitan area, but this fervor was not matched in the NHL office. When I phoned commissioner Bettman, I was inwardly furious and put the question bluntly to him: "Are they leaving?"

"I don't know," he replied matter-of-factly. "That's up to John McMullen."

At this point, I decided that it was important to get Bettman before the camera. He said he would be in Pittsburgh for Game Two and agreed that he would sit down with me. As always, his word was good and he visited the studio between periods of the game.

Never before had I been so pumped for an interview. My blood was boiling over the possible Nashville move, but I also realized that I had to maintain a reportorial self-control. But if Bettman had expected an amiable and bland interrogation, he was sadly mistaken. Here's exactly how it happened. I opened on camera with the following introduction:

FISCHLER: The Devils are averaging more than 16,000, they are developing a fan base very rapidly, they have excellent rivalries with the Rangers and the Flyers and they have a terrific future based on their championship farm team. That's why a lot of Jersey fans are distressed, commissioner, about the talk of a move to Nashville. And particularly because there is a feeling that the NHL does not care about their move to Nashville.

BETTMAN (sarcastically): We're doing the upbeat interview tonight, I see.

Fischler: I'm telling you, there are a lot of people out there who are upset.

Bettman: The fact is, no decision obviously has been made, and until one is, people may be getting prematurely based on what may turn out to be, or may not, speculation. The fact is, the Devils have some building problems, have some lease problems, have some disputes with the Authority that runs the Meadowlands. And as anyone involved in a very serious enterprise has to do when you're in such a situation, they're obviously exploring their options.

Fischler: One of the points that's been made in print is that the NHL feels that three teams in the metropolitan area is too much. I happen to think not, obviously. I'd like to know what you think about that.

Bettman: I think that if we have to ultimately pass on whether or not a move is advisable, and there's a big if there, we're going to have to look at the criteria you use for franchise relocation, but one of the things we're obviously going to be influenced by, or at least have to take into account, is that we've got three franchises in one geographic market, and no other professional sports league has that. Actually, the last time there were three teams in New York, two of them left, meaning the Giants and the Dodgers. And that poses some problems. As much as I'd like us to be the number one sport, we're still the number four sport, which means we have the seventh, eighth and ninth professional teams in New York, and since I think most hockey fans would tell you the Rangers have the number one position for hockey, so you're talking about the eighth or ninth team in the market. It's difficult for getting media attention, it's difficult for doing your television contracts, it's difficult for attracting fans to your buildings, so I think that presents some problems.

Fischler: There's also the feeling that the NHL is favouring the Rangers, that the NHL has not done anything to encourage, to help the Devils, and in this particular case, the Devils have nothing to be ashamed of; they make a profit. What I'm saying is, why isn't the NHL doing something positive, like perhaps, as Larry Brooks said in the *Post*, using your considerable influence on the Sports Authority?

Bettman: Well, first of all you don't know what it is I'm doing, and secondly, one of the problems when you have a team playing as well as this one does, and you take all the attention away from what's going on on the ice, and you do it on speculation on things that haven't transpired yet, I think you do a disservice to the game and to the players.

Fischler: But it is in the news and people want to know and there are NHL bylaws that cover the team, am I not right? One of them says you have to go to the people in that community and see whether they would like to buy it before the club is moved, am I not correct?

Bettman: That's what you do in the course of processing an application to move.

Fischler: Have you received one?

Bettman: No, not yet.

Fischler: Have you spoken with Dr. John McMullen, the owner of the Devils, and has he expressed any opinions to you?

Bettman: Well, actually I sat with him during the second period of this game.

Fischler: So what did he say about Nashville?

Bettman: Well, what he said is "We've got some game going on here."

Fischler: There's a lot of talk about franchise euthanasia, Winnipeg being one, Quebec being another. Will the Nordiques be moving out of Quebec, and what's the story with Winnipeg?

Bettman: Actually, Winnipeg's a very good example. The Jets are staying. So the hysteria that has mounted, the team's going to be there next year. And Quebec, Marcel Aubut, the president of the Nordiques, is working very hard to see what options he has to stay in Quebec. They've got an old building, one that's inadequate by 1990s standards, and there doesn't seem to be much inclination by anybody in the Quebec market, smallest market in professional sports, lowest per capita income, highest tax rate, fewest number of corporate headquarters, to do anything to help this team be economically viable in Quebec. And if it's not viable, we have to deal with it.

Fischler: Man, I wish I had an hour.

Bettman: Thank goodness you don't.

As the commissioner left the studio, I thanked him for coming on the air and did likewise to his media aide, Arthur Pincus. "Oh, by the way," Bettman said, turning to Pincus, "since you arranged this, you're fired!"

He was joking, of course, and we all laughed, wondering just how amused Bettman really was or whether this was a convenient way of paving over some pernicious potholes. In any case, the interview inspired the *New York Post's* Phil Mushnick to open a column about the tête-à-tête. "A DEAL WITH THE DEVILS" shouted the *Post* headline. "BETTMAN ADDS FUEL TO THE FIRE."

The interview infuriated Devils' fans because they interpreted some of Bettman's remarks as suggesting that their favourite team was disposable. Even Governor Whitman picked up on it when I cornered her for another interview a couple of days later in New Jersey.

"I don't think the NHL cares about keeping the Devils here because they don't like three teams here," she said. "I think some of the television networks would just as soon spread the teams around the country, so it's really us fighting for our Devils right now."

Apparently, the league office was feeling the heat and, sure enough, Pincus phoned the next day challenging me on my question to the governor. Meanwhile, SportsChannel printed a precise question-and-answer transcript of the Fischler-Bettman dialogue and distributed it to the media. By far the most pungent response came from the *New Jersey Record* which led off its editorial page with an open letter to Bettman:

Dear Mr. Bettman,

We heard with chagrin your comments last week about the Devils, who are threatening to abandon the Meadowlands for the allegedly greener pastures of Nashville. Your remarks were as infuriating as they were off the mark.

Perhaps you were merely providing cover for the Devils as they try to rewrite their lease for the third time in a decade and extract a better deal from New Jersey's Sports Authority. But don't try to kid anyone. If the Devils move, the reason will be greed, not demographics. Yes, Nashville may be throwing money at the Devils, but they have a loyal following here.

In a recent TV interview, you suggested that the New York metropolitan area may be too small to support the Rangers, the Islanders AND the Devils. As proof, you said that major league baseball was the only other professional sport that put three teams in the New York area, and two of them – the Brooklyn Dodgers and New York Giants – left town.

That's a catchy sound byte, but it makes two faulty assumptions: that North Jersey is merely a chunk of the metropolitan area and that you can equate Major League Baseball in the 1950s with pro hockey in the 1990s. The truth is, northern New Jersey qualifies as a big-league metropolitan area all by itself.

Here's a quick quiz for you.

"Of the following areas, which has the most households:

A. Miami
B. Pittsburgh
C. Houston
D. Minneapolis/St. Paul
E. Northern New Jersey

Answer: E., northern New Jersey, with 1.7 million households. Houston is second with 1.55 million. Minneapolis/St. Paul is third with 1.4 million. Miami is fourth with 1.31 million. And Pittsburgh is fifth with 1.16 million.

(Incidentally, Nashville – the town that's reportedly throwing so much cash at Devils' owner John McMullen – has 746,000 households. In other words, Music City isn't even a dot on the map.)

Your analogy to Major League Baseball is also a bit strained. Major League Baseball in 1957 had 16 teams, all east of the Mississippi. To have three of those teams in New York City and none in enormous markets like

Los Angeles and San Francisco made no sense. That's a far cry from the National Hockey League today, which has 26 teams in 23 North American cities, from Miami to Vancouver.

If you had bothered to check, Mr. Bettman, you'd see that the Devils are doing quite well here in the Garden State. The Devils drew almost 4,000 more fans a game than the Islanders did this season. Does that mean the Islanders should move instead?

The Devils may not fill every seat for most games, but even the Knicks didn't regularly sell every seat in Madison Square Garden until Pat Riley came to town. What's more, Devils' attendance has increased steadily in recent years, from 12,000 a game during the 1991-92 season, to more than 16,000 this year – in spite of your league's little hockey strike.

In fact, it would be in the NHL's best interests to keep the Devils where they are. The last time we checked, the Quebec Nordiques were carpetbagging their way to Denver. The Winnipeg Jets nearly jumped to Minneapolis. The Devils, meanwhile, have already moved twice in their 23-year history. First they were the Kansas City Scouts. Then they were the Colorado Rockies. If the Scouts/Rockies/Devils were to move again, to Nashville, perhaps you might have them call themselves the Ramblers and get Atlas Van Lines for a corporate sponsor.

For the sake of the league's stability, you should keep hockey clubs from picking up stakes whenever they smell a fresh greenback. Otherwise, the Devils and Nordiques might rightly be confused with Barnum & Bailey – just another road show coming to an arena near you, for a little while at least.

Finally, there's a certain irony in your apparent indifference to a relocation by the Devils. The league has done all it can to prevent its best players from becoming free agents and jumping from city to city, but apparently you look the other way when your team owners want to do the exact same thing.

Come on, commissioner. Greener pastures aren't usually what they're cracked up to be – unless you're a cow. The Devils belong in the Meadowlands. It's time you said so and showed some leadership.

Because of such editorials, the league's hypersensitivity over the Devils-to-Nashville story was growing by the day. When I requested league vice-president Brian Burke as a guest for a subsequent game, I was told by Pincus that he could come on the air provided no questions were asked about Nashville.

This didn't wear well with my producer, Roland Dratch, who suggested that I open the interview by stating that Burke would not address the Nashville issue. However, when Burke came to the studio and took his seat, I tipped him off about what we had planned. He said he preferred we get the question out of the way at the top and he would respond. Which he did.

It now was early June, the Devils had wiped out Pittsburgh and moved into the third playoff round against Philadelphia. Nashville wouldn't go away so I asked Bettman if he would do a return engagement. This time, he politely refused— although he would come later – but that wasn't going to get him off the hook.

Journalists who cared about the Devils and who knew that the NHL had bylaws that prevented the sudden transfer of a team, took aim at the commissioner for his failure to be more obviously proactive. My position was clear; if Nashville was such a terrific spot for an NHL team, fine. Put an expansion team there, but don't rob New Jersey of its maturing franchise. Larry Brooks put it best in the *Post:*

"Here's what the league seems to miss. That having three teams in New York triples the chance of keeping the league important in May and June. Triples the chance of having the largest market represented in the Stanley Cup finals. Instead of discrediting the idea of three teams, the league should be exploiting it. It should be searching for ways to maximize its impact, rather than hoping to find a way to erase it."

Easily the most ironic aspect of the seriocomic tableau was the Devils' relentless push forward. The more Nashville headlines, the more Devils' interest snowballed. It had become impossible to buy playoff tickets at Byrne Arena and Devils' merchandise became one of the hottest items among all the major sports teams.

"It has taken more than a decade," noted Brooks, "but there is now, finally, a generation of young Devils' fans growing in the Garden State. The next generation of ticket-buying, pay-per-view purchasing, demographically-correct hockey fans in New Jersey is an overwhelmingly Devils' generation. If the Devils leave, they have no team to cheer for. And more to the bean-counter's concern, no reason to buy expensive, licensed apparel. Take that to the bank."

If nothing else, McMullen was banking playoff money. His club opened the East Conference finals in Philadelphia winning two straight games against Eric Lindros and The Legion of Doom, but still Nashville wouldn't go away. Metropolitan area reporters jetted south to gauge hockey interest there and found that it ranged from nonexistent to tepid, while McMullen was stung by a Dave Anderson *New York Times* column that challenged him to keep his club in the Meadowlands.

Within days of Anderson's column, a spate of McMullen features suddenly blossomed in the local media. The embattled owner emphasized that his dispute was not with Devils' fans, but rather the Sports Authority which, as he had told me so many times, had mistreated him.

"I can't design a propeller or a ship anymore," he said. "Time has passed me by. But I don't need anyone to protect me either. Apparently a decision has been made that the way to settle this dispute we're having is to desecrate me and my reputation. It's not going to work. No decent person is going to submit to this kind of thing; harassment and slurs. I'm sorry we got into this argument, but it wasn't my fault.

"And as for me being greedy, it may be a valid argument that I have plenty of money so who cares if I'm making any off the Devils...But then, shouldn't somebody at least say, 'Thank you?' I think this team has been a great asset to the state."

It certainly has and that's why I expected Bettman to pull all the right strings and keep the Devils in New Jersey. But I was employing a different set of NHL standards than the kind I had learned when I worked for the Rangers as an assistant publicist in 1954-55.

If we had 13,000 fans in the 15,925-seat Garden, it was considered a successful evening. Now attendance was virtually meaningless. Both Winnipeg and Quebec played to more than 90 percent capacity, but that wasn't enough in the Bettman era. The accent was on new arenas, luxury boxes, merchandising and bigger TV deals.

Nashville might be a disaster at the gate, but who cares? Having cultivated Disney – who could drop out of the NHL picture as quickly as Huizenga or, for that matter, McNall – Bettman sought more corporate ownership. In Nashville Gaylord promised its own network, exclusivity as a major league city and another spot in the Sun Belt that would please the FOX Network in its quest for more southern exposure.

Business-wise it might make sense and Bettman, in his U-turning of a phrase, certainly built an impressive case for Nashville. But it all smelled bad to me and even worse on Tuesday night, June 20, 1995. This was at Byrne Arena, Game Six of the East Conference finals, New Jersey leading three games to two.

Never had I seen or felt the oversized rink throb with such anticipation. When Jacques Lemaire's Devils overcame a 1-0 deficit on Stephane Richer's power-play goal, I thought the tremors might collapse the ironwork right into the Meadowlands swamp. The noise was even greater when Randy McKay staked the home team to a 3-1 lead in the second period, sending the home club to the dressing room with an oversized cushion.

As Philadelphia desperately attacked midway in the third, Claude Lemieux was catapulted into the clear, one-on-one with Ron Hextall. The Devil faked, lured the goalie to his knees and then backhanded the puck into an opening at the right. All 19,040 fans knew that this was the clincher and they rocked the arena as never before. I peeked up at McMullen's box in the hopes of seeing his reaction to the mammoth orgasm of joy, but it was impossible to see anything but his shock of white hair.

With five minutes remaining I moved to our television slot between the benches. The Flyers scored a token power-play goal toward the end, but it meant nothing. Soon the fans were counting down the last seconds and finally the Jerseyites delivered their most ardent eruption. They were reacting the way I did as a 10-year-old when my favourite team, the Maple Leafs, won their Stanley Cup in 1942.

I went back to work, interviewing captain Scott Stevens in the aisle leading into the corridor.

Suddenly, Governor Whitman strode by followed by a big brown dog and McMullen; all headed into the dressing room. The dog was McMullen's pet, Hector, who had "watched" the game from the owner's box and now was going to "congratulate" the players. It was a bizarre scene, especially after Ms. Whitman entered the dressing room, catching a couple of semi-nude players completely by surprise.

"There was a rush for towels," said forward Bill Guerin, one of the more jubilant Devils.

As I went from player to player doing interviews for our post-game show, I couldn't stifle a feeling of exultation for the players who had emerged from the Rangers' shadow to take centre stageas they proceeded to the Stanley Cup finals.

When I interviewed the governor, I sensed that she felt genuinely thrilled by the event, but when I pressed her about a solution to the Nashville dilemma, she replied with the usual cliches. "We're still trying," was her theme.

I spotted McMullen on the other side of the room and he agreed to answer a few questions. After fielding the usual queries about the emotion of the moment, he addressed my pointed inquiry: "What does this victory mean in terms of the negotiations?"

McMullen picked it up on the short hop and shot back, "It means Lou (Lamoriello) is a helluva negotiator!"

Great line. The more his Devils' won, the more leverage they had in dealing with the Authority and Nashville. But where this tug of war would stop nobody knew so I phoned Harry Ornest the next morning for a clue.

"I don't know," he said, "but it sure would be tough to move."

My temptation was to believe that they couldn't move after going so far along the playoff trail with the hockey frenzy now at an all-time peak in New Jersey. But then I remembered how keenly McMullen felt about the Authority, not to mention the negative media he was receiving.

"Have you ever seen a favourable article?" he asked almost plaintively. "But it doesn't bother me anymore. I'm conditioned to it from experience. I expect it."

What I never expected, however, was to cover the New Jersey Devils in a Stanley Cup final, but it was happening. On the eve of the opener, Gary Bettman attended the annual hockey dinner hosted by the Canadian Society of New York. He was pressed about the Devils' dilemma.

"I can't talk. I can't talk. I can't talk." That was his response to the interview.

Then, someone pointed out that the NBA was about to avoid a lockout by working out a deal with its players' association. He whispered to a reporter: "They (the NBA) have a union that wants to work with you. Their players have a good thing going and they know it. We can't convince our players of that."

So, it was on to Detroit and the finals. As I headed for La Guardia Airport, I wondered whether the Devils as a New Jersey entity would survive July. Even at this late date there was no way of knowing, so I did the best thing I could do under the circumstances; I flipped a silver nickel – heads they stay, tails they go.

It came out heads.

17
•••

WILL THE DEVILS GET A
NEW JERSEY?
THE NHL MOVES FROM THE
RIDICULOUS TO THE BIZARRE

As a hockey newsman and historian, I can assure you that nothing –
absolutely nothing – is more fun than covering the Stanley Cup finals. But in
1995 it was different, much different. Juxtaposed against the joy of being with a
serious championship contender was the abject – and growing – depression over
the ubiquitous spectre of Nashville, the home of "Opryland" and "country-and-
western" music.

No matter how many games the Devils won; no matter how many spectacular clutch goals Claude Lemieux scored; no matter how brilliant the goaltending of 23-year-old Martin Brodeur; no matter how crunching and demoralizing
the body-checks of Scott Stevens, New Jersey's fast-growing list of accomplishments was diluted by questions about an incomprehensible plan to move the
Devils to Tennessee.

"We're trying to concentrate on the games," said Devils' defenceman Ken
Daneyko, "but people keep asking us about Nashville."

Although the Devils' general staff pleaded with the media to concentrate on
its excellent team, it was impossible not to discuss the possible move simply
because it was news – big news. And it kept getting bigger as the Devils emplaned
for Detroit and the opening of the 1995 Stanley Cup finals at Joe Louis Arena.

I flew to Detroit on the day before the first game. The series coverage provided by the Detroit newspapers was overwhelming. Both the *Detroit News* and
Detroit Free Press sports sections, ran story after story about the finals in obvious anticipation of the Red Wings first Stanley Cup victory since 1955.

For me there was a touch of irony in all this. In 1954-55 when the Wings
topped the NHL, I worked my first NHL hockey job as assistant publicist for the
New York Rangers. Once our club had been eliminated from playoff contention,

I was free to cover the playoffs. So I was in Montreal for the Stanley Cup finals between Detroit and the Canadiens. Ken McKenzie, who had been the NHL publicity director, employed me as a *Hockey News* aide in Montreal and allowed me to sleep in the Mount Royal Hotel press suite during the playoff run. This marvellous series ran seven games. It concluded at Detroit's Olympia Stadium. Since I wasn't given the opportunity to go to Detroit, I watched the final game on TV as centre Alex Delvecchio led the Red Wings to the title. Now, 40 years later, I was in Detroit for the title games.

Journalists throughout the world had gathered at Joe Louis Arena. After the teams held their first practices the NHL had scheduled interviews with the players. This was the most relaxed time anyone would enjoy during the finals.

For all the criticism the NHL received over the years, it finally learned something about public relations under Gary Bettman. It was clearly evident that Friday afternoon. Detroit Red Wings' coach Scotty Bowman and his stars, Paul Coffey, Steve Yzerman and Sergei Federov, were on the dais answering questions face-to-face from the media. This could not have happened under the regime of John Ziegler, who inexplicably feared open discussion.

It was Bowman's metier. If nothing else, Bowman can talk, ramble, digress and dissect the game. In that setting he is at his affable best. Plus, his team had just reached the finals and had not lost a game to New Jersey. Bowman was as loose as a hockey boss could be on the eve of the series.

The primary subject at hand was what the media had conveniently and simple-mindedly labelled "The Neutral Zone Trap." Originally, Roger Neilson was credited with – some would say accused of – devising this forechecking system which supposedly had created a boring type of hockey. Neilson, who as coach of the Florida Panthers, used the trap as a means of blocking the opposition's scoring potential against his brand-new expansion team.

Now late in the 1994-95 season, Jacques Lemaire was being targeted as a "trap-meister." Interestingly, the accusers among the media, had oversimplified the Lemaire strategy and also unfairly criticized it as some sort of hindrance to the game's progress. Actually, "trap" told very little about the intricacies of the New Jersey Devils' strategy nor its successful implementation. But while many beat writers can be shallow when it comes to hockey strategy – just blanketing a scientific defence-offence blueprint with a single word – "trap" made their work that much easier, although far from accurate.

Bowman would not be suckered into any easy rap at the trap. The ultimate strategist, Bowman acknowledged that his former pupil Lemaire, had devised a very effective checking style which featured a quick counterattack and, rather than being boring – as many erroneously claimed – it could be an exciting aspect of a game.

"Anaheim and Dallas have used it (The Trap)," said Bowman. "We did it. There's no sense forechecking so deep because the goalies are so active away from the net, you can't go in (deep in the enemy zone behind the net) now and forecheck foolishly. Now (with the Trap) there's selective forechecking. And, remember, the puck is still the fastest player on the ice."

The three Detroit stars and Bowman were patient and gracious, as were the other Red Wings who were sprinkled around various tables in the arena restaurant. I recalled Bowman as a rookie coach with St. Louis just after the first major NHL expansion in 1967. A particular vignette came to mind. Bowman's Blues were visiting New York and Scotty Bowman was invited to a hockey writers' luncheon. When it was over, he sat on a table, his legs dangling over the side, gabbing with a few writers until we exhausted our questions.

It was the same 28 years later. Bowman couldn't find enough media with whom to talk. He drifted over to a television interviewer, spent 10 minutes there, then found himself surrounded by Bob McKenzie, Roy Cummings of the *Tampa Tribune* and me. Most of the talk was analytical and not very printable. But it was certainly appetizing fodder for the hockey-minded.

"The Trap," Bowman concluded, "is like any other system. It's not unbeatable if you have the players."

After the Red Wings departed, New Jersey's contingent arrived. Jacques Lemaire, whose relationship as a player for Bowman had ranged from frigid to cool, took the podium. Having worked with him all season, I had developed a deep respect for him both as a hockey thinker and as a person. He disdained the limelight but nevertheless felt at ease talking hockey with me. Now he was centre stage as never before and facing a large curious assemblage.

"I never thought I'd coach. You see you can never enjoy winning when you're coaching because you're always worried about what's next," said Lemaire, his tanned, bald pate glistening under the television lights. "But here I am. I must tell you that there have been times when I would just sit in the corner, scratching my head, wondering why I'm doing this."

Lemaire's cerebral, yet down-to-earth approach captivated the media as it did his players. "Jacques is successful," said his captain, Scott Stevens, "because whenever he talks, he gets your immediate attention. He's honest. He's open with everyone. He has the believability and credibility to get every player to commit to his system."

His players were obviously pleased to get the attention. They understood that the reporters had an angle to pursue and it came down to an attack directed against the New Jersey-Lemaire style. While the Devils had become bored with the repetitive theme, they nonetheless parried the questions with uncommon grace.

"When we were in Pittsburgh, people criticized the way we played," said Stephane Richer, one of the NHL's true virtuosos. "But when we finished them off, the same people were saying that's the way Pittsburgh should play. It was the same story in Philadelphia. People said that the way we play isn't good or fancy enough. I can tell you that there are a lot of teams who would like to be in the same situation as we are today."

As a group, the media leaned heavily toward the Red Wings to win the series. In the *Toronto Sun*, for example, four out of five writers picked Detroit. (The exception was Dave Fuller who selected New Jersey in six games.) The Devils, who opened every one of the four playoff series on the road, laughed the underdog role off. In fact, they enjoyed it.

"Everybody is saying we don't have a chance," said Claude Lemieux, "that we don't have enough offensive players to compete with them. No one believed we could beat Pittsburgh either. Or Philly, or Boston. It doesn't matter to us though. Its time we were accorded some respect for the team we have."

Respect became the buzzword along with disrespect. Respect for New Jersey's hockey team; disrespect for Devils' fans who found themselves unwanted pawns in the battle for the hockey team between a northern hockey hotbed versus a non-descript southern state.

One New Jersey fan, Herman Zuker, a concert pianist from Manhattan, could not believe what was happening to his favourite team and his favourite game. "This NHL season is transcending The Game itself," Zuker wrote me during the playoffs. "It's overshadowed by off-ice problems – from the vacuum of the lockout to the dizzying drama of the Devils – and could be a script right out of Hollywood. I know there was a movie; what was it? A team has to win a championship to gain respect and not be relocated. But this defies credulity."

Yet, that seemed to be precisely the scenario. The more the Devils won and the closer they moved toward the Stanley Cup, the more logical it seemed that the franchise would have to remain in New Jersey. Certainly it would not be moved to Nashville, of all places. Thus, understandably, the Devils' fans became schizophrenic. One part of their personality became obsessed with the off-ice politicking and deal-making while the other part focused on the very important business of winning hockey games. Now the focus shifted to Michigan where the Jerseyites were regarded as big underdogs to winning the 1995 NHL championship.

On the eve of the series opener, I was excited by the hockey fever gripping Detroit. At the Hotel Ponchatrain, the media headquarters, an endless line of fans snaked around the sidewalk waiting for a glimpse of the Stanley Cup. It was on display in the lobby 24 hours a day. Red Wings' fans not only expected, but assumed, that Detroit would win the Cup in as few as four games.

This feeling was confidently evident in the bulging 20,000-seat arena during the pregame ceremonies. When the visiting team was introduced, each Devils' player stepped on the ice as his name was broadcast over the loudspeaker. With each name, the sellout crowd bellowed, "Who Cares? Who Cares?" Disrespect for the East champions carried from the stands to the press box high above the ice where the majority of the media favoured the home club.

The *Toronto Sun*'s Al Strachan, had a column headlined, "WINGS HAVE KEY TO DEVILS' TRAP." Strachan contended that the Trap was beatable, that the Red Wings had ample time to prepare for it and that the "Wings were smart enough to negate the Devils best defensive weapon."

Strachan and company were correct – for one period. Employing the old Montreal Canadiens' Fire Wagon style of hockey from the 1950s, the Red Wings repeatedly assaulted the Devils' defences, but were unable to penetrate goalie Martin Brodeur. The clubs remained scoreless until the second period. Then Stephane Richer beat Detroit goaltender Mike Vernon on a power-play shot from the left side. It was a very telling play because Richer's drive seemed harmless, yet the puck trickled through Vernon's legs for a cheap goal.

Detroit counterattacked with a power-play goal by Dino Ciccarelli and the second period ended with the teams knotted at one. Despite the tie score, the Red Wings seemed in complete command. New York sportscaster Dave Sims was standing with me during the intermission. He wondered what I thought.

"The Devils had better have steel fingernails," I said, "because they look like they're hanging from the edge of a tall building."

Remarkably, once the third period began, the ice tilted New Jersey's way. Tom Chorske dumped the puck into the Red Wing zone, and then headed to the bench on a line change. Meanwhile, John MacLean pursued the rubber against two Detroit players. Somehow, MacLean got the puck and backhanded a shot at Vernon who made the save. However, Vernon allowed the rebound to come directly out to Claude Lemieux, who promptly fired it past the goalkeeper.

With 10 minutes left in the game, I left my cat-bird perch high above the ice and headed to our studio in the bowels of Joe Louis Arena to prepare for the postgame show. My assignment was to cover the Devils' dressing room, while my colleague Matt Loughlin handled the Red Wings. As it happened, our makeshift studio was separated from the working press area by a portable curtain. Consequently, it was easy to watch the print media which gathered there.

The view was extremely meaningful from a comparative perspective. Dozens of writers were gathered in the room with their eyes riveted to the television screen situated in the middle. The people who you would have expected to report the game live – that is, by viewing it from the press box – were actually watching it on TV, as if they were in their home living rooms. Many had begun typing their stories as the third period unfolded on the TV screen.

What this demonstrated to me beyond a shadow of a doubt, was the obsolescence of the print media in terms of play-by-play reportage. Technically speaking, any one of these print reporters could just as easily have seen the game at a bar across the street from the arena, dashed to the dressing rooms for postgame quotes and then written his or her story about the Devil's surprise victory.

The game itself was filled with the tension that comes of two diverse but relatively equal teams. Working the Devils' locker room in the post-game segment of our SportsChannel show, I was surprised at the calm displayed by the winners. Tommy Albelin, the Swedish defenceman, was spread out on the floor while a trainer stretched his legs into a pretzel mold. Long-haired Mike Peluso, one of the most emotional of the Devils, refused to betray any feelings. The goalie, 23-year-old Martin Brodeur, smiled and smiled as he answered questions.

The Devils captivated the media with their total lack of airs. When their stars – usually Brodeur, Lemieux, Broten, Stevens, Richer – appeared at the NHL post-game press conferences their friendliness was in stark contrast to the well-known obnoxiousness of their Major League Basball counterparts.

"The image of three or four Devils reminded me of a scene from *The Right Stuff* about the Mercury astronauts," said one observer. "These players were extremely focused on the job at hand. Their mission."

Lemaire put it best in describing his club. "We played very well in our own end. We were trying to contain the puck-carrier to keep him to the outside and to also keep an eye on everyone who is moving." Others would have called it effective use of the Trap. Whatever, it worked.

The same could not be said for the Devils' attempt to quash the ever-growing Nashville exodus story. Time and again, I tried to get a handle on it. Just when it seemed that I "knew" the answer, another element would intrude to force me to reconsider.

Prior to the second game at Joe Louis Arena, this much was certain: NHL owners would be meeting on June 19, 1995, at the league's New York headquarters. At this time, the governors would be in a position to insist that the Devils' ownership make their position clear.

But the league's new balance of power had so markedly shifted to the commissioner's office and away from the governors that it now had become a matter between Gary Bettman and John McMullen. "A decision like this is left to the guidance of the league office," Pittsburgh chairman Howard Baldwin told me. "It's not like the old days when John Ziegler and the advisory committee ran the league. Owners no longer immerse themselves in league problems the way many used to do it."

Yet, the league had a clear-cut list of bylaws and other stringencies designed to curb carpetbagging. They were based logically on more than 75 years of existence.

Section 36.5 of the bylaws listed no less than 24 "considerations" requiring detailed review before a franchise can be transferred. For example, Item D asks "Whether the present owner of the club has made a good faith effort to find prospective purchasers who are prepared to continue operating the club in its present location," albeit there is no basis or formula to determine the price.

Or Item N: "The extent to which consent to the proposed transfer is likely to damage the image of the League as a major sports league."

Or Item O: "The extent to which the proposed transfer would adversely affect traditional rivalries that have been established between the club in its present location and other Member clubs."

Or Item T: "The extent to which the proposed transfer, if approved, would affect any contract or agreement in effect between the club and any public or private party."

If the NHL's bylaws had any teeth, there was every reason to believe that a move from New Jersey to Nashville could be and would be opposed by the board of governors.

In terms of Item D, Devils' owner John McMullen made it clear that he had no intentions of selling the team. Thus, even if a prospective buyer appeared – two did, but only one was considered serious – he would be rebuffed.

Item N was even more restrictive, if one presumes the NHL was serious about enforcing its bylaws. The league's image – often damaged and buffeted during the John Ziegler regime – would now be severely injured again as would Gary Bettman's role if a potential Stanley Cup winner was allowed to carpetbag out of town before the championship banner even was unfurled the following autumn. The league couldn't conceivably look more foolish if it allowed such a public relations obscenity to occur.

Item O was no less significant. Since 1988, when New Jersey enjoyed its first playoff run, the Devils had developed intense rivalries with the Islanders (1988 playoff), Rangers (1994 playoff), Flyers (1995 playoff) and Bruins (1988, 1994 and 1995 playoffs). Four excellent rivalries would be eliminated. Here, again, a bylaw demanded attention.

But it was Item T which packed the most explosive ramifications. After all, the Devils not only had a lease with the New Jersey Sports and Exposition Authority to remain in the Garden State, but it also had a contract with SportsChannel, among others. The Devils, of course, publicly claimed that the Authority had breached the agreement in several ways. Now the showdown was fast approaching with Gary Bettman – unlike the passive and fearful Ziegler of yore – playing a more pivotal, behind-the-scenes role than ever.

The first important question was: what would the NHL commissioner do if the Devils attempted to leave the Meadowlands before a court ruled on their breach-of-contract claim or before the lengthy appeal processes were concluded?

As Larry Brooks of the *New York Post* asked, "How can the NHL, which penalized Mike Keenan a year ago for skipping out on a contract, take a position in an ongoing legal process which supports contract-breaking?"

Meanwhile Bettman told me that he was awaiting the appropriate moment to intervene and that this moment had not yet arrived. But with each game the Devils won, the Stanley Cup moved closer to the Meadowlands. And with each victory came an added negotiating point for McMullen to use.

Brooks, who spoke for the Devils' fans better than any journalist on the beat, summed up the prevailing opinion from Trenton to Teaneck thus: "Still, though, it is time for Bettman to tell McMullen that the league will not support a franchise relocation if it takes breaking a lease to get the deed done. It is time for Bettman to tell McMullen that contracts apply to owners as well as to coaches and players.

"Time for Bettman to inform McMullen that if he attempts to break a lease, he'll face a trap far more distasteful than the one his championship team has already perfected."

But Bettman strategically continued to bide his time as McMullen's bargaining position grew stronger with each game of the finals. His warriors beat Detroit in Game Two, 4-2, at Joe Louis Arena. The next day NHL ownership convened at a midtown Manhattan hotel. McMullen didn't show up at the conference.

Instead, his president, Lou Lamoriello, attended and merely read an ambiguous statement indicating only that a status quo existed regarding a New Jersey move to Nashville.

"The governors were advised that no decision has been made. The issue wasn't going to be fully addressed, one way or the other, until the Stanley Cup finals are over," said Bettman. "I haven't even given them a date and I don't have one in mind. I'd rather the attention be focussed on the games that remain to be played. You see, I understand the Devils' desire to not address this right now.

"Obviously if the Devils came to the league on September 1st and said they'd like to move next season, that isn't going to work. I would expect that very shortly after the finals are concluded, this is going to have to be brought to a head. I'll inject myself when I think it will do some good in terms of bringing about a resolution one way or the other. You have to pick your spots carefully in terms of how you deal with these situations in an effective manner."

I had been reporting this story for SportsChannel since the spectre of Nashville appeared over Byrne Arena, so it was imperative that I keep my lines open to each side. My prime focus was on McMullen. Once during a playoff game between the Devils and Flyers at The Spectrum, I tracked him down in a private box. Seeking a scoop, I impolitely requested an interview then and there while his Devils and Flyers were fighting on the ice. Considering that I had barged into the luxury suite unannounced, McMullen was affable and reasonable. But he insisted that he wouldn't do any television interviews until the Devils' playoffs were over.

Thereafter, we did speak regularly on the telephone. It was during these conversations that I began to fully appreciate the depth of his feelings toward the Authority members. He also felt slighted by the media because he didn't think the Devils had gotten their just due for the club's outstanding accomplishments over the past several years. In my liberal-minded family we don't make a point of sympathizing with millionaires, but in this case McMullen was certainly making valid points. He had a right to make a profit; he had to keep up with rival teams such as the Bruins, Flyers, Blues and Blackhawks who either had brand-new buildings or soon would get them. As a result he couldn't make do if Byrne Arena was not properly maintained and luxuriously refurbished. Some of these points he had reiterated to me over the years – other comments were new.

I had somehow assumed that the popular election of his friend, Christie Whitman, as New Jersey governor would assure a better deal for him and the Devils at The Meadowlands. But the more McMullen and I talked, the more I realized that, for any number of reasons – some obviously political – Whitman no longer could be counted on as a major supporter.

One night I collared Whitman for an interview between periods at Byrne. I bluntly advised her that she would create public and political disdain if she was governor and New Jersey's favourite hockey team pulled up stakes for Tennessee.

"Actually," she bemoaned, "I'm stuck in a lose-lose situation. If they leave, I lose. But if they stay, my opponents, some of those Democrats, will accuse me of giving away too much in order to keep the team here."

Over the period of a month, from late May to late June, I conducted approximately a half-dozen personal interviews with Whitman. With each discussion, she seemed more frustrated by her pal, McMullen. "We've given him a proposal (more luxury boxes, etc.)," she said at the outset of the finals, "but we're still waiting for a counterproposal from him. We can't do anything more until we hear from John McMullen."

Several friends of mine, who were devoted Devils' fans, were equally frustrated. They knew they were backing a potential champion. They wanted to buy season tickets for 1995-96, but the Devils refused to put them on sale. Normally, next-season tickets were publicized by SportsChannel on the playoff telecasts. This time they were conspicuous by their total absence from the broadcasts.

"When you have a winning team the way they do, the best time to sell your season packages is while you're doing so well in the playoffs," said an NHL marketing executive. "That they're not sends some form of message to the fans."

There were reasons for withholding ticket sales: 1. Why sell tickets when a Nashville move is potentially imminent? 2. By not selling tickets for next season, the club reinforces its message to the New Jersey Sports Authority that it means business about moving. Ostensibly, this is designed to give the hockey club an even better bargaining position with its landlord.

That leveraged position was enhanced at the June 19th owners meeting in New York City. The board of governors quickly approved the relocation of the Quebec Nordiques to Denver.

Supposedly, a Canadian group had wanted to buy the Nordiques and keep them in Quebec. That group asked the board to delay approval of the move to Denver for 30 days, citing a provision of the NHL's constitution which requires consideration of any good-faith local offer to buy a team seeking to relocate. The board denied the request. Bettman logically claimed the unspecified offer came at "the eleventh-and-a-half hour" from "some unidentified group." In light of the months-long machinations of Quebec's managing partner, Marcel Aubut, nothing would surprise anyone about anything emanating from Quebec City, with or without Aubut. "Remember the Lindros auction?" one governor remarked.

Furthermore, Bettman asserted that there were some two dozen criteria which now must be weighed under the good-faith offer bylaw. What Bettman said was extremely important in terms of bylaw execution vis-à-vis the Devils:

"You look at the whole package and you make a businesslike decision on how you think these specific criteria have or haven't been met. But it's ultimately a decision, frankly, for the board of governors. It is the board that is charged with determining how decisions are made on franchise-ownership changes, and/or franchise relocations."

What if the Devils win the Stanley Cup and then move to Nashville? For the first time Bettman reacted with what appeared to be movement away from a Tennessee possibility and thus a bit closer to a New Jersey solution.

"Of course it presents a problem" he allowed. "Even on something like merchandise for the Stanley Cup champion. My guess is it's more difficult to get retailers to buy Devils merchandise if there's a concern the team may move and thus change its name and everything else.

"But we are where we are. We're in a difficult position created by many factors. The best thing we can do now, from the game's standpoint, is to put this matter to the side. Let's get through the finals. Then deal with it."

Now the finals were fast becoming a bigger story than even winning and losing. It seemed under Maestro Jacques Lemaire, the Devils had thoroughly confounded the Red Wings and all the analysts. At the outset, for example, the *Toronto Sun*'s erudite, Strachan, boldly predicted, "Scott Bowman certainly knows what (Lemaire's) Trap is. More importantly, he knows how to counter it."

While Strachan and others were wrong, Bowman was out maneuvered. The two-game deficit confronting the Detroit commander as he headed to New Jersey for Game Three underlined the point. Much of the media refused to see what their New York counterpart, Brooks, clearly understood – the Red Wings had become Dead Wings, destined for a sweep. In fact, Detroit was counted out before Game Three was half over. The Devils almost toyed with them, delivering four goals in the first 29 minutes, forcing goalie Mike Vernon to the bench. The final score, 5-2, was far too kind to the disorganized visitors who didn't even bother to hold a workout the next day or the morning of Game Four.

I was charged with doing morning interviews for our evening pregame show that (Saturday) night. I found the Red Wings at a nearby (Meadowlands) hotel where the NHL had arranged for Detroit stars and Bowman to meet the press. Under the circumstances, Bowman, Yzerman and Coffey were remarkably cordial. My only interview problem was with Slava Fetisov, an old friend from New Jersey, who was surrounded by Russian-language interviewers.

Normally, day-of-game interviews are relatively brief, allowing each of the reporters an opportunity to get his sound byte. Newsmen respect a colleague's needs for the most part. Rarely will anyone dominate above and beyond the call of duty. But this was different. The Russians went on interminably without any concern about others. So finally an NHL honcho intervened and I was able to pop a question at Fetisov.

Instead of giving me a normal reply in English, he answered in Russian – with a healthy touch of sarcasm. When he finally said a few words in English, they were banal to the point of insulting. I thanked him and moved on to Coffey who was typically eloquent and patient – nor did he speak any Russian.

Our crew left the Red Wings at their hotel and drove to a nearby restaurant for our pregame meal. Here we were just hours before Game Four and what could be a previously unlikely series sweep. The prime question being asked was not whether Bowman would start Mike Vernon or Chris Osgood in goal, but whether the Devils would move to Nashville a few days after they won the Stanley Cup.

In a matter of but two weeks the Devils had become *the* compelling story in the ravenous New York media market. This is where the Yankees fight the Mets for space; the Mets battle the Knicks, Rangers, Nets, Giants, Jets and so on. New Jersey rooters simply couldn't maintain their focus on the Stanley Cup. At least not as long as they knew that Gaylord Entertainment had offered their favourite club a $20 million relocation bonus, a generous share of all arena revenue and other financial sweeteners.

"The relocation situation made this so much more urgent, complex, dramatic and poignant," said pianist-fan Herman Zuker. "No player was terminally ill. There was no 'Win one for The Gipper.' But when a franchise is so wounded and yet its players are able to pull this off (with a great coach), it is a heroic story – full of daily drama."

The dénouement would come not in the evening but early in the afternoon. When I arrived back at Byrne, the parking lots were already alive with thousands of people. Tailgaters had set up their barbecues; teenagers were wheeling around on in-line roller skates, whacking hockey balls with their sticks; and miniature Stanley Cups were being fabricated out of pieces of tinfoil by some creative fans.

At our pregame TV production meeting, I slyly mentioned that Rangers' fans had similarly been carried away with such emotionalism after New York had taken a three-games-to-one lead against Vancouver a year earlier. The Rangers then proceeded to lose the next two games. Nevertheless, we prepared with confidence for the possibility of victory and a gala post-game dressing-room show. Two hours before game-time I went out to the parking area with a cameraman to do some fan interviews.

Bedlam had nothing on New Jersey at this moment. I could have used a phalanx of New Jersey State Troopers just to guide me through the overflowing, joyfully expectant throng. We did manage to reach a van whose roof was adorned with a mammoth replica of the Statue of Liberty and a Stanley Cup. I actually couldn't hear myself speak as the fans repeatedly chanted, "LET'S GO DEVILS! LET'S GO DEVILS!"

As I made my way back to the arena, I wondered whether this tremendous emotional surge and pride in the home club would have any effect on the hard-bitten negotiations which had screeched to a temporary halt. I realized, nevertheless, that it was the height of naivete to even consider for a moment that the business side of The Game would ever take a full backseat to the emotional part.

But once the players skated out on the ice for the beginning of Game Four, the raw pulsating emotion carried the evening. The roar from 19,040 mouths was the loudest, most intense I had ever heard at Byrne. It was accompanied by an assortment of placards reminiscent of the Mets 1969 World Series triumph at Shea. One cleverly read, "NASHVILLE ALREADY HAS ENOUGH PEOPLE WITHOUT TEETH." Another simply proclaimed, "THIS IS HELL."

Those of us who had spent time with the Red Wings that morning wondered what effect Bowman's verbal spanking (in public) would have on his charges. Hockey's winningest coach had indicted his players after the Game Three loss. He described the game – in pretty incisive adjectives – as "embarrassing," "humiliating" and "unacceptable."

Based on the first 15 minutes of the opening period, the rebuke had a palliative effect on Detroit. The Red Wings moved ahead, 2-1, and were more composed than the home club. But late in the period, New Jersey defenceman Shawn Chambers took a pass at the left point, glided into better position and then drilled an obscured shot into the upper right corner of the net. The Devils never trailed again. Neal Broten diligently worked the crease in front of goalie Mike Vernon, eventually lifting his own rebound over the goalie's pads for the go-ahead goal.

The goal was scored at 7:56 of the second period. Time was running out on the Detroit Red Wings. What 19,040 fans were still wondering was whether time was also running out on Byrne Arena as the home of their beloved Devils.

18

. . . .

CHAMPAGNE VERSUS THE COURTROOM:
CLIMAX OF THE NASHVILLE-NEW JERSEY NHL WAR

Between the second and third periods of Game Four of the 1995 Stanley Cup finals, New Jersey Devils' coach Jacques Lemaire was confronted with one of his most difficult assignments. His club owned a three-game cushion, was nursing a one-goal lead and, after having been outshot five minutes into the second period 13-8, had skated off the ice with a 16-15 lead in shots on goal.

"I didn't want them to get overconfident," said Lemaire. "I wanted them to keep their focus."

His Devils could have been forgiven for allowing their attention to falter. Game after game, they had taken the favoured Red Wings' best shots, counter-punched and then destroyed Detroit in every aspect of the game. They outshot the Red Wings, outhit them, outscored them and, seemingly, outcoached the Motor City skaters.

"Ten minutes into the first game I knew we were going to win this series," said Devils' centre Bobby Carpenter. "We hadn't played them. We saw they had the best record. We heard how good they were. We didn't know what to expect. But in those first 10 minutes we saw we could play with them and outcheck them. I knew then we were going to win."

But Lemaire knew that this game wasn't over. A one-goal lead against a desperate team like Detroit is but as firm as a gossamer string. He encouraged his troops to maintain their diligence and as they trooped out of the dressing-room door and through the vomitory to the ice, they were greeted with a roar which might have been heard in Cape May on the distant Jersey shore.

Observing the coach's dictum, the Devils became atrocious hosts, refusing to allow the visitors to handle the puck. The final shots-on-goal totals for the third period were 10-1 for the Devils. If there ever was a barometer of one-sided play, that was it. Yet, for more than seven-and-a-half minutes of the third period, Lemaire remained uneasy behind his bench. The score remained 3-2 in the Devils' favour. The Red Wings still had the great forward Sergei Fedorov, who had tied the game in the first period, taking his regular turn.

As the overhead clock ticked toward the eight-minute mark, The Kid Line of Bill Guerin, Brian Rolston and Sergei Brylin controlled the puck in the Detroit end. Back in November, a still-green Brylin skated for the Albany River Rats of the American League and appeared too inexperienced for NHL play. "What he needed," said Rats' coach Robbie Ftorek, "was lots and lots of ice time. That's what I gave him. We knew he was a comer."

Rolston had also been with the Rats, but because of a contractual technicality involving the NHL and the NHL Players' Association, he was forbidden to play in the AHL during the lockout. Instead, he practised with Albany and worked as a radio analyst for the River Rats games. "I worked as hard as I could in practices in case the lockout was settled and then I'd get a chance to play," said Rolston. "What I didn't want to happen was getting depressed about the whole thing. I stayed as positive as I could."

Guerin, who had been somewhat of a disappointment during the regular season, already had fashioned Broten's go-ahead goal. Now he and Rolston combined to pierce the Detroit defence. Then the puck skimmed to Brylin who had yet to score a playoff goal. The miniscule Russian pivoted from about 20 feet in front of Detroit goalie Mike Vernon and cleanly rifled the puck into the corner of the net for the third Devils' goal.

A majority of those in the house fully understood that a two-goal lead with 12 minutes remaining simply would not be overcome by Detroit. But if the game had to be irrevocably stamped, it was done so by the ubiquitous Chambers. Taking a perfect feed from Guerin which originally came from Brylin, the smiling veteran defenceman, who dresses faster in the post-game than anyone in the NHL, uncorked a missile from virtually the same spot he had shot late in the first period. Now it was 5-2. The game and series, for all intents and purposes, was over.

Already hoarse, Elaine Groh of Emerson, New Jersey, continued to cheer. A designer by trade, Groh epitomized the Devils' fan who felt emotionally torn as her team was about to annex the long-sought championship. "Being a Devils' fan," she would say later, "was like a roller-coaster ride; plenty of ups, mainly downs. But definitely a lot of laughter and many tears. It was hard to keep all of my emotions in check these last few weeks through what should have been one of the best times for long-suffering Devils' fans. We haven't had respect all this year, but the media treatment we received during the playoffs was the most despicable."

But Groh, like her seatmates in the corner of Byrne Arena – and, for that matter, everyone – put aside personal feelings of anger at the Sports Authority, Governor Whitman and even Dino Ciccarelli. They simply cheered lustily as their heroes suffocated the Red Wings until the final buzzer had sounded.

Preparing for the post-game festivities, I had moved into the corridor between the two benches during the last half-minute of play. The vomitory already was jammed with NHL security who protectively surrounded Gary Bettman. The commissioner had appeared as a FOX Network guest between periods in a visibly exposed area of the arena and thus had been roundly vilified by the fans. Now he would have to face them again – all of them – at centre ice; a prospect which was unmistakably daunting.

For a brief moment, my mind flashed back to that game 12 years ago between Edmonton and New Jersey immediately after Wayne Gretzky had delivered the now famous "Mickey Mouse" insult. My wife and I had taken our son, Simon, to that game. He sat close to the protective glass, almost suddenly becoming infatuated with a short goalie named Chico Resch, his goaltending and hockey. On this night Simon was again sitting in the stands roaring with the rest of them. My reverie was disturbed when a security guard pushed through carrying the Conn Smythe Trophy. He handed it to Bettman who stepped onto the rubber matting, quickly grabbed the microphone and presented the award to Claude Lemieux. The boos turned to cheers the moment Lemieux's name was heard.

Bettman retreated to the alleyway once more. This time he was handed the Stanley Cup. Momentarily, he again was showered with catcalls. His brief but cogent speech about the Devils epitomizing "teamwork in the best sense" was on target. He handed sport's most cherished team trophy to captain Scott Stevens, whereupon cacophony was the order of the day.

Just then, I noticed a white-maned figure step off the ice and onto the carpet next to the Devils' bench. It was McMullen. He noticed me, we shook hands and he said, "Whenever you want to do that interview, I'm ready."

I was surprised that he would think of such a seemingly unimportant matter such as that right in the midst of this monumental event in his ownership career. "I'll phone you Monday," I said. Then retreated back to my cameraman, who was preparing for the post-game show in the dressing room.

At this point it was difficult separating the professional part from the emotional. Having covered the Devils since their opening days, I had remained intrinsically close to the hockey club although this new Nashville business had begun mining some deep-seated cynicism within me. I was happy for many of the skaters I had come to know, especially Ken Daneyko, John MacLean and Bruce Driver, who had been with the club almost from its inception in New Jersey.

Then, there was my pal, Mike Peluso, always the first one in the dressing room on game days. In the midst of shaking hands, Peluso made a strange beeline off the ice to his locker. I later learned that Peluso was so overcome with emotion he had to compose himself in the room before returning to the ice minutes later.

When Scott Stevens, the Devils' captain, hoisted the glistening, silver Stanley Cup over his head in front of the vast, cheering throng, I was reminded of our first interview of the season at Hartford's Civic Center in mid-January. At the time the Devils' captain sounded so uncertain about the club. I thought of our trip to Philadelphia late in the season when Stevens lashed out at Larry Brooks of the *Post* for challenging his leadership and suggesting that he be traded – an idea which I considered sensible at the time. Now, it was totally impossible to imagine New Jersey winning the championship without Stevens' presence and leadership on the blue line.

Finally, after the handshakes and traditional Cup skate-around ended, the Devils trooped back to their quarters. This was the first time a SportsChannel-covered team had won the Stanley Cup since the Islanders captured their fourth straight championship in 1983. By that time, the Isles had become ever so slightly jaded about Cup wins – but not this Devils' club.

The tableau in the winners' quarters was right out of the Marx Brothers' chaotically funny stateroom scene from *A Night At The Opera*. Side by side with my cameraman, John Ackerina, I elbowed my way to whichever Devil might be available. The first was Bruce Driver with whom I had feuded years earlier. Driver had become much friendlier in recent years.

Driver had been team captain prior to Stevens' arrival from St. Louis four years ago, but he remained the club's union representative and a symbol of the beat-up Devil who got up off the canvas to triumph. "We're going to have a lot of fun the next couple of days," said the veteran defenceman. "A lot of people cracked jokes about where our victory parade would be if we won the Stanley Cup. It doesn't matter now."

Driver's wife, Tracy, was sobbing while her husband and I did the interview. Their cute eight-year-old daughter, Whitney, stood by smiling. "My wife was with me all the way," said Driver, who grabbed Tracy and hugged her to his chest.

The "pop" of champagne bottles echoed through the room. Peluso opened one and generously poured the bubbly over my head. It was the first time I had been doused with Korbel Brut. When my glasses became blurred, I stashed them in my pocket and plowed forward. Directly ahead was one of my favourite Devils, Bill Guerin, whose hair was being ruffled by his father, William Guerin Sr., a stockbroker from Hartford. I began interviewing them when, unexpectedly, Bill Guerin's mother, Ligia, an arresting, dark-haired professor of Spanish, appeared in the background.

I had met and chatted with the Guerins several times since their son had come to New Jersey and knew that Bill Guerin's mother was a terrific talker. While chatting with her son and husband, I waved her over to our side. Bill Guerin had not seen her until that moment. When Ligia Guerin came into view, the two – mother and son – collapsed in an uncontrollable, weeping embrace.

For a split second, I wasn't certain whether I should turn away and allow them a private moment or offer an on-air commentary as they tried to regain their emotional equilibrium. I chose the latter, which turned out to be the right thing because our camera caught the touching familial scene; easily one of the most poignant of the entire evening.

Typically, coach Jacques Lemaire ducked the limelight after the Cup presentation. I had been tipped off that he was hidden in the coach's cubicle, across from the dressing room. Roland Dratch, my producer, told me to try to persuade Lemaire to come on-camera for an interview.

I hustled through the crowd, across the corridor and banged on the door. Without waiting for an answer, I opened it to find the tiny room filled with Lemaire's family and assistant coach Larry Robinson. Lemaire unhesitatingly agreed to come back to the locker room. Lemaire had been burned by some who criticized his "Trap" and he hammered his point home during our chat.

"I thought the guys deserved a little more respect from their opponents," said Lemaire. "That's one reason our guys were aggressive. Because they got no credit."

Conn Smythe Trophy-winner, Claude Lemieux, was no less passionate in rebutting the critics. When one of them challenged the champions' style, Lemieux shot back, "Too bad you didn't like the show. You can go watch something else."

Despite the media critics a significantly high number of fans chose to watch Lemaire's intellectual brand of hockey, even after his team had amassed an unbeatable three-game lead. The proof was in the numbers most coveted by Bettman Inc. – U.S. television ratings. The FOX Network drew a 3.6 A.C. Nielsen rating, the highest-rated NHL broadcast on FOX in its first NHL TV season. It also tied the 1990 NHL All-Star game on NBC for highest-rated NHL telecast since 1990. It represented some 954,000 U.S. households who watched the game.

Once our post-game telecast was over, the dressing room had opened to all sorts of visitors, from family members to girlfriends. The Devils' Gallic trio – Claude Lemieux, Martin Brodeur and Stephane Richer – mounted a special platform that had been erected for TV interviews and lustily chanted victory songs in French.

A few minutes later my wife Shirley and son Simon drifted into the room and soaked up the joy if not the champagne. Throughout the Devils' Cup run, Simon had remained devoted to his Islanders, but admitted that he got a special charge out of watching long-haired Mike Peluso. Since Peluso was still sitting in front of his dressing area, I walked Simon over to him whereupon the lad said, "You made me a Devils' fan!" Peluso got a kick out of that, ruffled Simon's hair and assured us that after all the celebrations were over, we all would go to Brooklyn's fishing village at Sheepshead Bay and down cherrystone clams together.

It was an hour later when we traipsed through the parking lot, still filled with disbelieving fans. The Devils were Stanley Cup champions. It still was hard to digest. It was almost as difficult as accepting the transient potential of the new Cup winners. During their finest hour, the Devils were still bombarded with questions about a distant city they had not known. Nashville was on everyone's mind and especially that of John McMullen's.

During the afternoon after the championship night, McMullen startled me with a phone call. He repeated his willingness to do the television interview. I mentioned that I had planned to make the appointment on Monday. McMullen told me about his recent visit – he reluctantly and unavoidably missed Game Three of the finals because of it – to Annapolis for a class reunion at The Naval Academy. With a very audible quiver in his voice, this multi-millionaire, who had too often been unfairly mischaracterized for his insensitivity, choked up as he told me how many of his World War II classmates had been lost. I told him about my father's stint on the minelayer *U.S. San Francisco* during World War I. I promised him that I would bring a copy of my father's minelaying squadron's yearbook when we would next meet.

We arranged the interview for Monday afternoon at McMullen's business offices in Secaucus, New Jersey. It loomed as a big one for SportsChannel so I arrived early and carefully prepared my questions. When I arrived at the head-quarters of Norton Lilly (McMullen's firm), my cameraman already was setting up and McMullen invited us to partake of an enormous cake shaped in the form of a Stanley Cup.

That done, we began the interview which covered what I thought was every aspect of McMullen's dispute with the New Jersey Sports and Exhibition Authority. He was sharp, incisive, unwavering and articulate in his claim that his hockey club had been getting the short end of the fiscal stick from day one as a Byrne Arena tenant.

"The governor told me that she still was awaiting a counterproposal from you," I mentioned at one point. "What about the privatization plan?"

"What we'd like to do," McMullen asserted, "is lease the building."

Here was a concrete response that – as far as I knew – had never been artic-ulated before by McMullen. This would be the core of the interview which, according to early plans, might run in its entirety. That meant as much as an hour of air time. Despite the playoff run that consumed four rounds and nine sold-out home Stanley Cup dates, McMullen insisted that he was operating at a financial loss for the season. "I can't continue to do so any longer," he emphasized.

At one point, I seriously offered, "You don't strike me as a Nashville kind of guy."

He smiled, but then responded, "I'd rather make a profit in Tennessee than be debt-ridden in New Jersey." By the time we had concluded the session, I was convinced that: A. We had a meaty interview; B. The positive side of McMullen would be better revealed than ever before on television; C. He was dead serious about leaving unless he could strike a significantly better deal with the Authority.

After thanking him for the time, I got in my car and proceeded to buck the rush-hour traffic snaking its way to the Lincoln Tunnel toward Manhattan. Instinctively, I turned on the radio, tuning in to the all-news station WINS.

Having heard most of it on the trip out to Jersey, I listened with only half an ear until 5:45 p.m. when the sportscast was delivered.

It was then that I suffered a temporary case of lockjaw. The newscaster blurted, "...And the Stanley Cup champion Devils have announced that they will break their lease with the New Jersey Sports Authority next year."

Break lease. Next year. Devils announced.

Wait a minute! I had just spent an hour with John McMullen and never did the lease-ending come up in conversation. What was this all about?

My head was swimming as I drove up Broadway to our house. Try as I might, I couldn't explain why the saga was playing out this way. Naturally, when I walked into the apartment the phone was ringing off the hook. On one line I had Pete Silverman, my new boss at SportsChannel and a hard-nosed newsman if ever there was one. On the other was the network's publicist Paul Schneider, who only hours ago had notified all the sports-TV columnists that we were going to run a hot McMullen interview.

"We just heard on WFAN that the Devils are ending their lease in 1996," said Silverman. "Did McMullen tell that to you?"

"Not a word," I shot back. "But I'm going to call him right now to find out."

The Devils' owner had just left his office so I knew it would take a while before he reached his home in Montclair. About an hour later he picked up the phone and I explained my amazement at hearing about the lease termination on the radio.

"It's just a legal technicality," he said. "When we sent it to the Sports Authority, it was with the understanding that it remain a private matter. Then, they went public with it despite our agreement."

This was a key point. The original broadcast I had heard erroneously made it seem as if the Devils had made the announcement about the lease-breaking. Actually, it had come from the Sports Authority without McMullen's knowledge and that is what angered him.

I phoned the Authority spokesman John Samurjan and asked why the authority had gone public with the lease story when McMullen specifically had wanted it to remain private. "We had a document (the letter from the Devils) and apparently some members of the media learned about it," Samurjan explained. "They began asking questions so we decided we had to make a decision – to tell the truth or not. We chose to release the document that they sent us."

The one paragraph annoucement, which was enough to scuttle our grand plans for the "McMullen Interview Show with Stan Fischler," was released by the Authority while I had been closeted with the Devils' boss. Which meant that it was impossible for McMullen to know that Authority Chairman Michael D. Francis and President Robert E. Mulcahy III had gone public.

Their statement went as follows: "The New Jersey Sports and Exposition Authority today received a notice from the New Jersey Devils terminating their Franchise Agreement as of the 1996-97 season, based on their position that the

1991 Amendment to the Franchise Agreement is not valid. For the past four years, the Authority and the Devils have abided by the terms of that amendment which the Authority maintains is valid. The Authority's General Counsel is currently reviewing the termination letter."

Why did the Authority go against its agreement with McMullen to keep the matter under wraps?

In so many words, the Authority was saying that it broke its word simply because reporters were asking questions. No wonder McMullen was furious. From my viewpoint, his anger was completely justifiable but that didn't help us in terms of the validity of our interview. The late-breaking, lease-busting story pre-empted whatever good stuff I had from McMullen. Silverman told me he couldn't use the interview as we had originally planned.

Instead, he had me come to the studio to do a one-on-one with the *Game Time* news show host Matt Laughlin. The point of my being there was to explain why the original interview was killed while at the same time I would provide as much insight into the fast-breaking story as I could.

During the segment, we showed a couple of segments of the actual one-on-one I had with McMullen. Once it was over, I repaired to our offices to field the phone calls. One was from Nat Gottlieb, sports-TV columnist of the *Newark Star-Ledger*, who asked a number of questions about the sequence of events leading to the killed interview. Another was from Howie Rose, a probing newsman from WFAN and a friend.

I explained to both that I was very disappointed that the lease-breaking story hadn't come up in the interview but I reiterated that I believed McMullen was as much surprised by the Authority's breaking of the agreed-upon news blackout as I was by the announcement on the radio.

Gottlieb ran with the story, giving it considerable space in the next day's (Tuesday, June 27) edition. Others, such as the popular "Mike and the Mad Dog" (Mike Francesa and Chris Russo) jumped on it the next day, phoning me for yet another interview.

Needless to say, McMullen was less than thrilled that the interview was killed, but everyone at SportsChannel agreed that Silverman had done the right thing under the circumstances. Meanwhile, we sprinted ahead, keeping pace with a story that was exploding like an atomic chain reaction.

A day after announcing that it was terminating its franchise agreement after the 1996-97 season, the Devils pulled off another shocker. This time they said that as of July 6, 1995 – just 10 days away – they would terminate their lease with The Meadowlands!

Counterpunching as quickly as McMullen's attorneys could, the Authority's lawyers filed a complaint in Bergen County Superior Court. Francis and Mulcahy were seeking a preliminary injunction that, among other things, would prevent the Devils from moving to Nashville.

The July 6th target date made it appear that McMullen was dead serious about Tennessee. But several elements mitigated against the move: 1. The Sports Authority had the backing of Governor Whitman in seeking an injunction. A courtroom battle could prove embarRassing to the NHL; 2. In the hockey club's June 27th press release – titled "Devils Describe Actions Taken To Preserve Legal Rights" – a meaningful paragraph left room for compromise. "The Devils' organization does not intend to foreclose the possibility that an acceptable proposal may yet be forthcoming from the Authority; 3. Gary Bettman had entered the negotiations.

During a phone conversation with Bettman, he told me that there was little to nothing that he could say publicly. However, others told me privately that the commissioner had become an influential and, no less importantly, a calming influence on the negotiations. In our discussions, Bettman repeatedly used the term "leveraging" to describe the give-and-take.

An NHL owner put it another way: "When McMullen set the July 6th date, it was a case of 'ultimate hardball.' This was his best way of getting these Authority people to do some real negotiating and for him to get some meaningful concessions."

No doubt but the July 6th D-Day announcement came on the eve of the gala pep rally to celebrate the Devils' Stanley Cup championship. Some fans regarded it as an ironic and crushing point-counterpoint. At the time when they should be sharing their most joyous moments, they were now faced with a very real prospect that their favourite team would be departing

Making it even more personally confusing was the fact that SportsChannel had planned complete coverage of the celebration at The Meadowlands. Our broadcast team – Mike Emrick, Peter McNab, Matt Loughlin and myself – were scheduled to arrive at the arena at 3 p.m. for our production meeting and then prepare for the evening festivities which were due to kick off four hours later.

When I arrived at the sun-drenched parking lot that afternoon, I didn't know what to expect. Some fans were so furious about what seemed like a guaranteed Nashville move that they said they simply wouldn't show up for the party. There also were hints of violence to protest the July 6th ultimatum, yet what I saw throughout the concrete expanse were happy faces. Despite the early hour fans already were gathered around barbecues, enjoying their tailgate parties. True to the theme, they had come to celebrate, not denegrate.

But no sooner had I arrived at the TV truck, Pete Silverman was on the phone. A story was circulating that: 1. McMullen already had received a $25-million cheque from the Gaylord people in Nashville; and 2. Some Devils, purportedly led by Mike Peluso and Stephane Richer, knew about it and planned to boycott the event. Silverman wanted us to break the story, if we could have it verified.

The Devils had just finished their official team picture-taking in Bryne Arena and the dressing room now was open for interviews. Richer was nowhere to be found, but Peluso was sitting in front of his locker and soon was surrounded by newshounds. I waited about 10 minutes until they cleared away and then whispered the report I had heard. Puluso calmly denied it and I left the room convinced that he had levelled with me.

By the time I reached the pressroom down the hall, clusters of reporters were gathered around discussing a rumour that WFAN planned to run with virtually the same story that we were trying to unravel. Silverman had just arrived and phoned a contact at the radio station. "They're going with it as an unconfirmed report," he told me. "But we have to keep on it."

Unable to find Richer, I decided a call to Dick Evans at Gaylord headquarters in Nashville was in order. Evans and I had had a very distant relationship when he had been head honcho at Madison Square Garden several years earlier. When he got the call, Evans seemed surprised at the WFAN report and thoroughly ridiculed it as nonsense. I then phoned the commissioner and with typical Bettmanesque sardonic humour, he asserted, "And that's why they should ban sports-talk radio!" Both persuaded me that the move-to-Nashville rumour was fiction.

With his sharp news sense, Silverman knew we had to deal with the story on the show so he recommended that I open it with Emrick on the upraised SportsChannel platform amidst the crowd. The plan was for Emrick to immediately reveal the unconfirmed reports being circulated about the alleged transfer of a $25-million cheque and then for me to offer my analysis and any late update.

By 6:30 p.m. as we prepared to ascend the platform, a sea of humanity filled the vast parking lot. (The unofficial estimate later varied from 25,000 to 75,000, but most settled on the former. In either case it was more than anyone had expected under the circumstances.) As Emrick and I made our way through the crowd, fan after fan pleaded with us for information about the threatened move. At one point, when a youngster approached me, I was suddenly reminded of the classic episode involving Shoeless Joe Jackson of the White Sox who was accused, along with teammates, of dumping the 1919 World Series to Cincinnati. As Jackson ascended the courthouse steps in Chicago, the lad pleaded, "Say it ain't so, Joe!" In effect, the Devils' legion was urging, "Say it ain't so, John!"

But the unconfirmed reports heard on WFAN were scary. We all were thinking the same "Where there's smoke, there's fire" bromide, hoping against hope that no Nashville money had been deposited but also cynical enough to realize that it could have happened.

I asked one of our interns to place another call to Evans just in case he had anything further to add before airtime. Meanwhile, Emrick and I moved into our positions on the platform. We were in full view of the throng and, believe me, if they had taken a sudden disliking to us, we would have been in big trouble. Fortunately, many of the spectators had either seen or heard about my Bettman interview and my pro-Devils stance.

In 20 years of broadcasting – make that 40 years as a reporter-columnist – I had never been overwhelmed with such emotion. Frenzied over the celebration and furious over the threatened Devils' exodus, the fans began chanting "STAN, STAN, STAN," in deep-throated unison.

What could I do? I gave them the thumbs-up sign and that merely aroused them even more. Our stage manager, John McComb, suggested that instead of a thumbs-up, I give them a Papal wave instead. "Even better," he said, "just do what they do in the TV studios. Give them a 'c'mere wave,' for even more applause."

I settled for the thumbs-up since that seemed most appropriate and left it at that. Now it was 6:59 p.m. and we were ready to go on the air. As the final 10 seconds were being counted down, I noticed the intern, Rick DaCruz, rapidly climbing the platform steps, waving a piece of paper in his hand.

"Ten, nine, eight, seven, six..." the countdown continued.

DaCruz reached the top of the steps and, unaware that we were about to go on the air, pushed the paper toward Emrick. "...five, four, three, two, one."

Just as we went on, Emrick took the notes and quickly glanced at them. It was an update from Nashville. This time Evans was even more vehement in his denial that a cheque had been sent to McMullen. So forceful was the statement that I could only conclude that the story was false and I said as much in our pre-celebration discussion although there always was the concern that Evans was making a false denial.

That done, I left the platform and moved among the spectators for interviews until the players arrived for the Stanley Cup deliverance. On centre stage an upbeat band worked the crowd which sang along, "Go, Devils, go! Go, Devils, go!" Makeshift Stanley Cup replicas and banners were everywhere including one proclaiming, "NJ DEVILS FOREVER."

Finally, the player-carrying motorcade snaked around the arena toward the stage. I was particularly interested in two personalities, McMullen and Lamoriello; how they handled the crowd and vice versa. The Devils high command occupied the front-row seat in one of the open convertibles and seemed at ease as the motorcade moved to the stage entrance. I was there with Governor Whitman and interviewed her before she made her way up the steps. She was more intense than usual but emphasized that she remained hopeful because the warring parties were still talking.

When McMullen alighted from his car, he was accompanied by his pet dog, Hector, and suddenly surrounded by New Jersey State troopers who formed a flying wedge as he made his way to a special celebrity grandstand. It was a rather courageous move by McMullen who easily could have ducked the audience if he had so desired.

A circling helicopter then made a landing on a strip adjoining the stage whereupon captain Scott Stevens reached in and was handed the Stanley Cup. He carried it on stage, transporting the crowd into an even higher form of ecstacy. One by one, each player danced with the silver mug to the accompaniment of techno music. An even greater ovation overcame the throng when Bobby Holik stepped forward with the Cup and was accompanied by his fellow Crash Liners, Mike Peluso and Randy McKay.

It seemed as if there was even more energy being generated than one might have anticipated but it only was because a majority of the fans were seriously doubtful whether they would see this team play again at the rink in the background. Thus, they were determined to clear their lungs with unusual vigour.

However, when Whitman stepped forward, the cheers turned to jeers. With considerable aplomb, she easily hushed the dissenters and shouted, "They can play the Trap and they can do things other teams are just finding out about. And I look forward the same way every other fan does to watch them defend that Cup and bring it right back home here next year."

I was desperately trying not to get engulfed in the emotional whirlpool. To that end, I kept telling myself that hockey is a business and the Nashville threat is Exhibit A. Yet when Jacques Lemaire stepped forward, it was difficult to contain the goosebumps. Here was a "mensch," a gentleman, a man's man, a regular guy.

"I heard a lot of things during the season," he began as the lights brilliantly reflected off his bald pate, "but I never thought I'd ever hear about the Trap from the governor; I had enough of that all year."

Following the laughter, a fan raised a sign, "WHATEVER BO KNOWS, JACQUES KNOWS BETTER."

Lamoriello was an even more interesting study. How would he handle himself amid the tidal wave of doubt? What would he say to the growing legion of skeptics?

The club president grabbed the lectern as a coach would when he wants to shake some sense into a player. With a remarkable sense of conviction, he emphasized how much management wanted to remain in New Jersey. Then, he turned to goalie Chris Terreri and implored him to walk to centre stage and unfurl his makeshift sign. It read: "NASHVILLE. NO WAY!" The crowd went wild.

It ended after 10 p.m. on what had been an exquisitely clear, magnificently cool night. As we headed for our cars, we walked through minefields of beer cans and soda bottles any of which could have been armament for an ugly crowd. Instead decorum was the order of the day and now we wondered whether decorum would be the order of the courtroom.

Barring a sudden turnabout, the Devils and the New Jersey Sports and Exhibition Authority were due to face-off in court only five days after the last beer bottle was swept away from outside Byrne Arena.

19

....

AND THE FINAL VERDICT IS...

On the morning after the deliriously joyful Meadowlands celebration, two extremely significant events took place in two different states involving the New Jersey Devils.

At a press conference held in Nashville, Dick Evans, the man who ran Gaylord Enterprises, made it clear that he had no deal – as *Star-Ledger* columnist Jerry Izenberg put it, "with The Devil or the Devils." More than that, Evans uncharacteristically blasphemed the New York-New Jersey metropolitan area. When a reporter from the *Record* of Hackensack interviewed him, Evans snapped, "Why don't you go back to New Jersey? Why the hell would anyone want to go to New Jersey? It's a hellhole. I lived in New York for 10 years and I fought to keep from going through the tunnel to that hellhole." *New York Post* columnist Phil Mushnick, a New Jersey resident, retorted: "Dick Evans hates New Jersey? Good for New Jersey!"

Obviously, Evans was rapidly becoming disenchanted with negotiations. More than that, he apparently sensed that the New Jersey Sports Authority might very well launch a lawsuit against his firm for tampering with a major league team that had a major league lease with it. In fact the NJSEA had planned to sue both Gaylord and the National Hockey League, an event that must have been understood by lawyer Gary Bettman.

The second event was taking place behind closed doors in New Jersey where members of the Authority, John McMullen, Lou Lamoriello and Bettman were attempting to strike a deal. Only 24 hours after the Meadowlands celebration, the parties reportedly were extraordinarily close to forging a pact, but they adjourned for the evening without dotting any i's or crossing any t's.

Looming ominously ahead; like a detour sign on a road, was Judge Peter Ciolino in Hackensack, New Jersey Superior Court. On Monday, July 3, 1995,

Judge Ciolino was to hear the Sports Authority's lawsuit to bind the Devils to their contract. The word in legal circles was that there was a "shark-feeding frenzy" among judges who wanted to hear the case. "Every one of them wants to be *the* judge who keeps the Devils secure in his home state," was the way one New Jersey attorney put it.

Neither side relished the idea of going to court especially since the prospects for a long battle could have badly bruised both parties. In the meantime, the Devils were legally obligated to file their own papers rebutting the Authority's charges. As talks continued, the Devils asserted in court papers filed on Friday, June 30, 1995, "The Authority has continually and repeatedly represented that the Authority would deliver a base of 19,000 fans at the arena." The Devils have "lost millions of dollars" because of that unfulfilled albeit unwritten promise. "I was promised 19,000 fans and they never gave us a chance to produce them," McMullen said.

If there was to be an agreement, the Authority would have to concede to McMullen's basic demands. For example, just a few weeks earlier, he reminded me of a second trip he had made to see the new Boston NHL arena which still was under construction. He marvelled at the 104 suites which were included in the design. Byrne Arena sported 29.

"They don't give a damn about us," McMullen insisted. "Aren't I entitled to break even?"

McMullen knew whereof he spoke. In the NHL of the late 1990s, a club needs not only gate receipts and a good television deal, but monies from stadium ads, concessions and suites of which the Devils had far too few.

"Luxury boxes are critical," said Craig Simon, director of sports marketing for the Chicago consulting firm of Frankel and Company. "A stadium that doesn't have them is in danger of losing its team."

Which explains why the Nordiques abandoned Quebec for Denver. The antiquated Colisée couldn't compete with a brand-new arena in the Colorado metropolis that would be oozing with luxury boxes. At the United Center in Chicago, opened in 1994, owner Bill Wirtz boasts 216 suites selling for between $55,000 and $175,000 a year.

"The luxury suites are the financial engine that offsets the cost ($175 million) the Blackhawks and Bulls incurred in constructing the facility," said Steve Schanwald, vice-president of marketing for the Bulls.

The Authority was working out a plan to provide considerably more suites for Byrne Arena, but first there was a court date on Monday, July 3, 1995, at which time there would be either war or armistice.

I arrived in the sleepy and neatly-trimmed city of Hackensack about 20 minutes before the 9 a.m. court date accompanied by a cameraman and Anna Horton, an intern who had worked with us throughout the season at Byrne Arena. At least a dozen other media types were there for the event including my pal, Larry Brooks of the *Post*, and several local reporters.

Our advanced tip was that the Authority would ask the court for a postponement and the Devils would agree. This would be done only on the assumption that Judge Ciolino would receive assurances that both sides felt a negotiated settlement was near.

"The Judge will not ask this lightly," noted Jerry Izenberg of the *Star-Ledger*. "In this game, he is goalie, referee, head linesman and the only licenced Zamboni driver in the rink. If they say peace is just a couple of days away – and they will – they had better mean it."

Sure enough, Joel Kobert, the Authority's general counsel, did just as predicted and Judge Ciolino postponed a hearing until Tuesday, July 11, 1995. When I interviewed Kobert, one-on-one outside the courtroom, he made it clear that progress was being made. "Everyone is encouraged," he said, "and they'll keep talking this week."

The handsome old courthouse was bathed in pleasant sunlight when we stepped outside to do the on-camera opening for the TV segment. "Not so fast, Nashville," was my opener. "The Devils are still in New Jersey and appear to be here to stay."

Naturally, the operative word was "appear" since there still was a possibility of the talks erupting with the rancour that had pockmarked the earlier negotiations. And, as Izenberg so wittily noted, "The negotiations move forward with all the speed of a pair of herniated ants trying to drag a large potato chip back to their communal pantry."

I spent the rest of the week awaiting a resolution that never came. On Friday, the Devils' contingent, led by Lamoriello, was scheduled to leave for Edmonton and the annual Entry Draft on Saturday, July 8th. On Thursday, Lamoriello hosted a media conference call ostensibly to discuss the upcoming draft, but he also gave an unequivocally positive response when asked about the negotiations.

"We are making progress," said Lamoriello, who normally is cautious about such matters.

A day later, Izenberg wrote, "Logic dictates that the Authority and the Devils will settle this thing over the weekend before the Hon. Peter Ciolino settles it for them, starting Tuesday in Superior Court."

The weekend began with the NHL draft and no further news. On Sunday, McMullen was profiled in the *Star-Ledger*, a newspaper which he had continually claimed was in the Authority's corner. He sounded more optimistic than usual about a settlement.

Not wanting to be caught unawares, I urged my bosses to have a cameraman on hold just in case an announcement was made on Sunday. Early in the afternoon I received a call from the Authority's spokesman, John Samerjan. "They're still talking," he said.

I mentioned that the Devils were scheduled to meet President Bill Clinton at the White House on Monday afternoon. Might there be an announcement before then? "I'll let you know if there is," he politely replied.

By 9 p.m. on Sunday, I had not heard any further word so I assumed that the armistice would not be proclaimed until Monday; perhaps even by Governor Whitman at the White House. Now wouldn't that be a beauty.

I made an Amtrak reservation for 9 a.m. on Monday, still perplexed as to how this passion play was going to unfold in its final act. It now seemed obvious that Nashville was out of the picture and a deal would be made. But how and when would it be announced and what would the Devils get out of it?

While mulling over the possibilities, I could not help thinking about the effect these months of agonizing threats and counterthreats were having on the people who were directly involved or even tangentially affected. One of them was my colleague, Jiggs McDonald, with whom I had worked as part of the Islanders' SportsChannel broadcasts for 14 years.

McDonald's contract had expired with the network, but its other hockey play-by-play man, Mike Emrick, had a pact that extended through the 1995-1996 season. If Nashville claimed the Devils, SportsChannel would lose a team and have no need for two play-by-play broadcasters. From a purely business sense, the network would opt for Emrick since he already was under contract.

When McDonald was advised that his pact was put on hold pending resolution of the Devils' dispute, he decided to part with SportsChannel. He phoned me and we discussed his disagreement, but naturally, there was little I could do other than make mention of his availability in our weekly newsletter, *The Fischler Report*. On a personal level, I knew that I'd miss working with McDonald. Over the years, McDonald and I had a number of disagreements – about hockey ideas, not broadcasting – but they never adversely affected our on-air relationship. Quite the contrary; we bristled through a number of arguments, particularly Mario Lemieux versus Wayne Gretzky, and were all the better for them.

As the Metroliner rolled out of Pennsylvania Station for Washington on Monday, July 12, 1995, I thought about McDonald and the many big games we had covered together; especially the Stanley Cup winner in 1983 at Nassau Coliseum when the Islanders won their fourth straight championship. I felt more than a twinge of sadness at the breakup of our team and then was suddenly reminded of a remark made by old friend Marty Blackman.

The Madison Avenue marketing executive had closely followed the Nashville-Devils odyssey. One day I mentioned to Marty how emotional the New Jersey fans had become about the possible loss of their favourite team and how that emotional factor should be considered by owner John McMullen.

"Remember," said Blackman, "sports is big business. A hockey team in New Jersey is no different than a wire-cutting company. If the wire-cutting company got a fabulous offer to relocate to Tennessee the way the Devils did, the owner wouldn't think twice about moving south."

The Metroliner click-clacked over Newark Bay and braked to a stop in the grand art-deco station of New Jersey's largest city. Here I was en route to a presidential ceremony honouring that state's first championship team and still there were broad hints that the Devils might leave.

In the *New York Post*, Larry Brooks hinted at the possibility of a conspiracy between the NHL commissioner and Nashville. "Maybe," wrote Brooks, "Bettman, no advocate of the current metropolitan three-team market, is using his considerable influence to negotiate an out for the Devils they could not win through litigation.

"Maybe the Sports Authority, which will make every attempt to steal the Islanders if the Devils get away, can be bought off at this point. Maybe there are promises of which we know nothing, being traded in the modern version of the smoke-filled room."

If the Brooks' theory – and it was only based on maybes – held water, no NHL community would be immune from lease-busting. Each club would be open to the highest bid. Or, as Blackman kept saying, "It's a major business in a capitalist society."

But it was – and is – personal to all the fans involved, be they in Winnipeg, where the Jets were hanging by a thread, or Tampa Bay, Miami and Hartford. All these communities had supporters that passionately followed their big-league club, but who could easily wake up one day and learn that the Lightning, Panthers or Whalers were victims of a buyout, takeover or move-out.

In no time at all our train had rolled across the New Jersey countryside and pulled into Philadelphia's grand 30th Street Station. I watched passengers strolling along the platform and wondered something I never had thought about before; was there ever a championship hockey team that picked up and left its city after winning a title?

Sure enough, it happened in the Paul Newman movie, *Slapshot*. If the Devils left Jersey for Nashville it would be the most exquisite example of life imitating art.

But Paul Newman's club never enjoyed the honour of being greeted by the president of the United States and this was about to happen to captain Scott Stevens and his Devils. Accompanied by teammates Bill Guerin, Jim Dowd, Bruce Driver, Kevin Dean, Ken Daneyko, Martin Brodeur, Brian Rolston and Neal Broten, Stevens arrived in the East Room well before Bill Clinton.

The place was filled with familiar faces and people-watching was the order of the day. I noticed the venerable Helen Thomas, queen mother of the White House press corps who still was covering for *United Press International*, and Wolf Blitzer of Cable News Network. I found it amusing that Thomas was inconspicuously crammed behind a rope barrier with the New Jersey-New York hockey beat writers.

Seated in the high-powered guest section was Governor Christine Todd Whitman, looking attractive in a beige suit and accompanied by her husband, John, who supposedly had been brokering peace talks between McMullen and the Sports Authority. McMullen was sitting next to his handsome son, Peter, on the other side of the aisle. Since I had been tipped off that McMullen and Governor Whitman had been at odds recently, I watched carefully to see if there was any social byplay between the owner and the governor.

Sure enough, she graciously walked past six chairs to McMullen who rose and hugged her, then posed for a photo with his arm in a palsy-walsy grip around her shoulder. The Authority's Michael Francis and Bob Mulcahy wore appropriate smiles but kept their distance from McMullen.

Suddenly, a hush fell over the room and a voice blared, "The President of the United States."

A door opened to the left of the lectern and in walked the Chief Executive. He was wearing a dark suit with an intriguing red, yellow and blue tie, adorned with little human figures that I assumed were all Democrats. I had never seen Clinton up close and was instantly impressed with two aspects of his carriage: 1. He was bigger than I had imagined; 2. His nose was sunburned red.

Clinton's humour surfaced immediately and it was obvious that he had done his hockey homework. He knew that the Stanley Cup had once been left on a Montreal sidewalk after the Canadiens had stopped to fix a flat tire en route to a celebration. And he told about the time a member of the Ottawa Senators had drop-kicked the Stanley Cup into the frozen Rideau Canal. He made only one faux pas, calling the Conn Smythe Trophy (won by the absent Claude Lemieux) the Conn Smith Trophy.

When Devils' captain Scott Stevens thanked Clinton for inviting his team, Stevens added, "Like you, we've had a long, tough year."

Fielding the line on the short hop, Clinton immediately responded, "Hope mine comes out the way yours did."

Stevens presented the President with a Devils' jersey adorned with Clinton's name and the number one on the back.

"I identify with you because you were cast as classic underdogs, but your determination and teamwork paid off," Clinton added with telling sincerity.

Then, he compared hockey to the rough and tumble world of politics: "The difference is here we don't have a penalty box and sometimes the referees back there pile on, too!"

The ceremony was as pungent and tasty as sweet-and-sour soup. When it was over the president hung around shaking hands, mine included. (He has an engagingly firm handshake.)

But almost as quickly as he had appeared, the president disappeared behind the big doors of the East Room while the Devils moved out on the lawn for interviews and picture taking.

All things considered, it was a rather euphoric occasion. You could tell by the beaming rookie Brian Rolston that this was one of the best days of his young life. Even a seasoned veteran like Stevens was visibly moved.

"I'm still on cloud nine," said Stevens. "It'll take a while before I come down. I think it will last until the start of the season."

McMullen had moved among his players and I seized the opportunity to interview him. I wasn't sure how he would react since the problem we had after the post-Cup tête-à-tête in his office, but he was cordial, even to some of his adversaries such as Rich Chere of the *Star-Ledger*.

"It was a very nice ceremony," said McMullen. "This doesn't happen every year, although we'd certainly like it to."

Some of us wondered whether there would be an armistice announcement made before his Devils left the White House. McMullen made it clear that we would be covering the dispute in Hackensack court the next morning. "It won't get resolved until then," he added, but he steadfastly refused to admit that he would keep his club in New Jersey.

Then, he betrayed a rare emotional reaction; McMullen allowed that the rally and parade for the Devils outside Byrne Arena four days after they had won the Stanley Cup affected the negotiations to keep the team in his home state. "It was one of the greatest emotional outcries I've ever encountered," McMullen went on. "I was personally very affected by the rally and it definitely had an effect on the negotiations. It made it obvious to everyone how important it is to try and resolve this. A lot of people care."

Filtering through his comments, I tried to discern a pattern but it was difficult because McMullen uttered both positive – "We're holding out hope" – and negative – "What difference does it make (where we play next season)?" – remarks.

While we were gabbing on the White House lawn, word came down that the Devils' charter jet back to New Jersey was waiting at National Airport. "Do you want a ride?" McMullen asked.

I hesitated. My plans had been to return by train, but Amtrak wouldn't be leaving for another two hours. Besides, this was a chance to spend a last hour or so with some of the players, so I accepted. Before I knew it I was sitting in the charter, watching Daneyko chomp into an apple. Two of Daneyko's false teeth remained embedded in the core. He turned to me and grinned a semi-toothless smile. "All I was hoping for was that the teeth hung in there through the White House – and they did."

McMullen sat in an aisle seat across from Bettman at the front of the airplane. About a half-hour after takeoff McMullen walked to the rear, chatting with just about every passenger. Dr. Barry Fisher, the team orthopedist, along with trainer Ted Schuch were orchestrating a game of blackjack and motioned to the owner, "Doc, lemme relieve you of some of your millions," said Fisher. McMullen grinned and simply said, "No thanks."

McMullen and I chatted for a few more minutes after which he asked if I needed a car to take me to the city. It was a terrific offer but I figured I would just as soon take the bus. We agreed that it was a neat White House ceremony and then he repaired to his seat for more conversation with Bettman.

I had no doubt that they were discussing the ongoing negotiations which would continue later that evening and last until two in the morning. That meant another date for me in court and promptly, when the doors to the Superior Court opened, I was there along with the usual corps of print and electronic media.

Once again Joel Kobert, the Authority's counsel, and Frederick Lacey, who represented the Devils, agreed that the parties were closer than ever. Sources said the two sides were discussing the possibility of selling a corporation the right to put its name and symbol on the 14-year-old arena as a means to pay for renovations sought by the team. The Authority already had agreed to install more luxury suites and new, high-priced club seating in the arena and negotiators had been considering strategies to raise private-sector money to help pay for them.

"The deal is just about at the handshake stage," said one insider. "There's still some volatility, but the details are being worked out."

Some of the volatility was being generated by McMullen. He railed to the *New York Times* about what he called a "demeaning" negotiating process. Asked if he was feeling close to a deal, he shot back, "How can I be confident? It's a very undignified procedure."

Then, he elaborated: "It's demeaning to go over every little point for them to offer me anything. They should give me concessions without breaking my back. To lock myself into a 12-year deal with these people is difficult. We have a vast difference of opinion about the quality of the arena. It's tough to get them to understand what it takes for me to run the team profitably."

McMullen said he deserved givebacks that would produce profits for a team that he said lost $2 million while winning the Stanley Cup and $20 million since he acquired the team in 1982.

"I'm generating the hockey revenues, the money that can help me break even," he said. "Without the money, they can't generate those revenues." He also brought up Nashville again.

"There's no comparison, particularly as far as the future. Nashville creates a pleasant environment and we'd operate the arena and be our own landlord. No way this can approach Nashville. It's secondary."

I was due back in court on Thursday, July 12, 1995, unless a deal was hammered out before then, as most expected. On Wednesday morning I made my usual call to the Authority's public relations man John Samerjan and he cordially mentioned that "the wheels grind slowly." But he also indicated that there might be a break in the afternoon. At 3 p.m. I phoned him again.

"Does this mean I should be in Hackensack court tomorrow?" I asked.

"Not necessarily," he replied. "Sit tight and call me a bit later."

Meanwhile, I alerted SportsChannel to have a crew waiting should we have to move quickly to a press conference.

This was almost as exciting as the Stanley Cup finals.

20

· ·

D (AS IN DEVILS) – DAY:
THE FINAL "NO" TO NASHVILLE

One more phone call to the New Jersey Sports and Exposition Authority offices wouldn't hurt, I figured, so late on Wednesday afternoon, July 12, 1995, I dialed John Samerjan, the NJSE spokesman.

"Has a deal been done?" I inquired. "Are the Devils saved for New Jersey?"

Ever courteous and thoughtful, Samerjan insisted that there was no new news and, furthermore, he assured me that there would be nothing further to report today. This time he was emphatic so I took his word and phoned Gary Bettman at the National Hockey League.

The commissioner had been holed up all day trying to figure out ways and means of reviving the fiscally comatose Los Angeles Kings. Nevertheless, Bettman was amiable and patient as I prodded him for information. He had told me a few days earlier that he planned a trip on Thursday. I had assumed he was heading for the West Coast.

"When are you leaving?" I asked. "You are leaving for L.A., aren't you?"

"I'm not going to the coast and I'm not sure when I'm leaving," he cryptically answered.

"Does that mean you'll be around long enough for a (Devils-NJSE) press conference?" I asked.

There was a lilt in his voice. It was telltale without actually telling me anything specific. "I might," he said. "If there's a press conference and you have a camera there, I'll be happy to do an interview."

Without actually spelling it out, Bettman had told me that, yes, I had better be ready for the big announcement tomorrow, Thursday, and that the end of the saga was near.

In the meantime, SportsChannel arranged to have a mobile truck ready early the next (Thursday) morning. I would meet it in front of Byrne Arena in East

Rutherford, New Jersey, precisely where the Devils' victory party had taken place. If a deal had been cut, we would head for the press conference wherever it might be and if one had not been hammered out, we would drive to Superior Court in Hackensack where Judge Peter Ciolino was prepared to hear the Authority's request for a temporary restraining order to keep the team from terminating its lease at Byrne Arena.

But Samerjan had told me days earlier that when the pact had been signed, word would immediately leak to some well-connected media type. And, sure enough, at 6:05 p.m. on Wednesday, I received a call from a friend, Steve Viuker.

"Channel 13 is running with a story that a deal has been cut," said Viuker.

Sure enough, the station's political expert, Pat Scanlon, was saying it was a $25-million pact that would ensure the Devils stayed at Byrne Arena. Scanlon was well-connected enough to be trusted on this, but to be sure, I phoned Steve Hirsch, a political reporter at the *Record*. He checked with Samerjan who checked with his boss Bob Mulcahy. The latter offered a flat denial. Samerjan added that there was a one-in-a-hundred chance that an announcement would come later in the evening.

It was the classic scenario. Progress had been reported in court on Tuesday; the judge ordered everyone back on Thursday; if a deal had not been cut by then a messy legal battle would carry on through the next hockey season, embarrassing the Authority, the Devils and the NHL. There *had* to be an armistice and it was inevitable that word of the truce would leak before the actual, formal announcement was made.

From 6:15 p.m. to 7:15 p.m. the phone nearly rang off the hook with the usual follow-up calls from various sources. Scanlon, based at Trenton, the capital of New Jersey, had phoned Lou Lamoriello, but the Devils' president had not yet returned the call. Scanlon was staying with his story despite the NJSEA denial and even offered some details; the Devils would get considerable club seating; the Authority would provide more ad awareness; there would be a sizeable chunk of cash for selling the arena name to a corporation such as Bell Atlantic. Since Scanlon was based in Trenton, the assumption was that someone in the governor's office had provided the leak. It made sense.

All signs suggested that a formal press conference would be announced before the parties were due in court. Hockey's latest version of the Treaty of Versailles was rapidly reminding me of the famed Gary Bettman-Bob Goodenow peace parlay that I had witnessed across the Hudson River in the winter of 1995. But when I finally went to bed on Wednesday night, I still had no confirmation from any source and had no idea what would transpire the next morning.

David Kolb, a young man from Queens (New York) College, who had worked with me through the season on Devils' telecasts, drove up at 8 a.m. and we were off to our meeting with the SportsChannel truck in the Meadowlands parking lot outside the main entrance. Traffic flowed smoothly and we arrived at least a half-hour early, but to my surprise, the television truck already was there with several crew members. Obviously, our outfit was not fooling around today.

When my producer-director, Stu Wiener, and another aide, Anna Horton, pulled up a few minutes later, we laid out a battle plan. First we had to establish whether there was going to be a press conference or a meeting at the Hackensack courthouse. Then, we had to move all our equipment and trucks to the site for what would be a live telecast. Ironically, all of this breaking news was happening on the day when SportsChannel premiered its new logo and new image. For us, it was a big deal.

My prime contact was Samerjan at the Sports Authority whose offices were at the Meadowlands Racetrack about a half-mile from our site at the Byrne Arena. Samerjan had suggested I phone him at 9:30 a.m., but Keith Fernbach from my office already had checked with Samerjan who insisted he had nothing yet to report. The secret word was "yet."

Instead of waiting around, Wiener, Horton, Kolb and I drove over to the Sports Authority where we were stopped at the gate. A Samerjan aide came down to accept a book I had promised the Authority spokesman, but he would not give us any further information about whether we should be in court or somewhere else in the next hour. "Call me at 10," was the message so we headed back to our trucks and the crew in front of Byrne.

By this time the temperature was climbing toward 95 degrees. The parking lot was broiling, but this did not stop visitors who had come for a religious festival that night at the arena. Suddenly, one of our crewmen got a bright idea and walked over to the Winner's Restaurant inside Byrne where most of the major press conferences are held. A few minutes later he rushed back and breathlessly said, "They're setting up for something big. A couple of guys already are working on microphones. That's gotta be it!"

We dispatched another team of spies to double-check. One of them met a restaurant employee who confirmed that a press conference would be held there at noon. An Einstein wasn't required to deduce that it *was* the Devils-Sports Authority event, but still Samerjan didn't confirm it. This time Horton trekked to the Devils' office and, finally, got the official word; it was going to happen after all, at noon, in Winners not the Hackensack courthouse.

Great! We had the jump on everyone and immediately moved the television trucks and equipment to a location right outside the restaurant. Wiener immediately developed a plan of attack with the little information we had at hand. Our cameraman would hustle up to the podium and install our microphone and then he'd place the camera in the best position. That was considered a key strategic advantage and gave us enormous leverage in terms of our opposition.

According to Wiener, I would open the show live the moment it appeared that the press conference was close to starting. For however many minutes necessary, I'd elaborate on the events leading up to the armistice and then we'd turn it over to the speaker at the lectern.

Despite all the planning I was extremely nervous. So far, we had no official notice that the press conference was, in fact, happening and I had neglected to phone back Samerjan. Adding to my concern was the absence of any other media types. I returned to the Winner's Restaurant and immediately came upon a woman who I only know as Sue, who managed the Devils' pressroom and now was involved in preparations here. She confirmed that it was indeed the Authority-Devils armistice event for which they were preparing. That done, I exhaled deeply and prepared my opening for our live show.

By 11:30 a.m. a sprinkling of newsmen had drifted in and TV cameras were being mounted. Our SportsChannel people had planned to open the show as soon as any of the principals arrived, but that wouldn't happen for a while. In the meantime a crisis developed. Having been first on the scene, we planted our microphone in the middle of the lectern, but subsequent technicians had dislodged it and a minute before noon – the scheduled starting time for the event – we had no sound from the main microphone.

My right ear was nearly peeled off by decibels as Wiener demanded that we stall the start of proceedings until the mike was fixed and get the damn mike fixed before anything begins!

While this was being accomplished a camera suddenly appeared five feet behind me – closer to the dais – which blocked the view of our cameraman. My stage manager set a record for expletives while the intruding cameraman beat a hasty retreat to another portion of the room. Just then a Madison Square Garden Network cameraman blithely moved into the empty spot whereupon more expletives served to hasten his exit.

Our two go-fers, Kolb and Horton, were then given explicit instructions; Get Guests! We didn't expect to do interviews as they were coming in, but it was imperative that they grab whomever they could once the formal part of the press conference had ended.

About a minute later, Kolb, who was scouting the perimeter of the room, tipped us off that the entourage was making its way to the door. We gave the signal to Wiener who counted me down from the truck – "...four, three, two, one, Go Stan!"

Off to the right of the podium, I began my spiel: "D-Day has arrived. That is, D as in Devils-Day; the Stanley Cup champions are staying in New Jersey..." I continued until the principals were being introduced by Mike Levine, the Devils' PR man. Then, we cut to the dais microphone for the live conference.

Gary Bettman led off the speakers, confirming that he knew a day earlier, when I had spoken to him, that he would be in New Jersey. "The Devils are staying," said Bettman, appearing characteristically jaunty, "at least for the next 12 years. This marks the beginning of a new era in New Jersey."

The commissioner then spelled out how the hockey club would have new revenue streams, how the Byrne Arena would be renovated and how other goodies would provide John McMullen the fiscal wherewithal to compete with the Rangers, Red Wings and other big-money clubs.

McMullen was next and, typically, his theme was the recently-crowned Stanley Cup champions. "We beat the Bruins, Penguins, Flyers and Red Wings to win the Stanley Cup," said McMullen, "and the payrolls of every one of those teams was higher than ours!"

It was a wonderful line, but also profound in its simplicity. The buy-a-championship theory was refuted by McMullen's club and he wanted to underline that point. It was a lesson that the Blues, Rangers, Maple Leafs, Canadiens and other big spenders simply could not or would not acknowledge.

Eventually, the white-haired leader moved on to the traumatic topic at hand: the peace treaty. "We do need much more cooperation," said McMullen, "and I believe it will happen."

As the speakers came and went, a particularly fascinating aspect of the armistice was revealed. A condition of the Devils' declaration of intent to stay was that the New York Yankees, whose owner George Steinbrenner had for years been threatening to leave his Bronx turf for New Jersey, could not move into The Meadowlands until the year 2003, at the earliest.

"There can't be another major league team here," asserted Lou Lamoriello. "Not another pro football team, another pro basketball team, another NHL team or a baseball team."

The feud between McMullen and Steinbrenner was like a roller coaster, but the Yankees' boss never forgave McMullen for a remark the Devils' owner had made after being a "limited partner" of the Bronx Bombers. To wit: "There is nothing more limited than being a limited partner of George Steinbrenner."

It was not that the Yankees were barred from New Jersey forever but rather until the Bombers' lease with New York City runs out in 2002. What the anti-Yankees' clause did was buy time for Team McMullen to sell its new suites and take advantage of its new signage and other revenue deals before a fifth team of any kind could set up serious housekeeping in the neighbourhood.

"We are not about to do the whole Nashville thing," said Mike Francis, the New Jersey Sports Authority chairman. "We are not going to try to get any major league team to break its lease. We respect leases."

There was, however, an "if" involved and in the view of some observers it was a big "IF." The agreement to keep the Devils in New Jersey for a dozen years was contingent on the renegotiated lease being approved on September 15, 1995. If the deal was not completed by then, the Authority would reactivate its request in State Superior Court for a temporary restraining order to keep the team from terminating its current lease. Thus, if the lease was not approved, the warriors would return to the legal battlefield.

A major aspect of the agreement stipulated that if the Authority did not help the team secure a $25-million loan by September 15, 1995, the Devils could cancel the deal. "The pressure on the Authority is not a negative," added Lamoriello. "I believe pressure can be a positive. We put pressure on ourselves every day.

"But I'm very comfortable that the relationship is going to be better than ever before. And one of the major reasons for that is the way [Authority Arena and Stadium executive vice-president] Michael Rowe was involved in the talks, the manner with which he made us feel as though our needs were important. The communication and feedback we had with him was absolutely outstanding.

"The reality is that if the Sports Authority delivers what has been promised, the Devils have a 12-year lease and commitment to remain in New Jersey. This is not a one-year agreement with an 11-year option."

Bettman, who had inspired the ogre image in New Jersey after his appearance with me on television during the Penguins' playoff, suddenly had become a hero of sorts. Virtually every one of my sources credited him with persuading the Authority members of the need for compromise.

"On balance, each side left the table believing the commissioner was an advocate of their particular position," said Rowe. "If he were billing for his time, I'm sure we'd each be pleased to pay the bill."

Throughout the press conference, we anxiously awaited the moment that it would break into the one-on-ones that are so precious to television interviewers. In this case – since we were live – it was imperative that one of our go-fers latch on to a chief protagonist in this passion play. Suddenly, Bettman stepped forward and stopped further questions, signalling the end of the general give-and-take.

That was my cue to ad-lib on camera until someone was fetched for a live interview. Enough had taken place for me to cruise through the fiscal waters without capsizing and about 90 seconds after I had begun my peroration, out of the corner of my eye, I noticed that Horton had Lamoriello in hand. He moved right into camera formation and proved to be a solid opening interview.

Bettman followed, maintaining his upbeat style of the day. When I asked him to pinpoint the turning point in keeping the Devils in New Jersey, he wasted no time replying, "You may have accelerated the process when you interviewed me in Pittsburgh!" (I actually believed that he meant every word of it.)

It was evident that Bettman would not drop Nashville as a prospective NHL site and underlined it by saying, "I think it's a good market." Later in the day, Nashville Mayor Phil Bredeson said, "We want an NHL or NBA team in Nashville and I think when our arena opens next year, we'll have a team."

I was most interested in McMullen's reaction. This had been an extraordinarily trying few months for a man his age and he had been vilified beyond the call of duty, considering the losses he suffered along the way. When he had begun addressing the audience, he was upbeat and remained that way until the question-and-answer period began.

For the most part, he maintained a temperate flow of replies until someone mentioned the hostile reaction toward him expressed by some fans during the Stanley Cup celebration in front of Byrne Arena. What had been a positive mood began turning sour as reporters hammered away at this issue.

Exasperated, McMullen remarked, "Most of the negative impression comes from the press not the fans." By the time the leaders had broken up into separate groups, McMullen was in a foul mood and balked when one of his less charitable critics, Bob Page of Madison Square Garden Network, attempted to get him one-on-one. It was then that Horton intercepted him and mentioned that I was standing by hoping he would come over for a chat. He obliged while we waited out a station break. In a matter of seconds we were on camera and I began the interview.

"We're not guaranteed break-even," he declared. "That depends on salaries in the NHL. But I will say this; the NHL has the most constructive labour agreement in all of pro sports."

He was lavish in praising Bettman, insisting that the deal could not have been brokered without the commissioner's insights. "He has a knowledge about leases throughout the league that surpasses anyone's and that was a big help to us."

When McMullen was finished, I concluded the interviews with Authority members Mulcahy, Francis and Rowe. Having been tipped off about the infighting between Francis and McMullen – not to mention the fact that they hadn't talked for almost a year before the intense negotiating began – my attention was caught by his accent on peace in our time. "It's critical that we be able to work together," said Francis, "and we're genuinely looking to work jointly with the Devils."

I signed off the air about an hour after we had opened and, for the most part, I was satisfied with our show. It was live TV and we had covered it from the start, obtaining all the key individuals for interviews.

On the drive back to Manhattan over the George Washington Bridge, I began reflecting on the similarity in the two major off-ice hockey stories I had covered within a year; first the lockout and then the Nashville caper. They had a lot in common beginning with the acrimony shared by both sides and the same 11th-hour drama that kept newsmen in suspense. The owner-union war certainly was more bitter than sweet, whereas the Devils' Stanley Cup triumph was the honey that softened the unpleasant taste of Nashville.

Both wars were closely intertwined. The NHL Players' Association – with the encouragement of agents – had driven salaries to record levels. To keep pace with the salary spiral an owner such as John McMullen had to find additional sources of revenue. Nashville was such a terrific enticement that McMullen, the businessman, had to consider the offer and then demand a better deal from the Sports Authority. Surely, if salaries had been at a lower, more reasonable level, the battle would not have been fought.

It always has been terribly easy for sportswriters and sportscasters to criticize owners for being cheap, frugal or whatever. The knocks come from media which wouldn't spend a dime for a ticket. Had McMullen not invested a considerable fortune into the Devils through the years of fiscal abuse, New Jersey never would have had a big-league hockey club and surely never a Stanley Cup winner.

"He from day one has taken the hit, personally and financially," said Lamoriello. "He went through every lean year and no one helped him, not one dime. He sustained all of this. In past years no one wanted us. Now people want us. There's not any greed involved, but we're just trying to get back a little. He's never going to get whole."

By the time I had arrived home, there was a phone call from a repoter with the *Asbury Park Press*. She had been listening to radio station WFAN and was surprised at the vituperation of hosts Chris Russo and Mike Francesa. "They're saying that the Devil thing is all a joke," said Wall, "because they could be out of New Jersey in a year. What do you think?"

I was taken aback by their vehemence and when she asked me for a comment, I suggested that the Russo-Francesa shtick was cynicism and I didn't for a second believe them. It seemed to me that the Sports Authority had too much at stake to allow the Devils to leave now and that it would only require a few months to iron out the bumps in the agreement.

In any event their negativism, followed by some dubious comments made by *New York Times* columnist Dave Anderson had me wondering again. Just when it appeared that there was cause for celebration, another reason for doubt intruded.

There was only one thing to do, contact the journalist I considered the most tuned in to this story from the start. I called Jerry Izenberg from the *Star-Ledger* and he immediately dismissed Russo and Francesa out of hand. He pointed out that there was too much for either party to lose – including a serious trip to Superior Court in Hackensack – by reneging on the pact.

"This is a deal where everyone can make money," said Izenberg, "and that's why everyone was involved in the first place. You cannot fault the New Jersey Devils for that."

I certainly couldn't, not when the bottom line in the NHL clearly had switched from pucks to bucks.

AFTERWORD:
THE LIFE OR DEATH OF HOCKEY

If I have witnessed one change that has troubled me more than any other in my four decades of professional hockey chronicling, it is the dramatic change in values from the advent of the 1990s.

Teamplay has given way to individuality. A form of runaway greed has replaced prudent fiscal management. Loyalty has become almost an anachronism. Money has become everything. Almost. But the NHL is only the latest league to enter this phase of development.

When the NHL was a less complicated business, trades were made to improve hockey clubs. In 1964, the Toronto Maple Leafs traded five players to the New York Rangers for Andy Bathgate and Don McKenney. General manager/coach Punch Imlach believed that he could win another championship with Bathgate firing goals, so he made the trade. That was always Imlach's modus operandi.

As it happened, Imlach was right. The Maple Leafs won their third straight Stanley Cup. The Rangers didn't win anything even though the additions of Bob Nevin, Arnie Brown, Rod Seiling and Dick Duff turned the Broadway Blueshirts into a playoff contender. That's why trades were made in those days. It's only partially the case now.

The economic chaos that continued the escalation of salaries has totally changed the NHL as we once knew it. Nowhere is it more apparent than in the trade department. Once based on calculated daring and logic, trades now are almost always predicated on salaries; that is, what a player is earning now and what his future demands are. It is a sorry state of affairs, to be sure, but it is a fact of life that has contaminated the thinking of every club owner and general manager.

Moreover, it has now even affected the haves as well as the have-nots. The Rangers, who played to automatic sellout crowds at high prices throughout the

1994-95 season, were affected by the new "money" game. General manager Neil Smith knew that Teemu Selanne wanted $3 million a year from the Winnipeg Jets. In order to obtain the coveted superstar, Smith knew he first had to balance the budget which meant he would have to trade the likes of Pat Verbeek, who wanted $2 million, and Sergei Zubov, who sought more than $1 million.

It didn't matter that in my opinion none of the above were actually worth the amounts they were demanding. That's irrelevant in today's hockey economy where a young defenceman such as Chris Pronger is obtaining more than $1 million a year and on the best day he ever had, wasn't worth half that figure (again, my opinion). Nor was it surprising that in July 1995, the Hartford Whalers were offering Pronger to any team that would take him (and his paycheque) because in contemporary hockey, the bottom line is the bottom line.

Pick any team at the 1995 Entry Draft in Edmonton and you would find one that was focusing as much on the fiscal as the physical. Desperately trying to work their way out of the doldrums, the New York Islanders coveted their 1993 draft pick Todd Bertuzzi, whose agent was demanding more than $1 million for an unproven youngster who had not played a single NHL game. Minutes before the deadline, general manager Don Maloney capitulated. He signed the lad for a million-plus but then had to face the demands of freeagent veterans Steve Thomas and Ray Ferraro who were asking for equally considerable amounts.

The NHL Players' Association, which so assiduously fought ownership's demand for a salary cap, seems oblivious to the league's traumatic economic conditions. By July 1995, the average player's salary had skyrocketed to $700,000 while the Los Angeles Kings, once mistakenly considered viable, had rolled up a debt of more than $100-million. It started with the implausible actions of Bruce McNall, and got worse under Joe Cohen in 1995.

The Buffalo Sabres, a club that forever fails to get past the opening playoff round, lost two of its marquee players – Dale Hawerchuk and Alexander Mogilny – simply because of the fiscal fanaticism. Hawerchuk was signed by the St. Louis Blues, the most profligate underachieving team in NHL history, while the over-paid Mogilny was dealt to the Vancouver Canucks for a collection of no-names. Buffalo was left with one-time star Pat LaFontaine whose ability to perform at the highest level has been rendered dubious by knee surgery. Meanwhile, the Sabres wasted no time following the trend, raising ticket prices for the umpteenth time.

By the start of the 1995-96 season runaway salaries had forced owners to price the NHL out of the range of most blue-collar fans and many white-collar ones as well. Many of the governors wondered whether there was any room for more ticket hikes. The answer was negative. Viewing hockey in the arena had become geared to the upper-middle class, corporations who can't feel the costs, and the diehards who were able to scrape together enough cash to afford an occasional game, if not a season ticket. As far as the league was concerned, the rest could watch the NHL on television.

While Gary Bettman's knee-jerk reaction that the NHL was "doing great" still could be heard through the summer of 1995, there were enough suggestions that "grate" might be the more applicable term. The Kings' finances were in such a state of disarray that even Wayne Gretzky was not paid monies due him in June and July. In Dallas, owner Norman Green was scrambling to find a partner who would purchase his club so he could be bailed out of a mountainous real estate debt in Alberta. The Winnipeg Jets remained in Manitoba as a lame-duck club after a plan to seek funds for a new arena died in August 1995. Oddsmakers figured the Jets would be at a stateside location in 1996.

Even the very rich Wayne Huizenga, the former Blockbuster Video tycoon who had planted the Panthers in Miami, was rightly or wrongly agonizing over his club's problems. Huizenga had sought to have Florida taxpayers' money build him a new arena as a replacement home for the inadequate Miami Arena. It is one of the smallest NHL facilities (14,500 seats) with only 18 luxury boxes. The building was only seven years old in 1995, yet it was considered obsolete. Floridians rebelled against Huizenga's financially self-serving tactics and by the summer of 1995 he was publicly projecting a $7-million loss for his club in 1995-96 in Miami, while broad hints were heard that the Panthers might relocate to Atlanta, Phoenix or whichever city might present one of the country's richest men with a better deal. After all, Nashville was still offering a $20-million relocation bonus and a sweetheart lease if any NHL club would become tenants in the new Nashville Arena due to open in the fall of 1996.

All of this has had a direct affect on the attitudes of hockey fans. Cynicism and skepticism have become the operative buzzwords, and for good reason. "We devote years of allegiance to a team like this, and then they tell us they're going to Nashville?" moaned one devoted, yet disgruntled, New Jersey Devils' fan during the Stanley Cup champions' moving crisis early in July 1995. "Where the bleep are they going to hang the Stanley Cup banner – in the Grand Ole Opry?"

But fans should remember that Devils' owner John McMullen did not want to move his club. The native New Jerseyite simply was tired of taking a fiscal bath brought on by the combination of escalating player salaries and an unfair lease. When McMullen stated, "I have a right to make a profit," no one could dispute him.

Unfortunately, the NHL Players' Association and its leader Bob Goodenow have placed increased player salaries as their number one priority. If Goodenow had any sense of history, he would have studied the continent-wide manner in which fans have rejected Major League Baseball and its overpaid players. The players' strike combined with their wealth and apparent insensitivity to the general public scarred the spectators' psyche. If it could happen in baseball, it could happen in hockey as well. Several small-revenue clubs will be forced to move, albeit at a nice profit.

What fans are seeking is a good game, energetically played at a fair ticket price. Owners in the International Hockey League came to that conclusion a few years ago. They have turned what once was a backwater minor league into one of the most sensibly-operated, fastest-growing organizations in professional sports.

I watched with amazement as the International Hockey League spread across the continent from Houston to Kansas City to Cincinnati, finally invading NHL turf in Chicago and Detroit. Now it has moved into Los Angeles and the San Francisco Bay area to further compete with the NHL for hockey's dollars.

Entrepreneurs in the International League who once had designs on the NHL changed their mind as they studied the evolution of the big league. One of them was Richard Adler, co-owner of the IHL's Atlanta Knights. "When we got into this," said Adler, "the idea was to grow into NHL ownership. But the NHL the last three years has become suicidal. It's the Chapter Eleven (as in bankruptcy) League."

Adler's was not an idle comment but rather an observation based on research. The average NHL ticket price was $35 in 1995. In three years, his researchers determined, it would be $40 to $45 which would result in NHL crowds averaging no higher than 12,000. By contrast, the IHL's average ticket in 1995 was less than $12 and that remained the key to the league's success. Ironically, Adler could be out of business in Atlanta if and when the NHL expands in 1996-97.

While the St. Louis Blues' payroll climbed over the $25-million mark, team salaries in the International League remained fixed at approximately $1.5-million, which is less than an average NHL player like Ray Ferraro was earning.

"Why would anyone go into a business like the NHL," asked Adler, "when a club like the Nordiques were going to lose $25-million in the next two years?"

The Nordiques' purported dilemma was beautifully solved by a sale to the Comsat Corporation and a move to Denver. Other blue chip companies have expressed an interest in NHL investment. Yet, for every Comsat, there appear to be others espousing concern because of the increasing price of hockey players.

Where salaries have been more rigidly controlled, hockey has boomed. The East Coast League has become a cash cow. Florida, which once was considered out-of-bounds for pro hockey, had no less than seven professional hockey teams in 1995. Meanwhile, the venerable American Hockey League, which set an attendance record during the 1994-95 season, continued to add new franchises to slake the thirst of fans in the southeastern tier of the United States. Huntsville, Alabama, once known as "Bear Bryant Country," now boasts one of the largest youth leagues in America.

There can be no arguing with hockey's immense popularity as a participant sport, nor as a spectator sport on levels other than the NHL. And one could make a good case suggesting that the NHL can only grow bigger and stronger as it reaches toward the new century.

But if this is to happen, an entire reorganization of the salary structure must be accomplished. This was the message delivered by John Ziegler to Bob

Goodenow in 1992 and by Gary Bettman to Goodenow during the NHL's Civil War in 1994-95. At no time did the players display any real interest in coming to terms with runaway inflation and the result is a future clouded with uncertainty and threatened by the same popular backlash that resulted in the fan boycott of Major League Baseball.

If America's "national pastime" could lose millions in rejected television contracts and millions in loyal spectators, imagine what will happen to the National Hockey League if its players continue to maul the goose that laid their golden eggs.

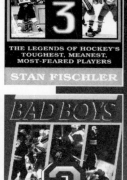
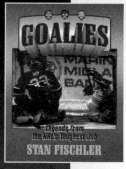

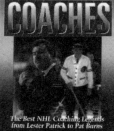